RECIPE RESCUE COOKBOOK

RECIPE RESCUE COOKBOOK

Healthy New Approaches to Traditional Favorites

From

The Magazine of Food & Health
EATINGWELL

Edited by
Patricia Jamieson & Cheryl Dorschner

Camden House Publishing
A division of Telemedia Communications (USA) Inc.

Camden House Publishing
Ferry Road
Charlotte, Vermont 05445

© 1993 by EATING WELL: The Magazine of Food & Health™

Library of Congress Cataloging-in-Publication Data

Recipe rescue cookbook : healthy new approaches to traditional favorites from
Eating well: the magazine of food & health / edited by Patricia Jamieson & Cheryl Dorschner.
p.   cm.
Includes index
ISBN 0-944475-48-5 : $24.95. — ISBN 0-944475-47-7 (pbk.) : $18.95
1. Cookery.   I. Jamieson, Patricia.   II. Dorschner, Cheryl.
III. Eating well.
TX714.R4222   1993
641.5—dc20   93-17814
                                                                   CIP

Editorial Director: Julie Stillman
Cover and interior design by Eugenie Seidenberg Delaney
Front cover photograph by Steven Mark Needham
Back cover photographs by Brian Hagiwara (left and center) and Alan Richardson (right)
Illustrations by Dorothy Reinhardt

Trade distribution by
Firefly Books Ltd.
250 Sparks Avenue
Willowdale, Ontario
Canada M2H 2S4

Printed and bound in Canada by
D.W. Friesen & Sons
Altona, Manitoba

To EATING WELL Magazine Readers

Acknowledgments

Like the labor that brings our food from the field or garden to the table, this book is the work of many hands. As editors of this project, we recognize with gratitude the extraordinary efforts of the following people.

The EATING WELL readers who sent us their families' favorite recipes, trusting that we would transform them into something more healthful but still scrumptious.

Nutrition Editor Elizabeth Hiser and Food Editor Susan Stuck, whose solid work is evident on every page of this book.

The tireless, innovative, even-spirited Test Kitchen staff of Susan Herr and Susanne Davis, who are not only adept in the kitchen but seemed to juggle with equal aplomb, creating and preparing recipes for this book and the bimonthly magazine. And Lisa Cherkasky, Linda Clark and Marie Piraino who were able to step into the whirlwind of kitchen activity as needed for this project.

The amazing Production Editor Wendy Ruopp, whose long-time experience and computer expertise combine to define EATING WELL language and style. Suzanne Seibel, who proofed the final manuscript.

The Camden House Publishing staff, particularly Darcy Charbonneau, whose behind-the-scenes efforts smoothed the process; Howard White, who made it all make financial sense; and Editorial Director Julie Stillman, who knew just when to nudge us and when to give us free rein to do our best.

Cheryl Dorschner & Patricia Jamieson

Contents

Preface

This book is the result of the kitchen alchemy that has made EATING WELL Magazine such a popular success since its launch in 1990. The point of the magazine, and of the RECIPE RESCUE COOKBOOK, is to prove that healthful cooking is not about giving up our favorite foods. Instead, we modify our favorite foods with cooking techniques that we have perfected in our own test kitchen. We don't stop working with a recipe until we love the result. We don't ditch good taste on the road to good nutrition. We love to eat well.

But we know, and we know that our readers know (because they ask us to "Rx" so many of their favorite recipes), that much American cooking has been needlessly laden with fat. When in doubt, add another stick of butter, another cup of cheese, another half-pound of bacon; we grew accustomed to food that was, frankly, greasy.

Food need not be that way. Low-fat cooking actually *reveals* the flavors of many fresh foods; smart use of herbs and spices compensates when cream sauces are cut back; new low-fat dairy products make superb substitutes; and new cooking techniques produce delightful results after they are put through our kitchen-testing crucible. It would be silly to pretend that low-fat food tastes exactly the same as high-fat food. Rather, it tastes *as delicious* as high-fat food—when it's properly done. And the potential health benefits are substantial.

The recipes in this book fit into the approach to healthy low-fat eating that is explained in the Introduction. But even if you're not following a low-fat diet every day, these recipes can inspire you to move in the right direction. We hope they will find a home in your kitchen as they have in ours.

Scott Mowbray, Editor
EATING WELL Magazine

Introduction

The Basics of Eating Well

This is not a diet book. It is a book about a new way of cooking that has been evolving in America since Americans have become concerned about heart disease rates, obesity and other symptoms of a too-rich food supply. Weight-loss diets fail; *changing one's whole diet* is the solution, and EATING WELL Magazine is leading the way. The magazine is dedicated to the philosophy that a new, healthier American cuisine can include all the favorites—from barbecued hamburgers and cheesecake to the French, Italian and Asian foods that have become so popular over the past 25 years. This *inclusive* approach to healthy eating stands opposed to the dieting mania that has caused so much heartbreak and frustration, and to the health-food extremism that has scared so many people away.

We cook according to a simple goal: lower the fat, but keep the food delicious and remember that the word "delicious" describes not only the flavor but also the texture, aroma, appearance and "soul" of a dish. The work is not finished when the fat has been reduced; in many cases it has just begun—we tinker and refine until the food is completely satisfying.

The recipes in this book are also in line with public health consensus on the need for Americans to use far more grains and other complex carbohydrates as a base in their diets, to add generous amounts of fruits and vegetables, and to reduce the amount of full-fat dairy foods, meat, added fats and sweets. This doesn't mean that every *recipe* follows that pattern precisely; rather, it means that when you put a meal together using the RECIPE RESCUE COOKBOOK dishes, these important dietary goals can be easily met.

How Do We "Rx" a Recipe?

The recipes in this book came from three sources.

From the start, EATING WELL Magazine asked its readers to supply favorite recipes for the magazine's *Rx for Recipes* column. Here, readers challenge the Test Kitchen to trim the fat from tried-and-true kitchen favorites. Recipes contributed by readers are marked in this book with an R_X. Response to the *Rx* call has been overwhelming; sheer numbers dictated that we couldn't include them all here. Some recipes were not fixable because fat played an integral role: we wouldn't mess with them. Others used so many shortcut processed foods that making the recipe from scratch would be too laborious. The recipes chosen for this book were the standouts, the dishes that taste wonderful in their lower-fat guise and are classic and easy enough to become part of a cook's basic healthy repertoire.

Meanwhile, our Test Kitchen staff, with its expertise and training in classical cooking, is always updating or creating its own healthful versions of culinary classics. Some of these recipes have appeared in EATING WELL, on the Cable News Network "On the Menu" program and in syndicated columns in newspapers throughout North America. Others were developed expressly for the RECIPE RESCUE COOKBOOK.

Finally, we regularly test and publish the latest low-fat creations of some of the country's best chefs and food writers. Some of those recipes, too, are in this book.

The method for *"Rxing"* a recipe begins with cooking the full-fat version and analyzing it, both for nutrition content and taste. Then we consider the best method of reducing the fat content; we have many techniques to choose from—including substituting low-fat products, supplementing meats with grains, using lower-fat cuts of meat, adding more vegetables, boosting or adding seasonings and simply cutting back on the amount of added fat. Those methods can be understood by simply cooking from this book, and we have highlighted our fat-cutting techniques in the recipe headnotes.

Sometimes fat reduction is straightforward; more often a combination of techniques and ingredients is required to right the imbalance that fat removal causes. Rarely does the first version of an *"Rxed"* recipe satisfy, but each version builds upon what the Test Kitchen learns from the comments of the recipe-tasting panel. Sometimes a dozen versions are tried before the final recipe is written.

The One Big Rule, and Reading the Fine Print

Today's nutrition advice can be summed up this way: Eat more plant-based foods, and eat less fat. That simple rule needs to be understood before you can choose your new, healthier diet—even when you base that diet on the RECIPE RESCUE COOKBOOK recipes. Consider the *daily* grain and vegetable and fruit contents that a healthy diet should contain: six to eleven servings of bread, cereal and other carbohydrates; three to five servings of vegetables; and two to four servings of fruit (refer to the new USDA Food Pyramid for more detailed guidelines about servings). This is far more than most Americans now eat. Then calculate the limit of the amount of daily fat that you ought to observe (see fat guidelines below). Having this basic knowledge, you will be able to make better use of the nutritional fine print on the RECIPE RESCUE COOKBOOK recipes.

The breakdown of calories, protein, fat, carbohydrate, sodium, and cholesterol for one serving that follows each recipe in this book is, therefore, not just of interest to nutritionists and diet fanatics. Everyone should make this part of their recipe browsing, because it is easier to *think* that one is eating a healthier diet—by eating an extra apple here, cutting back to low-fat milk there—than to do so over the long term. Here is a brief explanation of the nutrition information for our recipes.

---

467 CALORIES PER SERVING: 33 G PROTEIN, 12 G FAT, 52 G CARBOHYDRATE; 929 MG SODIUM; 55 MG CHOLESTEROL.

CALORIES: Cutting calories is not the goal; eating the amount to maintain an ideal body weight and getting optimum nutrition from every calorie are the essential points. Calorie needs vary enormously among individuals; contributing factors include age, gender, genetics and activity levels. On average, most people need to take in about 15 calories per pound to maintain their present weight.

PROTEIN: Few Americans have to worry about getting enough protein, because the typical diet provides two to three times the amount required. In fact, eating smaller amounts of high-protein foods helps lower fat intake because fat and protein often occur together in foods.

FAT: Minimizing the amount of fat in each recipe helps people stay below the recommended limit—30 percent of total daily calories from fat. Reducing fat in the diet not only lowers risk of heart disease and cancer, but is the best way to maintain a healthy weight because fat is the most concentrated source of calories.

Easier than counting calories and calculating percentages is to use EATING WELL Magazine's simple shortcut method to estimate your fat limit: divide your ideal body weight (or the weight you would *like* to be) by two. For example, an average person with an ideal weight of 150 pounds should eat no more than 75 grams of fat per day. This helps put the grams of fat in a recipe in perspective.

We are mindful of not only the amount, but also the sources of fats. Most recipes specify monounsaturated oils—usually olive oil and canola oil. Saturated fat should make up less than a third of total fat. Saturated fats raise blood cholesterol, and although both polyunsaturated and monounsaturated fats lower blood cholesterol when they replace saturated fats in the diet, new evidence suggests that monounsaturates are the healthier of the two.

CARBOHYDRATE: In a healthy diet, foods high in complex carbohydrates outnumber high-fat foods while offering more vitamins, minerals and dietary fiber. Simple sugars add to the carbohydrate counts in nutritional analysis, but don't contribute much in the way of nutrition.

SODIUM: Our recipes vary greatly in sodium content but contain the minimum amount that we judge necessary to enhance food flavor.

CHOLESTEROL: It is recommended that intake of dietary cholesterol be kept below 300 milligrams per day. Fat (particularly saturated fat), rather than dietary cholesterol, is most implicated in raising blood cholesterol.

How to Use Less Fat in the Kitchen

Creating great-tasting low-fat dishes is a matter of carefully balancing flavors and textures, creatively compensating for the contribution that fat makes to a dish, and wisely budgeting the fat that you do use. In the course of testing recipes for EATING WELL Magazine and the RECIPE RESCUE COOKBOOK, we have developed formulas and techniques that can be applied to a wide variety of dishes. But from the beginning we found that every recipe has nuances. Often adjusting a single ingredient can throw the entire recipe out of balance. Only with thorough testing do we achieve results that live up to the EATING WELL name. The following are guidelines, not rules. When using any of these ideas to revise your own favorite recipes, understand that delicious revisions are the product of repeat experimentation, frequent error and serendipity.

DAIRY FOODS

- If the flavors of a dish are delicate, try substituting skim milk for whole milk or cream; thicken it with cornstarch or flour to compensate for the lack of body.
- To enrich sauces and soups, evaporated skim milk can replace cream or whole milk when paired with robust flavors that mask its slightly sweet, canned flavor. Because about half of the water has been removed, the consistency of evaporated skim milk is similar to that of cream. Mix it with regular skim milk for baked custard and quiche.
- When a slightly tart flavor is desirable, finish a soup or sauce with nonfat yogurt or skim-milk buttermilk. Yogurt or buttermilk may curdle when overheated, but this can be prevented if cornstarch is added *(page 143)*. When a slightly richer, less tart flavor is appropriate, reduced-fat sour cream may be a better substitute.
- For dips, spreads, lasagna and cheesecakes, *fromage blanc* or pressed low-fat cottage cheese *(page 26)* are excellent replacements for high-fat fresh cheeses like cream cheese or ricotta. Balance the flavor and texture with the addition of a small amount of reduced-fat cream cheese.
- As a substitute for whipping cream, you can whip *chilled* evaporated skim milk *(page 179)*. This works best in recipes that contain vibrant flavors and are stabilized with gelatin, such as Frozen Lemon Mousse *(page 185)*.
- Another alternative to whipped cream as a dessert topping is lightly drained yogurt. Allow vanilla nonfat yogurt to drain in a cheesecloth-lined colander in the refrigerator for about 1 hour, until slightly thickened.
- For dessert toppings and fillings that call for whipped cream, try making an Italian meringue filling *(page 185)*. This cooked meringue has a lovely creamy consistency and contains no fat.
- We have not found satisfactory substitutes for high-fat firm and semi-firm cheeses in cooking. In dishes in which cheese plays an integral role, we reduce the quantity and use high-quality cheeses that deliver maximum flavor, such as aged Parmigiano-Reggiano, Asiago or Gruyère. In cheese sauces, pureed cottage cheese boosts the dairy flavor, allowing us to use less hard cheese.

MEATS

- Choose lean cuts, such as beef round or rump steak, rather than chuck, pork tenderloin rather than loin or shoulder, and chicken or turkey breasts rather than thighs.
- Control portion size. Allow a maximum of four ounces raw meat (which will shrink to three ounces when cooked) per portion. In casseroles, saucy meat dishes and even burgers, you can usually reduce the meat portion significantly if you compensate with additional vegetables and grains. We have used bulgur to successfully replace some of the ground meat in meat sauces. It absorbs the meaty flavors and often is unnoticeable.
- Trim meats carefully of fat. Removing poultry skin saves about five grams of fat per three-ounce portion. If the poultry will be marinated or braised, remove skin before cooking, but if it will be roasted, remove the skin after cooking.
- You can recreate the smoky rich flavor that ham or salt pork contributes to dishes such as baked beans or chili if you substitute dried tomatoes for the pork.

BAKING

- Treats like carrot cake, brownies, muffins and plum pudding can easily be converted into lower-fat versions when a fruit puree, such as prune puree or apple butter, is used to replace much, but not all, of the oil or butter. Match the flavor of the fruit puree to the flavors in the recipe: prune puree works well in a spicy carrot cake, but apple butter is better suited to more delicate zucchini muffins.

- Fat makes baked goods tender and moist. Low-fat baked goods will be more tender if you switch from all-purpose flour to cake flour. Milled from soft wheat, cake flour contains less gluten than all-purpose flour, which comes from hard wheat. Gluten turns baked goods tough and elastic—desirable in yeast breads but not in quick breads or cakes. If you'd like to boost the fiber content in a quick bread or muffin, replace about half of the white flour with whole-wheat pastry flour.

- Virtually fat-free, egg whites are the low-fat baker's best friend because of their ability to incorporate air when beaten. Because of the risk of salmonella contamination, adding raw meringue to a mousse or filling is no longer recommended. Avoid this problem by making Italian meringue, a procedure that heats the egg whites with a very hot sugar syrup *(page 185)*.

- When a recipe calls for whole eggs, reduce the amount of yolks (all the fat and cholesterol is in the yolks) by using a mixture of eggs and egg whites. Replace four whole eggs with two whole eggs and two egg whites. You may need to increase the amount of moisture in the recipe slightly.

- Nuts are a critical element in many recipes. In toppings and crusts, nuts can be mixed with a crunchy toasted nonfat cereal, such as Grape-Nuts. (Inside a cake, however, the flavor and texture of the cereal gets lost.) Toasting nuts intensifies their flavor so you can use fewer in a recipe.

- Pastry is one of the low-fat cook's greatest challenges. The pastry recipes in this book use a combination of canola oil and a little browned butter rather than solid shortening or lard. Phyllo pastry, moistened with a mixture of canola oil and egg white, is a wonderful alternative to flaky or puff pastry in both savory and sweet pastries.

QUICK TRICKS IN EVERYDAY COOKING

- Store canned chicken stock in the refrigerator rather than in the cupboard. That way it's easy to remove the fat that solidifies on the surface.

- To moisten sandwich fillings, cut the mayo by mixing equal parts of reduced-fat mayonnaise with nonfat plain yogurt. Tart yogurt adds a welcome refreshing note.

- In vinaigrette salad dressings, replace about half of the oil with defatted chicken stock, fruit or vegetable juice or water.

- Because fat not only provides richness but amplifies flavor, it is often necessary to increase seasonings in a low-fat dish.

- Toasting, roasting and even caramelizing ingredients are great ways to boost flavors. When the flavor of butter seems essential to a dish, we cook it until it turns a light nutty brown. The flavor from a small amount of this brown butter carries much further.

- Spend your "fat budget" wisely by selecting the best ingredients available. A small amount of good-quality extra-virgin olive oil will contribute more and better flavor than pure or "light" olive oil, while offering the same amount of fat.

MENUS

These 10 menus are offered for inspiration and as a springboard to your own combinations. The recipes were not created specifically for these menus, so in some cases you may need to double the recipes; in others, you may have leftovers.

Picnic by the Brook

This simple menu for four features food that can be made ahead, packed and carried to that stream-side site where you spotted the great blue heron last year. Expect plenty of extras on the potato salad and brownies.

Bedeviled Eggs, page 58
Mama's Potato Salad, page 85
Oven-Fried Chicken, page 153
Tricolor Coleslaw, page 85
Better-For-You Brownies, page 238
Fresh Fruit

All-Season Breakfast

This brunch for six will be a big hit and not a big deal to prepare. Everyone can be part of the waffle making.

Clear-Conscience Waffles, page 20
Turkey & Apple Sausage Patties, page 21
Sliced Oranges
Pear Tatin, page 218

Pizza Party

*A casual get-together for about eight hungry friends.
Just double the salad recipe and make two batches of the frozen yogurt.*

Wonton Chips, page 63
Salade Niçoise Nouvelle, page 81
Pizza Selection — Pesto, page 108, Tex-Mex, page 112 or Caramelized Onion, page 110
Peach-Melon Frozen Yogurt, page 198

Elegant Company Dinner

Two couples can enjoy this winter selection. You will have extra soup.

Cheese Puffs, page 61
Curried Butternut Squash Bisque, page 77
Pork Medallions With Port & Dried-Cranberry Sauce, page 138
Bulgur With Celery & Sage, page 123
Braised Winter Vegetables With Thyme, page 101
Crème Caramel, page 190

Vegetarian Chili Supper

An ideal informal meal for four with plenty of corn bread and lemon squares to spare.

Half-Hour Vegetarian Chili, page 124
Quick Corn Bread, page 43
Mixed Greens With Buttermilk Dressing, page 94
Luscious Lemon Squares, page 237

Easy Summer Outdoor Dinner

*Here is a versatile menu that is easy to prepare "as is" for four with extra (easy-to-store) pita crisps and cobbler.
Or double the chicken, fries and coleslaw for dinner for eight.*

Hummus With Pita Crisps, page 60
Barbecued Chicken, page 153
Oven "Fries", page 102
Tricolor Coleslaw, page 85
Cherry & Nectarine Cobbler, page 193

Make-Ahead Entertaining

*Dinner for eight could not be easier than this meal in which everything
but the tossed salad can be prepared in advance. Double the salad recipe.*

Spinach-Feta Rolls, page 56
Greek Revival Salad, page 81
Pastitsio, page 141
Profiteroles, page 196

Christmas Dinner

The centerpiece turkey will easily serve 12.
Expect leftovers. Double the potato and onion dishes and triple the salad recipe.

Smoked Trout & Cucumber Tartlets, page 54
Romaine, Red Onion & Orange Salad, page 86
Turkey With Madeira Gravy, page 158
Rutabaga & Potato Puree, page 103
Baked Stuffed Onions, page 99
Peas
English Trifle, page 189
Plum Pudding, page 186

Simple Dinner Party

This is perfect for six people. Just double the dressing recipe.

Parmesan Straws, page 62
Mixed Greens With Ginger-Orange Dressing, page 94
Sauté of Shrimp With Fragrant Indian Spices, page 173
Basmati Rice
Banana Cream Pie, page 225

Sunday Dinner

The special treatment given the beef elevates this meal for four
beyond the typical weekend meat and potatoes fare. Expect extra pie.

Romaine Salad With Parmesan-Pepper Dressing, page 93
Braised Beef With Brandy & Mustard, page 136
Buttermilk Mashed Potatoes, page 102
Steamed Carrots
Light Lemon Meringue Pie, page 226

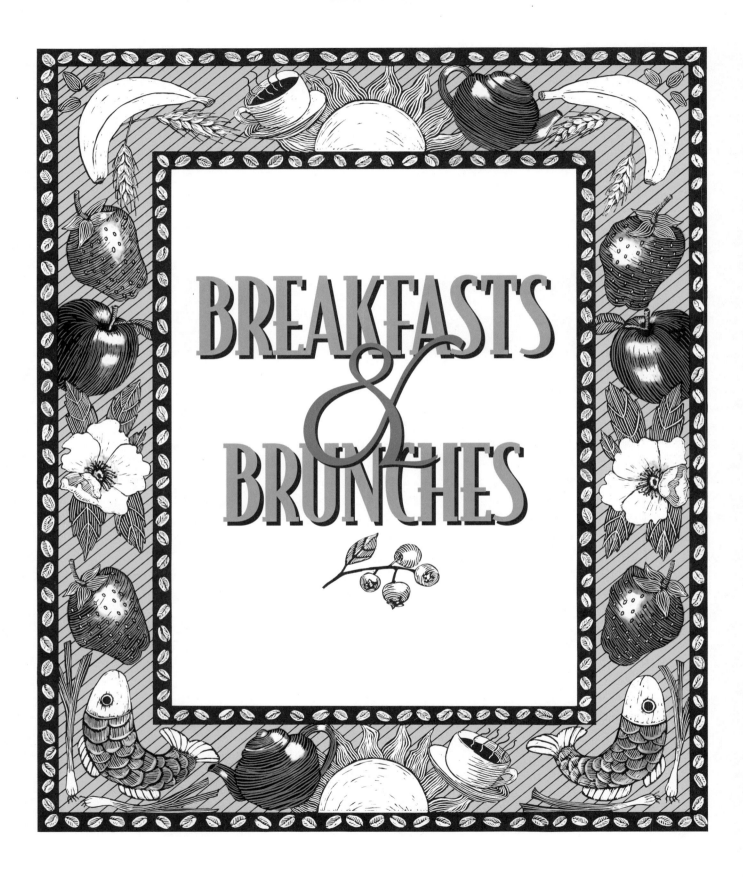

CHAPTER ONE

BREAKFASTS & BRUNCHES

RECIPES

Banana-Raisin French Toast

*French toast conjures images of family breakfasts with the main dish slathered in butter
and dripping with syrup. Memories begone! With a nutritious surprise filling,
this low-fat French toast is sure to please children and adults.*

1   ripe banana, peeled
2   tsp. frozen orange-juice concentrate
4   slices cinnamon-raisin bread
2   large egg whites

¼   cup skim milk
¼   cup nonfat or low-fat plain yogurt
1½ Tbsp. maple syrup or honey
1   tsp. butter

In a small, shallow bowl, mash banana coarsely with a fork. Stir in orange-juice concentrate. Spread the banana mixture over 2 slices of bread and top with the remaining 2 slices of bread, forming 2 sandwiches. In a pie plate, whisk together egg whites and milk; add sandwiches and soak for about 20 seconds. Turn sandwiches over and soak for 20 seconds longer. Transfer the sandwiches to a plate.

In a small bowl, stir together yogurt and maple syrup or honey. Set aside. In a nonstick skillet, melt ½ tsp. butter over low heat. Tilt the pan to swirl the butter around the skillet. With a metal spatula, place the sandwiches in the pan, and cook until the underside is browned, 5 to 7 minutes. Lift the sandwiches and add the remaining ½ tsp. butter. Turn over and cook for 5 to 7 minutes longer, or until browned. Serve with the sweetened yogurt.

Serves 2.

302 CALORIES PER SERVING: 11 G PROTEIN, 4 G FAT, 57 G CARBOHYDRATE; 317 MG SODIUM; 7 MG CHOLESTEROL.

Eat Your Breakfast or Else...

For as long as anyone can remember, mothers, nutritionists, school nurses, troop leaders, home economics teachers, managers and coaches all warned of dire consequences if we didn't eat our breakfast. Skipping breakfast ensured a sluggish brain and body, bad posture, poor grades—and much worse. Has the breakfast adage gone the way of "the earth is flat," "potatoes are fattening" and "eat meat at every meal"?

No: The old breakfast saw is still true. The Iowa Breakfast Studies of the 1970s showed that when people went without breakfast their mental reactions were slower and their performance was poorer. More recent research concludes that people who do not eat breakfast have *higher* blood cholesterol levels than those who do, even if the breakfast skippers consume less total fat during the day.

Without breakfast, it is hard to get all the necessary nutrients each day. Traditional breakfasts contain fiber, minerals and vitamins not plentiful in routine lunch and dinner fare. Now that the fat-laden breakfast of bacon, eggs, buttered toast and hash browns is less acceptable in the American diet, it is time to shed a little morning light on the delicious alternative. There is no excuse for skipping breakfast anymore.

Buttermilk-Oatmeal Pancakes

Here is a hearty, high-grain way to start the day. Maple syrup is a perennial favorite atop a stack of these pancakes; sliced bananas would also complement their oat flavor.

2½ cups skim-milk buttermilk
¾   cup rolled oats
1   cup all-purpose white flour
½   cup whole-wheat flour
¼   cup toasted wheat germ
¼   cup packed light brown sugar
2   tsp. baking powder

1   tsp. baking soda
1   tsp. ground cinnamon
½   tsp. salt
1   large egg
2   large egg whites
2   tsp. vegetable oil, preferably canola oil
    maple syrup (optional)

Combine buttermilk and rolled oats in a small bowl; let rest for 20 to 30 minutes to soften oats. In a medium-sized bowl, stir together flours, wheat germ, brown sugar, baking powder, baking soda, cinnamon and salt. In another bowl, mix together egg, egg whites and 1 tsp. oil with a whisk or fork. Add the oat mixture and the flour mixture and stir with a wooden spoon until just combined. *(The batter can be stored, covered, in the refrigerator overnight.)*

Heat a large nonstick skillet over medium heat and brush lightly with a little of the remaining 1 tsp. oil. Using ¼-cup batter for each pancake, pour batter onto the skillet and cook until the underside is browned and the bubbles on top remain open, 2 to 3 minutes. Turn the pancakes over and cook until the underside is browned, about 1 to 2 minutes. Transfer to a platter and keep warm in a 200-degree F oven. Repeat with remaining batter, brushing skillet with a little of the remaining oil as needed. Serve hot, topping with maple syrup if desired.

Makes 12 pancakes, serves 6.

307 CALORIES PER SERVING: 14 G PROTEIN, 5 G FAT, 53 G CARBOHYDRATE; 510 MG SODIUM; 37 MG CHOLESTEROL.

Clear-Conscience Waffles

"We were appalled to see that recipes for basic waffles are very high in eggs and butter," wrote Susan Fillion, asking for our help. Indeed, a single waffle contained 19 grams of fat. Our waffles contain a fifth of the fat. Top with fresh berries or sliced peaches and yogurt—you'll never miss the butter.

1   cup whole-wheat flour
1   cup all-purpose white flour
1½   tsp. baking powder
½   tsp. salt
¼   tsp. baking soda
2   cups skim-milk buttermilk

1   large egg, separated
1   Tbsp. pure vanilla extract (optional)
1   Tbsp. vegetable oil, preferably canola oil, plus more for preparing the waffle iron
2   large egg whites
2   Tbsp. sugar

In a large bowl, stir together flours, baking powder, salt and baking soda. In a separate bowl, whisk together buttermilk, egg yolk, vanilla (if using) and oil. Add to the dry ingredients and stir with a wooden spoon just until moistened.

In a grease-free mixing bowl, beat the 3 egg whites with an electric mixer until soft peaks form. Add sugar and continue beating until stiff and glossy. Whisk one-quarter of the beaten egg whites into the batter. With a rubber spatula, fold in the remaining beaten egg whites.

Preheat waffle iron. Brush the surface lightly with oil. Fill the iron two-thirds full. Cook for 5 to 6 minutes, or until the waffles are crisp and golden. Repeat with the remaining batter, brushing the surface with oil before cooking each batch.

Serves 6.

220 CALORIES PER SERVING: 10 G PROTEIN, 4 G FAT, 38 G CARBOHYDRATE; 368 MG SODIUM; 37 MG CHOLESTEROL.

R_x *Susan P. Fillion of Baltimore, Maryland*

Turkey & Apple Sausage Patties

Instead of the pork links of yore bursting with fat, these lean patties are full of flavor.
To ensure a moist sausage, use homemade fresh breadcrumbs.

2 tsp. vegetable oil, preferably canola oil
1 onion, finely chopped
2 tart apples, such as Granny Smith, peeled and grated
1 lb. ground turkey
1 cup fresh breadcrumbs *(see below)*

2 large egg whites
2 tsp. rubbed dried sage
1½ tsp. salt
½ tsp. freshly ground black pepper
¼ tsp. freshly grated nutmeg
¼ tsp. allspice

Preheat oven to 450 degrees F. Spray a baking sheet with nonstick cooking spray or line it with parchment paper.

In a medium-sized nonstick skillet, heat oil over medium heat. Add onions and sauté until softened, about 3 minutes. Add apples and sauté for 3 to 5 minutes longer, or until the apples are very tender. Transfer to a large bowl and let cool completely. Add turkey, breadcrumbs, egg whites, sage, salt, pepper, nutmeg and allspice; mix well. Divide the sausage mixture into 16 portions and form into ¾-inch-thick patties. *(The patties can be prepared ahead and stored, well wrapped, in the freezer for up to 3 months.)* Place the patties on the prepared baking sheet and bake until the outside is golden brown and the interior is no longer pink, about 10 minutes for fresh patties or 20 minutes for frozen patties.

Makes 16 patties, serves 8.

92 CALORIES PER SERVING: 12 G PROTEIN, 5 G FAT, 16 G CARBOHYDRATE; 552 MG SODIUM; 36 MG CHOLESTEROL.

Making Fresh Breadcrumbs

Fresh breadcrumbs are called for in some recipes because they contribute moisture to the recipe. Substituting dried crumbs would pull moisture from the other ingredients and yield unsatisfactory results.

3 slices fresh or day-old sandwich bread (3 oz.)

In a food processor or blender, process bread until fine crumbs form.
Makes about 1 cup.

Quiche Lorraine Light

Transforming this traditionally high-fat favorite was one of the EATING WELL Test Kitchen's greatest challenges. There were countless unsuccessful efforts before we were happy. Evaporated skim milk turned out to be the key to maintaining quiche's custardlike texture. For maximum flavor with a minimum of cheese, we opted for nutty Gruyère rather than milder varieties of Swiss cheese.

CRUST
- 1 cup all-purpose white flour
- ¼ tsp. salt
- 1 Tbsp. butter
- 3 Tbsp. vegetable oil, preferably canola oil
- 1-2 Tbsp. ice water

FILLING
- 2 large eggs
- 4 large egg whites
- ¾ cup skim milk
- ¾ cup evaporated skim milk
- ¼ tsp. salt
- ¼ tsp. freshly ground black pepper
- ¼ tsp. freshly ground nutmeg
- pinch cayenne pepper
- 1 tsp. Dijon mustard
- ½ cup shredded Gruyère cheese (about 1½ oz.)
- ¼ cup diced smoked ham (about 1 oz.)
- ¼ cup chopped scallions (about 3 scallions)
- 1 Tbsp. freshly grated Parmesan cheese

To make crust: Set rack in the lower third of the oven; preheat to 425 degrees F. In a medium-sized bowl, stir flour and salt together. In a small saucepan, melt butter over low heat. Cook for about 30 seconds, swirling the pan, or until the butter is a light, nutty brown. Pour into a small bowl and let cool. Stir in oil. Using a fork, slowly stir the butter-oil mixture into the flour mixture until it is crumbly. Gradually stir in enough ice water so that the dough will hold together. Press the dough into a flattened disk.

Place between two sheets of plastic wrap and roll into a circle about 12 inches in diameter. Remove the top sheet and invert the dough into a 9-inch pie plate. Remove the remaining wrap. Fold the edges under at the rim and crimp. *(The crust can be prepared ahead and stored, covered, in the refrigerator for up to 2 days or in the freezer for up to 1 month.)*

Line the dough with a piece of foil or parchment paper large enough to lift out easily; fill evenly with pie weights or dried beans. Bake for 7 minutes. Remove paper and weights and bake for 3 to 5 minutes longer, or just until lightly browned. (The pastry will not be fully baked.) Cool on a rack. Reduce oven temperature to 350 degrees F.

To prepare filling: In a large bowl, whisk eggs and egg whites well. Add milk, evaporated milk, salt, pepper, nutmeg and cayenne, stirring gently to avoid creating many bubbles.

To assemble and bake pie: Spread mustard over the bottom of the prebaked pie crust. Sprinkle with Gruyère, ham and scallions. Carefully pour in the custard mixture. Sprinkle with Parmesan cheese. Bake for 30 to 35 minutes, or until a knife inserted near the center comes out clean. Transfer to a rack and let cool for 10 to 15 minutes before serving hot or warm.

Serves 8.

202 CALORIES PER SERVING: 11 G PROTEIN, 10 G FAT, 16 G CARBOHYDRATE; 330 MG SODIUM; 67 MG CHOLESTEROL.

R_x *Mary Jo Marsh of Antigo, Wisconsin*

Hash Browns Revisited

The secret is the skillet. A heavy nonstick skillet allows the cook to cut as much as 7 teaspoons of fat from traditional hash brown recipes. We used fresh potatoes here, but this is a great way to use last night's leftovers.

3   medium-sized russet potatoes (1 lb. total), peeled and cut into quarters
2   tsp. olive oil
1   small onion, finely chopped

½   tsp. salt or to taste
¼   tsp. freshly ground black pepper or to taste pinch paprika
1   Tbsp. chopped fresh parsley

In a medium-sized saucepan, cover potatoes with cold, lightly salted water. Bring to a boil and boil for 5 to 10 minutes, or until potatoes are just tender. Drain and cool. Cut into ½-inch cubes. (You should have 2 cups of cubed potatoes.)

In a large nonstick skillet, heat olive oil over medium heat. Add onions and sauté until they are limp and translucent, about 5 minutes. Add potatoes and continue to sauté until golden brown, about 10 to 12 minutes. (Lower heat slightly if pan becomes too hot.) Season with salt, pepper and paprika. Stir in parsley and serve immediately.

Serves 4.

115 CALORIES PER SERVING: 2 G PROTEIN, 2 G FAT, 22 G CARBOHYDRATE; 273 MG SODIUM; 0 MG CHOLESTEROL.

Beurre Noisette

Beurre noisette, "nutty butter," is the French cooking term for butter that is heated until it turns light brown. In dishes where the taste of butter is essential, you can get away with using much less if you use *beurre noisette.* You will see this technique used in many recipes throughout the book.

Breakfast Burritos

You can make these hearty fast-food favorites the night before and reheat them in the microwave at medium power the next morning.

4   corn or flour tortillas
1   tsp. vegetable oil, preferably canola oil
½   cup chopped scallions (4-6 scallions)
2   red potatoes, cooked, peeled, if desired, and diced (1½ cups)
1   tomato, seeded and diced
1   4-oz. can chopped green chilies, drained
    salt & freshly ground black pepper to taste

2   large eggs
2   large egg whites
    pinch of cayenne pepper
2   Tbsp. chopped fresh cilantro
½   cup tomato salsa
¼   cup grated low-fat Cheddar or Monterey Jack cheese (1 oz.)

Preheat oven to 325 degrees F. Wrap tortillas in aluminum foil and place in the oven for 5 to 10 minutes to warm. In a large nonstick skillet, heat oil over medium heat. Add ⅓ cup scallions and potatoes and sauté 1 minute. Add tomatoes and chilies and sauté until heated through, about 2 minutes. Season with salt and black pepper.

Push the vegetables away from the center of the skillet. In a small bowl, beat eggs, egg whites and cayenne pepper together with a fork. Pour the egg mixture into the center of the skillet and cook, stirring the egg mixture with a wooden spoon, until some curds have formed but the mixture is still creamy, 1 to 2 minutes. Sprinkle cilantro over and stir the eggs and vegetables together. Taste and adjust seasonings. Divide the egg mixture among the warmed tortillas and roll each one into a log. Top each one with a spoonful of salsa, a little cheese and some of the remaining chopped scallions. Serve immediately.

Serves 4.

234 CALORIES PER SERVING: 12 G PROTEIN, 7 G FAT, 33 G CARBOHYDRATE; 680 MG SODIUM, 112 MG CHOLESTEROL.

Potato & Smoked Fish Frittata

It's especially important to cook this pancake-style omelet slowly and to avoid overcooking, because protein-rich egg white coagulates at a lower temperature than yolks or whole eggs. In plain English, it can turn as tough as leather in seconds, but with a careful hand you'll dazzle the brunch crowd with this recipe.

4   new potatoes, unpeeled, scrubbed
3   large eggs
3   large egg whites
3   Tbsp. skim milk
¼   tsp. salt
¼   tsp. freshly ground black pepper

2   tsp. olive oil
1   onion, thinly sliced
3   scallions, trimmed and sliced
6   oz. smoked fish (sturgeon, trout or whitefish), skin and bones removed, flaked

In a saucepan, cover potatoes with cold, salted water. Cover, bring to a boil and boil 15 to 20 minutes, or until just tender. Drain, cool in cold water, peel and slice.

In a medium-sized bowl, whisk together eggs, egg whites, milk, salt and pepper; set aside.

Heat 1 tsp. oil in a 10-inch nonstick, ovenproof skillet over medium heat. Add onions and scallions and sauté until the onions begin to soften, about 5 to 6 minutes.

Add the potatoes to the skillet, spreading them gently to cover the bottom of the pan. Add remaining 1 tsp. oil. Toss briefly and sauté on medium heat for 3 to 5 minutes, or until they are lightly browned and crisp. Scatter the smoked fish over the potatoes.

Reduce the heat to low. Carefully pour the egg mixture over the potatoes and fish, covering them evenly. Cover the pan and cook until the egg mixture has set around the edges but the center is still fairly liquid, about 6 to 10 minutes. (Adjust the heat if necessary; the mixture should sizzle gently but steadily as the egg cooks.) Meanwhile, preheat the broiler and place the rack so that the top of the skillet will be about 1 inch from the flame.

Place the skillet under the preheated broiler and cook just until the surface is light golden, about 1 to 2 minutes. Watch carefully to prevent overcooking, or the egg mixture will toughen. Cut the frittata into 6 wedges and serve hot or warm, passing the pepper mill at the table.

137 CALORIES PER SERVING: 12 G PROTEIN, 6 G FAT, 9 G CARBOHYDRATE; 185 MG SODIUM; 107 MG CHOLESTEROL.

Cut the Yolks: Omelets and Scrambled Eggs

Each egg yolk adds 5 grams of fat and 213 milligrams of cholesterol to a recipe. Most dishes can take the reduction without affecting flavor or texture, although it is trickier in baking.

For example, to make a **French omelet** for one:

Combine 1 large egg, 1 large egg white and salt and freshly ground black pepper to taste in a small bowl and stir briskly with a fork until blended. Heat a small nonstick skillet over medium-high heat. When hot, remove from the heat, spray with nonstick cooking spray, and return to the heat. Pour in the egg mixture and cook until the bottom layer has set (this will take about 10 seconds). Tilt the pan and use the fork to lift the outer edge of the omelet, allowing the unset egg to flow underneath. Continue until the omelet is almost completely set. If using a filling, place it down the center. Use the fork to fold the sides in to the center, then turn the omelet out onto a plate. Suggested fillings: Diced tomatoes with basil; smoked salmon and reduced-fat sour cream; salsa; sautéed mushrooms with dill.

To make **low-fat scrambled eggs** for one:

Combine 1 large egg, 1 large egg white, 1 Tbsp. skim milk, salt and freshly ground black pepper to taste and chopped fresh herbs, if desired, in a small bowl. Stir briskly with a fork until well blended. Heat a small nonstick skillet over low heat. When hot, remove from the heat, spray with nonstick cooking spray, and return to the heat. Pour in the egg mixture and cook, stirring with a wooden spoon, until the eggs have thickened into soft creamy curds.

Cheese Blintzes

Using low-fat dairy products, cutting down on egg yolks and baking the filled pancakes, rather than frying them, lightens these Jewish favorites considerably.

PANCAKES

¾ cup all-purpose white flour
1 cup skim milk
2 large egg whites
1 large egg
¼ tsp. salt

FILLING

1 lb. low-fat cottage cheese (2 cups) pressed to make 1 cup *(see below)*

1 oz. reduced-fat cream cheese (2 Tbsp.)
1 large egg white
2 Tbsp. sugar
1 tsp. grated lemon zest
½ tsp. pure vanilla extract

TOPPING

½ cup reduced-fat sour cream
¼ cup fruit preserves, applesauce or fresh berries

To make pancakes: In a blender or food processor, combine all ingredients; process until smooth and transfer to a bowl. Spray an 8-inch nonstick skillet with nonstick cooking spray and heat it over medium heat. Pour in 2 Tbsp. of the batter, tilting the pan slowly to cover the bottom. Cook until the underside is golden, about 15 seconds. Slip the pancake onto a plate and set aside. Repeat with the remaining pancake batter, stacking the cooked pancakes.

To make filling and bake blintzes: In the food processor or blender, combine pressed cottage cheese, cream cheese, egg white, sugar, lemon zest and vanilla; blend until smooth.

Preheat oven to 400 degrees F. Spray a 9-by-13-inch baking dish or a baking sheet lightly with nonstick cooking spray. Spoon about 2 Tbsp. filling in the center of each pancake. Fold bottom of pancake up over filling. Fold opposite sides of pancake in toward center. Roll up to completely enclose the filling, forming a cylinder. Place the blintzes seam-side down in the prepared baking dish. *(The blintzes can be prepared ahead to this point and stored, covered, in the refrigerator overnight.)* Bake for 15 to 20 minutes, or until a knife inserted in the center of a blintz feels hot. To serve, top each blintz with sour cream and preserves, applesauce or berries.

Makes about 12 blintzes, serves 4.

302 CALORIES PER SERVING: 24 G PROTEIN, 6 G FAT, 35 G CARBOHYDRATE; 748 MG SODIUM; 70 MG CHOLESTEROL.

Pressed Cottage Cheese

Pressed cottage cheese is sold as farmer cheese or pot cheese; it contains 24 grams of fat per cup. Until a low-fat pot cheese is available, it is best to make your own. At 5 grams of fat per cup, low-fat or nonfat pressed cottage cheese is a practical way to cut back on cream cheese in recipes.

To make pressed cottage cheese: Place the amount of cottage cheese called for in the recipe in a sieve lined with a double thickness of cheesecloth. With a spoon, press well to remove as much moisture as possible (or gather ends of cheesecloth and squeeze out moisture). The volume will reduce to about one half.

New Generation Granola

A little number-crunching reveals that granola's image as a health food is undeserved.
Like most granolas, the recipe submitted by Susan Kirby derived nearly all of its calories from fat.
To transform granola into a truly wholesome food, we shifted the balance
toward fruits and whole grains and shaved the almonds and coconut to a minimum.
Apple-juice concentrate replaces the sweetened condensed milk of the original.

2½ cups rolled oats
1 cup wheat flakes
½ cup toasted wheat germ
¼ cup chopped almonds
¼ cup unsweetened shredded coconut
½ tsp. salt

1 12-oz. can apple-juice concentrate, thawed
¼ cup packed brown sugar (optional)
2 Tbsp. vegetable oil, preferably canola oil
1 cup raisins
½ cup pitted prunes, chopped
½ cup dried apricots, chopped

Preheat oven to 300 degrees F. In a large bowl, combine oats, wheat flakes, wheat germ, almonds, coconut and salt. In a small bowl, stir together apple-juice concentrate, brown sugar (if using) and oil; add to the oat mixture and mix thoroughly. Spread on a baking sheet and bake, stirring occasionally, for 40 to 50 minutes, or until golden brown. Stir in raisins, prunes and apricots. Bake for 5 minutes longer. Cool and store in an airtight container in a cool, dry place for up to 2 weeks.

Makes 8 cups.

202 CALORIES PER ½-CUP SERVING: 6 G PROTEIN, 5 G FAT, 37 G CARBOHYDRATE; 195 MG SODIUM; 1 MG CHOLESTEROL.

R_x *Susan Kirby of Buffalo, New York*

Cantaloupe Smoothie

If on a hurried morning you eat nothing but this smoothie, you will still be doing your body a favor.
The drink is rich in potassium, calcium, vitamin C and beta carotene.

1 ripe banana
¼ ripe cantaloupe
½ cup nonfat or low-fat plain yogurt
2 Tbsp. skim-milk powder

1½ Tbsp. orange-juice concentrate
2 tsp. honey
½ tsp. pure vanilla extract

Place unpeeled banana in the freezer overnight or for up to 3 months. Remove banana from the freezer and let it sit for 2 minutes, or until the skin begins to soften. With a paring knife, remove the skin. (Don't worry if a little fiber remains.) Cut the banana into chunks and put in a blender or food processor. Seed the cantaloupe quarter and cut the flesh from the rind. Cut the flesh into chunks and add to the blender. Add the remaining ingredients and blend until smooth.

Serves 1.

427 CALORIES PER SERVING: 21 G PROTEIN, 1 G FAT, 86 G CARBOHYDRATE; 290 MG SODIUM; 8 MG CHOLESTEROL.

CHAPTER TWO

MUFFINS, QUICK BREADS & BREADS

RECIPES

Blueberry Muffins

A light and healthful version of an old favorite. These muffins have a hearty rather than a cakelike texture. If using frozen blueberries, partially thaw them, then pat them dry with paper towels.

1⅓	cups all-purpose white flour		1	cup skim milk
¾	cup whole-wheat pastry flour		3	Tbsp. vegetable oil, preferably canola oil
6	Tbsp. sugar		1	large egg white
1	Tbsp. baking powder		1	tsp. pure vanilla extract
½	tsp. salt		½	tsp. grated lemon zest
¼	tsp. baking soda		1	cup fresh or partially frozen blueberries

Set rack in the upper third of the oven; preheat oven to 425 degrees F. Spray 12 muffin cups with nonstick cooking spray.

In a large bowl, whisk together flours, sugar, baking powder, salt and baking soda. In a small bowl, whisk together milk, oil, egg white, vanilla and lemon zest.

Gently stir blueberries into the flour mixture until evenly incorporated. Stir the milk mixture into the flour

mixture just until the dry ingredients are moistened; do not overmix. Using a ¼-cup measure or a large spoon, immediately divide batter among 12 muffin cups.

Bake the muffins for 14 to 17 minutes, or until golden and springy to the touch. Let cool on a rack for 5 minutes before serving.

Makes 12 muffins.

151 CALORIES PER MUFFIN: 4 G PROTEIN, 4 G FAT, 25 G CARBOHYDRATE; 214 MG SODIUM; 1 MG CHOLESTEROL.

For Good Measure

If measuring flour correctly seems obvious to you, good for you—and your baking results. You would be surprised how many recipe failures can be traced to using liquid-measuring cups for flour.

Standardized metal or plastic dry measures have a flat lip and come in graduated sizes from ¼ cup to 1 cup. Dry ingredients may settle or become compact from long storage periods, and should be stirred in their containers before being measured. Place the appropriate measuring cup on a piece of wax paper and gently spoon the dry ingredient to overflowing. Using a knife or any flat-edged utensil, level the dry ingredient by scraping off any excess. Some dry ingredients are affected by the amount of moisture in the air: during the cold, dry months, a little less may be needed than when using the same recipe during the hot, humid season.

Apple-Oat Muffins

The hint of cinnamon in these muffins complements the faintly nutty taste of oats and sweet-tart apples.

1⅓ cups rolled oats
1 cup skim milk
⅓ cup packed light brown sugar
¼ cup dark corn syrup
3 Tbsp. vegetable oil, preferably canola oil
1 large egg white
¾ cup all-purpose white flour
½ cup whole-wheat flour

1½ tsp. baking powder
1 tsp. ground cinnamon
½ tsp. baking soda
½ tsp. salt
¼ tsp. ground nutmeg
1¼ cups finely chopped, unpeeled tart apples, such as Winesap or Granny Smith (1 large apple)

Set rack in the upper third of the oven; preheat oven to 425 degrees F. Spray 12 muffin cups with nonstick cooking spray.

In a medium-sized bowl, whisk together oats, milk, sugar, corn syrup, oil and egg white, and let stand for 5 minutes. In a large bowl, whisk together flours, baking powder, cinnamon, baking soda, salt and nutmeg. Stir apples into the flour mixture until evenly distributed.

Stir the milk mixture into the flour mixture just until the dry ingredients are moistened; do not overmix. Using a ¼-cup measure or a large spoon, immediately divide batter among 12 muffin cups. (They will be quite full.)

Bake the muffins for 15 to 20 minutes, or until golden brown and springy to the touch. Let cool on a rack for 5 minutes before serving.

Makes 12 muffins.

168 CALORIES PER MUFFIN: 4 G PROTEIN, 4 G FAT, 24 G CARBOHYDRATE; 188 MG SODIUM; 1 MG CHOLESTEROL.

Zucchini-Oatmeal Muffins

*These are good enough to make you wish you had an abundance of zucchini in the garden in August.
Toasting the rolled oats alongside the pecans enhances the nutty character.*

1½ cups all-purpose white flour
1   cup whole-wheat pastry flour
1½ cups sugar
1   Tbsp. baking powder
1½ tsp. ground cinnamon
1   tsp. salt
½   cup rolled oats, toasted *(see below)*

¼   cup pecan halves, toasted *(see below)* and chopped
2   large eggs
3   large egg whites
½   cup apple butter
¼   cup vegetable oil, preferably canola oil
2   cups grated zucchini (1 medium)

Set rack in the upper third of the oven; preheat oven to 375 degrees F. Spray 16 muffin cups with nonstick cooking spray. In a large bowl, stir together flours, sugar, baking powder, cinnamon, salt, oats and pecans. In a medium-sized bowl, whisk together eggs, egg whites, apple butter and oil. Stir in zucchini. Fold this mixture into the dry ingredients with a rubber spatula just until well combined. Spoon the batter into the prepared muffin cups, filling them about ¾ full. Bake for 20 to 25 minutes, or until the tops are golden and spring back when lightly pressed.

Makes 16 muffins.

233 CALORIES PER MUFFIN: 5 G PROTEIN, 6 G FAT, 42 G CARBOHYDRATE; 215 MG SODIUM; 27 MG CHOLESTEROL.

R_x *Beverly Parker of Austin, Texas*

Toasting Nuts

Nuts are essential to many recipes. They add flavor to baked goods, crunchy texture to toppings, and, alas, fat. Toasting nuts intensifies their flavor so you can use fewer. You can toast them in a small, dry, heavy skillet over medium-high heat on the stove top or on a baking sheet in the oven. Most recipes that call for nuts will be using the oven anyway, so here is the oven method.

Preheat the oven to 350 degrees F. Spread the nuts on a baking sheet and bake, stirring occasionally, for 5 to 15 minutes (depending on the size of the nuts), or until lightly toasted. Let cool.

Blueberry Muffins, page 30

New Generation Granola, page 27

Nectarine-Raspberry Coffee Cake, page 49

Cinnamon Rolls, page 47

Rum-Raisin Spice Muffins

These moist, tender muffins are best when made with rum,
but sweet apple juice is an appropriate substitute.

1 cup raisins	1 cup all-purpose white flour
3 Tbsp. rum or apple juice	⅔ cup whole-wheat pastry flour
1 cup skim-milk buttermilk	⅓ cup plus 1 tsp. sugar
⅓ cup wheat bran	1¼ tsp. baking powder
3 Tbsp. vegetable oil, preferably canola oil	1⅛ tsp. ground cinnamon
1 large egg white	¾ tsp. baking soda
1½ tsp. pure vanilla extract	¼ tsp. salt

Set rack in the upper third of the oven; preheat oven to 425 degrees F. Spray 12 muffin cups with nonstick cooking spray.

In a small bowl, combine raisins and rum or apple juice and let stand for 10 minutes. In a medium-sized bowl, whisk together buttermilk, bran, oil, egg white and vanilla. In a large bowl, whisk together flours, ⅓ cup sugar, baking powder, 1 tsp. cinnamon, baking soda and salt.

Stir raisins and rum or apple juice into the buttermilk mixture. Stir the buttermilk mixture into the flour mixture just until the dry ingredients are moistened; do not overmix. Using a ¼-cup measure or a large spoon, immediately divide batter among 12 muffin cups. (They will be nearly full.) Combine 1 tsp. sugar and ⅛ tsp. cinnamon in a small bowl and lightly sprinkle over muffin tops.

Bake the muffins for 12 to 16 minutes, or until golden brown and springy to the touch. Cool on a rack for 5 minutes before serving.

Makes 12 muffins.

166 CALORIES PER MUFFIN: 4 G PROTEIN, 4 G FAT, 30 G CARBOHYDRATE; 159 MG SODIUM; 1 MG CHOLESTEROL.

Storing Low-Fat Muffins

Low-fat baked goods go stale quickly. Muffins are best fresh but may be wrapped in plastic and frozen for up to a month. To reheat, wrap frozen muffins in foil and bake in a 375 degree F oven for 30 minutes, or until heated through.

Flour Power

There is a great deal of controversy surrounding the merits of bleached and unbleached flour. The debate has little to do with the nutrition profiles of either. Flour boasting an "unbleached" label may conjure a superior nutritional image, but both bleached and unbleached flour are refined flours made from the starchy part of the wheat kernel after it is stripped of its fiber- and nutrient-rich components.

The color of flour has no practical or nutritional significance; white flour is bleached simply to appeal to consumers who desire whiter baked products. Bleaching removes the light yellow color in flour caused by the same carotenoid pigments that are found in potatoes and onions. Although the flour loses the yellow tinge naturally over time, most flour producers use chlorine dioxide, a suspected carcinogen, to speed the bleaching process up. The chemical residue that remains in the finished product falls well below the limits set by the FDA. Opponents of chemical bleaching claim that it is unnecessary and imparts a slightly medicinal taste to food. Unless home cooks desire the whitest possible baked goods, unbleached flour is an appropriate, less-processed option.

An even better option, when recipes will allow it, is whole-wheat flour. Using whole-wheat flour as a partial substitute for white flour is an option in many quick bread, muffin and cookie recipes, although a better alternative often lies in whole-wheat pastry flour. Standard wholewheat flour is high in gluten, the protein that traps the gas bubbles formed by yeast in bread dough and gives the dough its elasticity, causing it to rise. Whole-wheat pastry flour, milled from softer wheat, contains little gluten and consequently lends a more tender, pastrylike texture to baked goods.

Enlightened Banana-Breakfast Muffins

Two breakfast standards, bananas and bran, team up in these tasty muffins. Overripe bananas can be frozen and used for baking. Thaw them just long enough to easily peel and mash.

1	cup skim-milk buttermilk	⅔	cup wheat bran
¾	cup mashed overripe bananas (about 2)	1	cup all-purpose white flour
½	cup packed brown sugar	1	cup whole-wheat pastry flour
3	Tbsp. vegetable oil, preferably canola oil	1	tsp. baking powder
1	large egg white	1	tsp. baking soda
1¼	tsp. pure vanilla extract	½	tsp. salt

Set rack in the upper third of the oven; preheat oven to 425 degrees F. Spray 12 muffin cups with nonstick cooking spray.

In a blender or food processor, combine buttermilk, bananas, brown sugar, oil, egg white and vanilla. Process for about 30 seconds, or until completely smooth. Transfer to a medium-sized bowl and stir in wheat bran until well incorporated.

In a large bowl, whisk together flours, baking powder, baking soda and salt. Stir the banana mixture into the flour mixture just until the dry ingredients are moistened; do not overmix. Using a ¼-cup measure or large spoon, immediately divide batter among 12 muffin cups. (They will be about ¾ full.)

Bake the muffins for 14 to 17 minutes, or until golden brown and springy to the touch. Let cool on a rack for 5 minutes before serving.

Makes 12 muffins.

174 CALORIES PER MUFFIN: 4 G PROTEIN, 4 G FAT, 31 G CARBOHYDRATE; 215 MG SODIUM; 1 MG CHOLESTEROL.

Morning Glory Bran Muffins

Thick, sweet apple butter is rich in pectin and other soluble fibers, making it a suitable replacement for much of the fat in these wholesome muffins. Use dried fruits of your choice.

¾ cup wheat bran	1 cup skim-milk buttermilk
¾ cup all-purpose white flour	⅓ cup molasses
½ cup whole-wheat flour	⅓ cup apple butter
1½ tsp. baking powder	1 large egg white
½ tsp. baking soda	3 Tbsp. vegetable oil, preferably canola oil
¼ tsp. salt	1 Tbsp. fresh lemon juice
½ cup golden raisins	1½ tsp. grated lemon zest
½ cup chopped dates	1 tsp. pure vanilla extract
½ cup chopped dried apricots	

Set rack in upper third of the oven; preheat to 425 degrees F. Coat 12 muffin cups with nonstick cooking spray. In a large bowl, stir together bran, flours, baking powder, baking soda and salt. Stir in raisins, dates and dried apricots. In a medium-sized bowl, whisk together buttermilk, molasses, apple butter, egg white, oil, lemon juice, lemon zest and vanilla. Stir into the flour mixture just until the dry ingredients are moistened; do not overmix. Divide the batter among the prepared muffin cups. (They will be nearly full.) Bake for 15 to 20 minutes, or until a cake tester inserted in the center comes out clean. Turn the muffins out onto a rack and let cool for 5 minutes before serving.

Make 12 muffins.

182 CALORIES PER MUFFIN: 4 G PROTEIN, 4 G FAT, 36 G CARBOHYDRATE; 145 MG SODIUM; 1 MG CHOLESTEROL.

Proper Scottish Oat Scones

What alchemy gives scones their crumbly, buttery texture?
And what wizardry it took to maintain that texture, after a little more than half the fat was cut from
the original recipe. These are nutritionally superior to their forebears and offer 81 fewer calories.

2   Tbsp. butter
1¼ cup rolled oats
¾   cup all-purpose white flour
¾   cup whole-wheat pastry flour
¼   cup sugar
1   Tbsp. baking powder

½   tsp. baking soda
½   tsp. salt
½   cup raisins
1   large egg, lightly beaten
½   cup nonfat plain yogurt
2   Tbsp. vegetable oil, preferably canola oil

Preheat oven to 425 degrees F. Spray a baking sheet with nonstick cooking spray or line it with parchment paper. Melt butter in a small saucepan over low heat and cook until it begins to turn light brown, about 2 minutes. Skim foam and pour into a small bowl.

In a large bowl, stir together oats, flours, sugar, baking powder, baking soda and salt. Stir in raisins and make a well in the center of the dry ingredients. In a small bowl, combine the browned butter, egg, yogurt and oil; add to the dry ingredients, stirring just until moistened.

Turn out onto a lightly floured surface and gently knead several times to form a ball. Pat the ball into an 8-inch circle and cut into 8 wedges.

Place the wedges on the prepared baking sheet and bake for about 12 minutes, or until lightly browned and firm to the touch. Transfer to a rack and let cool slightly. Serve warm.

Serves 8.

254 CALORIES PER SERVING: 7 G PROTEIN, 7 G FAT, 40 G CARBOHYDRATE; 412 MG SODIUM; 35 MG CHOLESTEROL.

R$_x$ *Edna McNamara of Bedminster, New Jersey*

Light & Fluffy Biscuits

A combination of all-purpose flour and cake flour produces a light, tender low-fat biscuit.
Serve with meals or for breakfast or tea with fruit preserves.

1   cup all-purpose white flour
1   cup sifted cake flour
1   Tbsp. baking powder
½   tsp. baking soda
¼   tsp. salt

3   Tbsp. reduced-fat cream cheese
2   Tbsp. cold butter, cut into small pieces
¾   cup skim-milk buttermilk
1   Tbsp. skim milk

Preheat oven to 400 degrees F. Line a baking sheet with parchment paper or coat lightly with nonstick cooking spray.

In a mixing bowl, stir together flours, baking powder, baking soda and salt. Using a pastry blender or two table knives, cut in cream cheese and butter until pea-sized lumps form. Stir in buttermilk with a fork. Gather the dough into a ball and knead it several times in the bowl until smooth.

Turn the dough onto a lightly floured surface. Pat into a smooth, ½-inch-thick disk. With a 3-inch cutter, cut out rounds. Repeat with dough scraps until you have 10 biscuits. Brush tops with skim milk. Place on the baking sheet and bake for 15 to 20 minutes, or until golden.

Makes 10 biscuits.

122 CALORIES PER BISCUIT: 3 G PROTEIN, 3 G FAT, 20 G CARBOHYDRATE; 250 MG SODIUM; 8 MG CHOLESTEROL.

Pumpkin Popovers

Preheating the muffin pan before baking makes these rich-tasting popovers rise to dramatic heights.

¼   cup canned pumpkin puree
3   large eggs
3   large egg whites
2   cups skim milk
2   Tbsp. vegetable oil, preferably canola oil

2   cups all-purpose white flour
½   tsp. salt
¼   tsp. pumpkin-pie spice
⅛   tsp. cayenne

Place a 12-cup muffin pan on a baking sheet in the oven; preheat oven to 400 degrees F. In a bowl, whisk together pumpkin puree, eggs, egg whites, milk and vegetable oil until smooth. In a large bowl, combine flour, salt, pie spice and cayenne. Add the pumpkin mixture to the dry ingredients and whisk until smooth.

Remove the muffin pan from the oven and coat it with nonstick cooking spray. Divide the batter among the prepared cups. Bake the popovers until they are puffed and browned, about 25 minutes. Do not open the oven door while baking, or the popovers will collapse. Remove the popovers from the oven and reduce the oven temperature to 350 degrees. With a small knife cut small slits into the sides of the popovers, about 3 or 4 per popover. Bake an additional 7 to 10 minutes. Serve hot. *(The popovers can be baked earlier in the day and reheated at 325 degrees for 7 minutes.)*

Makes 12 popovers.

135 CALORIES PER POPOVER: 6 G PROTEIN, 4 G FAT, 19 G CARBOHYDRATE; 140 MG SODIUM; 54 MG CHOLESTEROL.

Pumpkin-Wheat Bread

"Delicious with festive meals," wrote Ellen Davis when she asked us to make this bread healthful. Baked goods using pumpkin are excellent candidates for revision because pumpkin contributes an especially moist texture. After increasing the amount of the original recipe's pumpkin, reducing the number of eggs and substituting oil for butter, we struggled to bring out the flavor. Finally, we replaced white sugar with brown and were rewarded by a delicious bread with half the fat of the original.

2½ cups all-purpose white flour
2 cups whole-wheat flour
1 Tbsp. baking powder
2 tsp. baking soda
2 tsp. salt

2 large eggs
2 large egg whites
2 cups packed brown sugar
3 cups canned pumpkin puree
½ cup vegetable oil, preferably canola oil

Preheat oven to 350 degrees F. Spray two 9-by-5-inch loaf pans with nonstick cooking spray. In a large bowl, stir together flours, baking powder, baking soda and salt. In a separate bowl, whisk together eggs, egg whites, brown sugar, pumpkin and oil. Add the pumpkin mixture to the dry ingredients and mix until just combined. Turn the batter into the prepared pans and smooth the tops. Bake for 50 to 60 minutes, or until the tops are golden brown and a cake tester inserted in the center comes out clean. Let cool for 10 minutes in the pans on racks. Turn the loaves out onto the racks to cool completely.

Makes 2 loaves, 12 slices each.

204 CALORIES PER SLICE: 4 G PROTEIN, 5 G FAT, 37 G CARBOHYDRATE; 306 MG SODIUM; 18 MG CHOLESTEROL.

R_x *Ellen W. Davis of California, Maryland*

Going With the Grain

EATING WELL Magazine and RECIPE RESCUE COOKBOOK readers won't find many yeast-bread recipes among our pages. The reason is simple: most bread recipes are already low in fat and not in need of repair. In fact, breads and other grain-based foods should make up the bulk of our diets.

Americans harbor a deep-rooted suspicion of starchy foods, however. Whenever the topic of weight control comes up, someone invariably claims the problem is one of eating too much bread; diners, trying to avoid temptation, commonly ask waiters to hold the bread; and some people still follow bizarre low-carbohydrate diets that forbid bread. Even now, with all the indicators pointing to high-carbohydrate diets as the route to optimum health, bread is still regarded as fattening, an unnecessary filler—it is often the first food to be banished.

In reality, research has shown that when given 8 to 12 slices of bread a day and a free choice of other foods, overweight college students lost an average of 14 pounds in one study and 19 pounds in a similar study. The generous bread allowance allowed the volunteers to lose weight because it displaced fattier, higher calorie foods. And high-fiber breads were shown to be even more effective for weight loss because they are more filling.

Now health experts, backed by overwhelming research evidence, say the more carbohydrates in the diet the better. For weight control, heart health, lower cancer risk and overall nutritional balance, Americans are advised to eat 6 to 11 servings of breads, cereals and grains each day.

Quick Corn Bread

Pleasant with soup or chili, this simple corn bread is sweet enough to serve for dessert.

1⅓ cups skim milk
1 cup cornmeal
3 Tbsp. vegetable oil, preferably canola oil
1 large egg white
1 cup all-purpose white flour

3 Tbsp. sugar
1 Tbsp. baking powder
½ tsp. salt
¼ tsp. baking soda

Preheat oven to 400 degrees F. Spray an 8-inch square baking pan with nonstick cooking spray.

In a small bowl, whisk together milk, cornmeal, oil and egg white. In a medium-sized bowl, whisk together flour, sugar, baking powder, salt and baking soda. Stir the cornmeal mixture into the flour mixture just until the dry ingredients are moistened; do not overmix. Immediately pour batter into pan, spreading to edges.

Bake for 20 to 25 minutes, or until golden and springy to the touch. Cool on a wire rack for 5 minutes before serving.

Serves 9.

167 CALORIES PER SLICE: 4 G PROTEIN, 5 G FAT, 26 G CARBOHYDRATE; 289 MG SODIUM; 1 MG CHOLESTEROL.

Blueberry-Cornmeal Loaf

*A buttery, dense loaf with a lemony flavor and a slightly crunchy texture
is all the better with wild Maine blueberries, but any kind will do.*

⅔ cup fresh or frozen (not thawed) blueberries
1½ cups all-purpose white flour
⅓ cup cornmeal
1½ tsp. baking powder
½ tsp. salt
½ cup plus 1 Tbsp. nonfat plain yogurt
1 Tbsp. fresh lemon juice

1 large egg
1 large egg white
⅔ cup plus 2 tsp. sugar
¼ cup vegetable oil, preferably canola oil
1 tsp. grated lemon zest
¼ tsp. ground cinnamon

Preheat oven to 350 degrees F. Spray an 8-by-4-inch loaf pan with nonstick cooking spray. Toss blueberries with 1 Tbsp. of the flour and set aside.

In a small bowl, stir together the remaining flour, cornmeal, baking powder and salt. In another small bowl, combine yogurt and lemon juice.

In a mixing bowl, whisk together egg, egg white, ⅔ cup sugar, oil and lemon zest. Alternately add the dry ingredients and the yogurt mixture to the egg mixture, beginning and ending with the dry ingredients. Mix until just combined. Gently fold in blueberries. Spoon batter into the prepared pan. In a small bowl, combine the remaining 2 tsp. sugar and cinnamon and sprinkle over the batter.

Bake for 25 minutes uncovered, then loosely cover the pan with aluminum foil and bake for another 25 to 30 minutes.

Cool the cake in the pan on a rack for 10 minutes, then turn out onto rack and cool completely. (For best flavor, wrap the cake and store overnight before serving.)

Makes 1 loaf; 10 slices.

205 CALORIES PER SLICE: 4 G PROTEIN, 6 G FAT, 34 G CARBOHYDRATE; 180 MG SODIUM; 22 MG CHOLESTEROL.

Banana Bread

Coffee is a surprise ingredient here, lending a rich flavor. Banana bread is the perfect vehicle for using bananas once they are past their prime. This recipe shows it need not be oily to be rich.

⅔ cup packed brown sugar
⅓ cup hot, strong brewed coffee
1½ cups mashed overripe bananas (about 4)
1 large egg
1 large egg white
3 Tbsp. vegetable oil, preferably canola oil
1 tsp. pure vanilla extract

1 cup all-purpose white flour
1 cup whole-wheat flour
1½ tsp. baking powder
1 tsp. ground cinnamon
1 tsp. ground ginger
½ tsp. salt
¼ tsp. baking soda

Preheat oven to 350 degrees F. Spray a 9-by-5-inch loaf pan with nonstick cooking spray.

In a medium-sized bowl, dissolve brown sugar in coffee. Stir in bananas. In a large bowl, whisk together egg, egg white, oil and vanilla. Add the banana mixture. In a separate bowl, whisk together flours, baking powder, cinnamon, ginger, salt and baking soda. Add to the ba-

nana mixture and stir just until combined.

Pour into the prepared pan and bake for 40 to 50 minutes, or until a toothpick inserted into the center comes out clean. Let cool in the pan on a rack for 10 minutes. Invert the loaf onto a rack and let cool completely.

Makes 1 loaf; 12 slices.

163 CALORIES PER SLICE: 4 G PROTEIN, 4 G FAT, 37 G CARBOHYDRATE; 163 MG SODIUM; 18 MG CHOLESTEROL.

Apricot-Orange Loaf

*This easy quick bread tastes wonderful toasted
and maintains its tang when reheated. For best results, use moist plump apricots.*

1   cup skim-milk buttermilk
1   cup diced dried apricots
¾   cup packed light brown sugar
2   large egg whites
3   Tbsp. vegetable oil, preferably canola oil
1¼   tsp. pure vanilla extract
1   tsp. grated orange zest

¼   tsp. pure almond extract
1½   cups all-purpose white flour
1   cup whole-wheat pastry flour
1½   tsp. baking powder
1   tsp. baking soda
½   tsp. salt

Preheat oven to 350 degrees F. Spray a 9-by-5-inch loaf pan with nonstick cooking spray.

In a medium-sized bowl, stir together buttermilk, apricots, brown sugar, egg whites, oil, vanilla, orange zest and almond extract. Let stand for 5 minutes.

In a large bowl, whisk together flours, baking powder, baking soda and salt. Stir the apricot mixture into the flour mixture just until the dry ingredients are moistened; do not overmix. Immediately turn out mixture into prepared pan, spreading to edges and smoothing top.

Bake for 45 to 55 minutes, or until the top is well browned and a cake tester inserted in the center comes out clean. (If loaf top begins to brown too rapidly, reduce heat to 325 degrees F for the last 15 minutes of baking.) Let cool on a rack for about 20 minutes in the pan. Turn the loaf out onto the rack to cool completely.

Makes 1 large loaf; 16 slices.

160 CALORIES PER SLICE: 4 G PROTEIN, 3 G FAT, 30 G CARBOHYDRATE; 177 MG SODIUM; 1 MG CHOLESTEROL.

Cinnamon Rolls

Donna Meinecke dared us to take the fat from her delicious cinnamon rolls and still retain the buttery goodness. We slimmed down the yeast dough with pressed nonfat cottage cheese, fewer egg yolks and skim milk. But it is the rich, sticky sweetness oozing from cinnamon rolls that makes them truly memorable. We managed to eliminate the butter from the filling and slash 13 grams of fat from each roll, yet retain the gooey lusciousness.

DOUGH

3½-4 cups all-purpose white flour
1 cup whole-wheat flour
1 pkg. active dry yeast (1 Tbsp.)
½ cup nonfat cottage cheese, pressed *(page 26)*
1 cup plus 1 Tbsp. skim milk
⅓ cup sugar
2 Tbsp. vegetable oil, preferably canola oil
½ tsp. salt
2 large eggs, lightly beaten
1 large egg white

FILLING

½ cup packed light brown sugar
¼ cup dark corn syrup
1 Tbsp. ground cinnamon
½ cup golden raisins
¼ cup toasted pecans *(page 32)*, chopped

GLAZE

1¼ cups confectioners' sugar
1-2 Tbsp. skim milk
1 tsp. corn syrup
½ tsp. pure vanilla extract

To make dough: In a large mixing bowl, combine 1½ cups white flour, whole-wheat flour and yeast. Puree the pressed cottage cheese by pressing it through a sieve into a small saucepan. In the saucepan combine pressed cottage cheese, 1 cup milk, sugar, oil and salt; heat, stirring, until warm (120-130 degrees F). Stir into the flour mixture. Add eggs and egg white; beat with an electric mixer on low speed for 30 seconds, scraping the sides of the bowl. Beat on high speed for 3 minutes. Using a wooden spoon (or dough hook of mixer), stir in 2 cups white flour. Turn the dough onto a lightly floured surface and knead for about 5 minutes, adding enough of the remaining flour to make a soft, smooth dough. (It will be slightly sticky.) Place the dough in a lightly oiled bowl and turn once. Cover with plastic wrap and let rise in a warm place until doubled in bulk, about 1 hour.

To make filling and bake rolls: Spray a 9-by-13-inch baking dish with nonstick cooking spray. In a small saucepan, combine brown sugar, corn syrup and cinnamon; heat gently, stirring, until smooth. Set aside to cool.

Punch dough down. Turn out onto a lightly floured surface. Cover and let rest for 10 minutes. Roll or pat into a 12-by-18-inch rectangle.

Spread the brown sugar mixture over the dough. Sprinkle with raisins and pecans. Starting at the long edge, roll up jelly-roll fashion. Pinch the edges of dough together along the length of the roll. With a sharp knife, slice the roll into 12 pieces. Place the cinnamon rolls, cut-side up and slightly apart, in the dish. Cover with plastic wrap and let rise in a warm place until nearly doubled, about 45 minutes. *(Alternatively, refrigerate for 2 to 24 hours, then let stand in a warm place for 30 minutes.)*

Meanwhile, preheat oven to 375 degrees F. Brush rolls with 1 Tbsp. milk. Bake for 25 to 30 minutes, or until light brown. Transfer to a rack and let cool slightly in the pan.

To make glaze: In a small bowl, stir together confectioners' sugar, 1 Tbsp. milk, corn syrup and vanilla. Add more milk, if necessary, to make a drizzling consistency. Drizzle the glaze over the rolls and serve them warm.

Makes 12 rolls.

367 CALORIES PER ROLL: 9 G PROTEIN, 5 G FAT, 73 G CARBOHYDRATE; 127 MG SODIUM; 36 MG CHOLESTEROL.

R$_x$ Donna T. Meinecke of Denton, Texas

Stollen

EATING WELL Magazine subscriber Debbie Boyken wanted to do her grandmother's traditional German Christmas bread justice when she asked for our help. With half the fat of the original, our updated version should keep future generations happy and healthy.

2   cups skim milk
3   envelopes active dry yeast (3 Tbsp.)
2   cups whole-wheat flour
2   cups nonfat cottage cheese, pressed
     (page 26)
⅔   cup sugar
2   large eggs, beaten lightly with a fork
3   egg whites, beaten lightly with a fork
¼   cup plus 1 Tbsp. vegetable oil, preferably
     canola oil

1   Tbsp. grated lemon zest
1   tsp. salt
     approximately 7 cups all-purpose white
     flour
1   cup raisins
1   cup dried currants
1   cup chopped candied orange, lemon and/or
     citron peel
¼   cup toasted blanched almonds *(page 32)*,
     chopped

Heat milk until steaming; pour into a large mixing bowl and let cool to lukewarm. Sprinkle in yeast and let stand for 5 to 10 minutes, or until dissolved. Whisk in 1 cup whole-wheat flour, cover with plastic and set aside in a warm, draft-free place for ½ hour, or until foamy.

Puree the pressed cottage cheese in a food processor. Stir cottage cheese, sugar, eggs, egg whites, ¼ cup oil, lemon zest and salt into the yeast mixture. With a wooden spoon, gradually beat in the remaining 1 cup whole-wheat flour and enough of the white flour to make a soft, sticky dough. Turn out onto a lightly floured board, sprinkle raisins, currants, candied peel and almonds over it and knead for about 10 minutes, or until the fruits and nuts are evenly distributed and the dough is smooth and elastic, adding just enough additional white flour to prevent the dough from sticking. Place the dough in a lightly oiled bowl and turn to coat it with oil. Cover with plastic and let rise for 1 to 2 hours, or until doubled in bulk.

Punch the dough down and knead for about 1 minute on a lightly floured board. Divide it into 4 portions. Roll each portion into an 8½-by-10-inch oval. With the side of your hand, crease the dough down its length just off center. Fold the smaller side over the larger and place the loaves at least 4 inches apart on two large, lightly oiled baking sheets. Brush the remaining 1 Tbsp. of oil over the top of the loaves. Cover with plastic and let rise in a warm, draft-free place for about 45 minutes, or until almost doubled.

Preheat oven to 350 degrees F. Bake the loaves, one sheet at a time, for 30 to 35 minutes, or until tops are golden brown and the bottoms sound hollow when tapped. *(The stollen can be prepared up to 1 month ahead and stored, well wrapped, in the freezer. To reheat, wrap frozen loaves loosely in foil and heat at 300 degrees F for 30 to 40 minutes.)*

Makes 4 loaves, 8 slices each.

224 CALORIES PER SLICE: 8 G PROTEIN, 4 G FAT, 41 G CARBOHYDRATE; 151 MG SODIUM; 14 MG CHOLESTEROL.

R̽ *Debbie Boyken of Denville, New Jersey*

Nectarine-Raspberry Coffee Cake

Cereal supplements the nuts in the crunchy fruit topping on this moist buttermilk-based cake.
The flavors can't be beat when the fruit is in season.

CAKE

1½ cups all-purpose white flour
½ cup whole-wheat pastry flour
¾ cup sugar
4 tsp. baking powder
1 tsp. ground cinnamon
½ tsp. salt
1 large egg
1 cup skim-milk buttermilk
3 Tbsp. vegetable oil, preferably canola oil
1 tsp. pure vanilla extract

FRUIT TOPPING

2 nectarines, cut into ⅛-inch thick slices (1 cup)
½ cup fresh raspberries or frozen unsweetened raspberries
¼ cup Grape-Nuts cereal
3 Tbsp. sugar
2 Tbsp. chopped pecans
¼ tsp. cinnamon

To make cake: Preheat oven to 400 degrees F. Coat the inside of a 9-inch springform pan with nonstick cooking spray.

In a medium-sized bowl, stir together flours, sugar, baking powder, cinnamon and salt. In a large bowl, whisk together egg, buttermilk, oil and vanilla. Add the flour mixture to the egg mixture and stir the batter just to blend. Turn the batter into the prepared pan.

To prepare topping: Arrange nectarines and raspberries over the batter. In a small bowl, stir together Grape-Nuts, sugar, pecans and cinnamon; sprinkle over the fruit. Bake for 40 to 45 minutes, or until the top is golden and a cake tester inserted in the center comes out clean. Let cool in the pan on a rack for 10 minutes. Loosen edges and remove from pan. Serve warm.

Serves 10.

248 CALORIES PER SERVING: 5 G PROTEIN, 6 G FAT, 45 G CARBOHYDRATE; 278 MG SODIUM; 22 MG CHOLESTEROL.

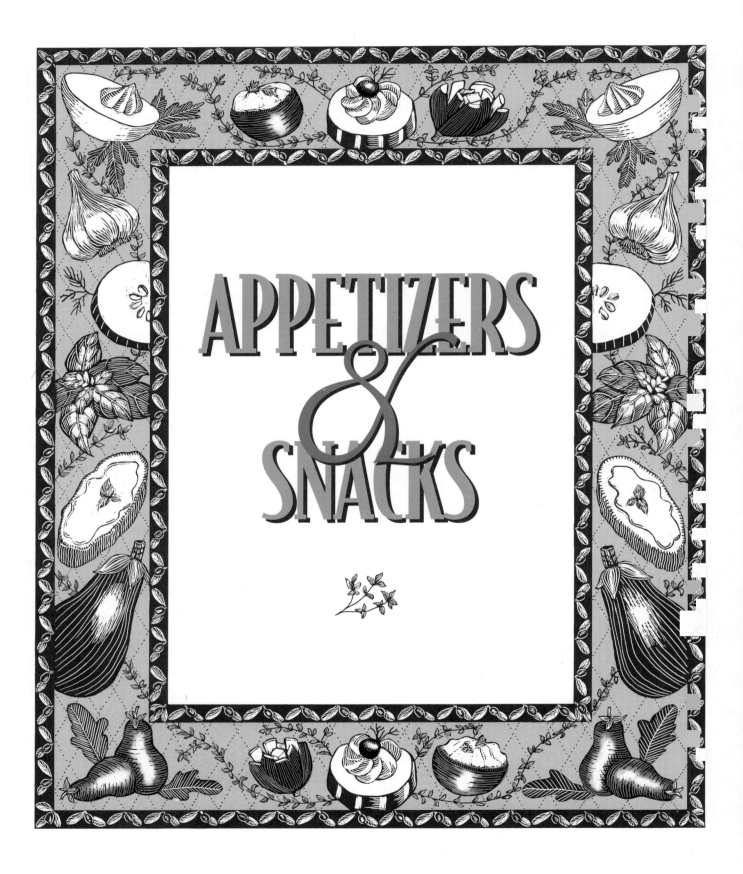

APPETIZERS & SNACKS

RECIPES

Hot Crab Dip

Crab-loving Maryland resident Ora Williamson submitted her recipe for Hot Crab Dip, and it was simplicity itself — eight ingredients stirred together and heated. But with 7 grams of fat in every tablespoon, it cried for serious fat reduction. Our version, with only 1 gram of fat per tablespoon, lets the unmistakable crab flavor step forward while surprising the palate with a little zing of cayenne and lemon.

½   cup nonfat cottage cheese, pressed
(page 26)
4   oz. reduced-fat cream cheese
2   small cloves garlic, minced
¼   tsp. Worcestershire sauce
¼   tsp. Old Bay seasoning

¼   tsp. cayenne pepper
¼   tsp. freshly ground black pepper
½   lb. fresh or frozen and thawed crabmeat, well drained and patted dry
1   Tbsp. fresh lemon juice

Place pressed cottage cheese and cream cheese in a food processor or blender and blend until smooth. Transfer to a medium-sized saucepan and add garlic, Worcestershire sauce, Old Bay seasoning, cayenne and black pepper. Heat over low heat for 2 to 3 minutes, stirring frequently until warm. Add crab and lemon juice; stir well. Heat for 30 to 40 seconds until warm. Remove from heat and serve immediately with French bread.

Makes about 1½ cups.

22 CALORIES PER TABLESPOON: 3 G PROTEIN, 1 G FAT, 1 G CARBOHYDRATE; 29 MG SODIUM; 7 MG CHOLESTEROL.

R_x *Ora Williamson of Silver Spring, Maryland*

The Nutritional Benefits of "Grazing"

There's nothing sacred about three meals a day. In fact, research suggests that we may be better off grazing throughout the day instead of taking in all of our calories and nutrients at mealtimes. People who eat smaller, more frequent meals have lower blood-cholesterol levels and healthier distributions of body fat than people who confine their eating to three or fewer meals a day.

Eating small amounts of food more often allows the body to process nutrients smoothly and efficiently. Presenting the body with a third or more of its daily calories at one time can tax systems and result in higher levels of fats and sugars circulating in the blood.

Serving a variety of low-fat appetizers during a leisurely gathering can be a healthful (and relaxing) alternative to a large sit-down meal. Begin by borrowing finger-food ideas from other cuisines—Sicilian Caponata, Middle Eastern Hummus with Pita Crisps and Greek Spinach-Feta Rolls. Add a large platter of crudités and bite-sized chunks of crusty bread for a nourishing afternoon meal.

Plum Tomato Tart

The tangy mustard is a pleasing accent to the sweet tomatoes in this easy-to-prepare appetizer.

1   large egg white
3   Tbsp. olive oil
6   sheets phyllo dough (14x18 inches)
5   tsp. fine dry breadcrumbs
⅓   cup Dijon mustard
¼   cup freshly grated Parmesan cheese

1   lb. plum tomatoes (about 8), cored and sliced
    ¼ inch thick
2   Tbsp. chopped fresh parsley
2   cloves garlic, finely chopped
1   tsp. chopped fresh thyme or ½ tsp. dried

Set oven rack on the upper level; preheat to 400 degrees F. Lightly coat a baking sheet with nonstick cooking spray or line with parchment paper. In a small bowl, whisk together the egg white and 2 Tbsp. olive oil.

Lay a sheet of phyllo on the prepared baking sheet. Keep remaining phyllo sheets covered with plastic wrap or wax paper. With a pastry brush, lightly coat the surface with the egg-white mixture. Sprinkle with 1 tsp. breadcrumbs. Repeat this step, layering 4 more sheets of phyllo on top. Lay the sixth sheet of phyllo on top and brush with the egg-white mixture. To form an edge to the tart, carefully roll over the edges toward the center, using the blade of a knife to help you get started.

With a rubber spatula, spread mustard over the sur-

face of the dough and sprinkle with cheese. *(The tart can be prepared ahead to this point. Wrap and freeze for up to 2 months. Do not thaw before continuing.)* Arrange tomato slices on top in 5 rows of 8 slices each. Bake for 15 to 20 minutes, or until the pastry is golden brown. Let cool in the pan for 5 minutes. In a small bowl, combine the remaining 1 Tbsp. olive oil, parsley, garlic and thyme. With your fingers or a fork, dab some of the herb mixture onto each tomato slice. Slide the tart onto a serving platter or, if you wish to serve bite-sized appetizers, slide it onto a cutting board and with a sharp knife or pizza cutter, cut the tart into squares between the tomato slices. Serve warm or at room temperature.

Makes 40 appetizers.

32 CALORIES PER PIECE: 1 G PROTEIN, 1 G FAT, 4 G CARBOHYDRATE; 40 MG SODIUM; 1 MG CHOLESTEROL.

Smoked Trout & Cucumber Tartlets

The rich, creamy filling contrasts with the pleasant crunch of the tartlet shell.
You can substitute smoked salmon for trout.

PHYLLO TARTLET SHELLS

- 1 large egg white
- 2 Tbsp. olive oil
- ¼ tsp. salt
- 8 sheets phyllo dough (14x18 inches)

SMOKED TROUT FILLING

- 1 cup nonfat cottage cheese, pressed *(page 26)*
- 1 8-oz. pkg. reduced-fat cream cheese
- ½ lb. smoked trout fillets (2 fillets), skin and pin bones removed
- ⅓ cup chopped scallions (2 scallions)
- 4 tsp. well-drained prepared horseradish
- 1 cup shredded cucumber

To make phyllo tartlet shells: Preheat oven to 325 degrees F. Lightly coat 2 mini-muffin pans with nonstick cooking spray. In a small bowl, whisk together egg white, oil and salt.

Lay a sheet of phyllo on a work surface. Keep remaining phyllo sheets covered with plastic wrap or wax paper. With a pastry brush, lightly coat it with the egg-white mixture. Lay a second sheet smoothly on top, taking care to line up the edges before setting the sheet down. (Once you set down the sheet, it cannot be moved.) Brush with the egg-white mixture and repeat with 1 more sheet. Lay a fourth sheet on top but do not brush it.

With a knife, cut the dough into 4 strips lengthwise and 6 strips crosswise, making 24 squares. Press squares into muffin cups and bake for 8 to 12 minutes, or until golden brown and crisp. Transfer the tartlets to a rack and let cool. Repeat the procedure with the remaining 4 sheets of phyllo and egg-white mixture. *(The baked tartlet shells may be stored in a closed container at room temperature for 1 week or in the freezer for up to 2 months.)*

To make smoked trout filling: In a food processor, combine pressed cottage cheese, cream cheese and smoked trout; process until fairly smooth. Add scallions and horseradish and pulse until just combined. *(The smoked trout filling may be made ahead and refrigerated for up to 2 days.)* Shortly before serving, spoon or pipe about 1 heaping tsp. of filling into each tartlet shell and garnish with shredded cucumber.

Makes 4 dozen appetizers.

37 CALORIES PER PIECE: 2 G PROTEIN, 2 G FAT, 4 G CARBOHYDRATE; 62 MG SODIUM; 4 MG CHOLESTEROL.

Smoked Salmon Spread

If plain vodka is substituted for the pepper-flavored vodka, season generously with cracked pepper.

- ½ lb. smoked salmon
- 1 cup nonfat cottage cheese, pressed *(page 26)*
- 1 8-oz. pkg. reduced-fat cream cheese
- 3 Tbsp. pepper-flavored vodka, such as Absolut Peppar
- 2 Tbsp. fresh lemon juice
- 2 tsp. Dijon mustard
- 3 tsp. well-drained prepared horseradish freshly ground black pepper dill sprigs for garnish

Cut half of the salmon into chunks. Dice the remaining salmon. Placed pressed cottage cheese, cream cheese, salmon chunks, vodka, lemon juice, mustard and horseradish in a food processor. Process until smooth. Transfer the mixture to bowl and fold in the diced salmon. Refrigerate until chilled. *(The spread may be prepared ahead and stored, covered, in the refrigerator for up to 2 days.)*

To serve, spread on crostini *(page 59)* and garnish with a generous sprinkling of pepper and dill.

Makes about 2½ cups.

24 CALORIES PER TABLESPOON: 2 G PROTEIN, 1 G FAT, 1 G CARBOHYDRATE; 82 MG SODIUM; 4 MG CHOLESTEROL.

Spinach Pesto Appetizer

The original pesto appetizer contained 18 grams of fat, about one-third of the recommended daily limit for an average-sized woman. That doesn't leave much room for the main course, let alone dessert. This version boasts about half of the calories and a quarter of the fat of the original recipe.

2½ cups nonfat cottage cheese, pressed
      (page 26)
1 10-oz. pkg. frozen, chopped spinach, thawed
      and squeezed to remove excess moisture
1 8-oz. pkg. reduced-fat cream cheese, cut into
      pieces
¼ cup grated Romano cheese (1 oz.)
1 large egg

2 large egg whites
2 cloves garlic, minced
2 tsp. dried basil
¼ tsp. salt
⅛ tsp. freshly ground black pepper
      cherry tomatoes and fresh basil leaves for
      garnish (optional)

Preheat oven to 325 degrees F. Spray a 9-inch springform pan with nonstick cooking spray and set aside.

Place pressed cottage cheese, spinach, cream cheese, Romano cheese, egg, egg whites, garlic, basil, salt and pepper in a food processor. Process until smooth. Spoon the spinach mixture into the prepared pan and smooth the top with a spatula. Bake for about 1 hour, or until firm. Cool on a wire rack.

(The recipe may be prepared ahead and stored, covered, in the refrigerator for up to 2 days. Allow to come to room temperature before serving.)

To serve, place the pan on a serving plate, run a knife around the outer edge and remove pan sides. Garnish with tomatoes or basil leaves, if desired, and serve with crostini *(page 59)*, crackers or French bread.

Serves 16.

73 CALORIES PER SERVING: 8 G PROTEIN, 3 G FAT, 3 G CARBOHYDRATE; 252 MG SODIUM; 23 MG CHOLESTEROL.

R_x *N. Thies of Osceola, Missouri*

Phyllo Facts

Phyllo pastries can have a lot of style and—if prepared by our method—a little fat. The paper-thin sheets of phyllo dough can be rolled, folded, shaped, seasoned or filled in countless ways. In typical phyllo recipes, however, the layers are freely brushed with melted butter; when baked, the butter keeps the thin sheets separate, producing a flaky—and fat-saturated—result. We developed a technique in which the leaves of phyllo are lightly coated with a blend of egg white and olive oil. During baking, the egg white becomes crisp while the oil keeps the leaves separate. The pastries turn out crisper than those made with pure fat, and filled pastries don't become soggy.

Frozen phyllo is available in most supermarkets. One pound of dough averages 25 large sheets of pastry. The recipes in this cookbook were developed for full-sized sheets, either 14 by 18 inches or 12 by 17 inches.

Spinach-Feta Rolls

Inspired by the Greek appetizer spanakopita, these rolls are easy to make for a crowd.

SPINACH-FETA FILLING
1¼ lbs. fresh spinach, stemmed and washed
1 Tbsp. olive oil
3 bunches scallions, trimmed and chopped (1½ cups)
¼ cup crumbled feta cheese, preferably imported
2 Tbsp. freshly grated Parmesan cheese
2 Tbsp. chopped fresh dill
1 Tbsp. fresh lemon juice

salt & freshly ground black pepper to taste
2 large egg whites

PHYLLO PASTRY
8 sheets phyllo dough (14x18 inches)
1 large egg white
2 Tbsp. olive oil
¼ tsp. salt
1 tsp. poppy or sesame seeds, or a combination (optional)

To make filling: Put spinach with water still clinging to the leaves in a large pot. Cover and cook over medium heat until the spinach is wilted, about 5 minutes. Drain and refresh with cold water. Squeeze the spinach quite dry and chop. In nonstick skillet, heat oil over medium heat. Add scallions and sauté until softened, 2 to 3 minutes. Transfer to a medium-sized bowl and stir in spinach, feta, Parmesan, dill and lemon juice. Season with salt and pepper. Beat egg whites lightly with a fork and stir into the spinach mixture.

To form phyllo rolls: Set oven rack on the upper level; preheat to 350 degrees F. Coat a baking sheet lightly with nonstick cooking spray or line with parchment paper. In a small bowl, whisk together egg white, oil and salt.

Lay one sheet of phyllo on a work surface with a short side toward you. Keep remaining phyllo sheets covered with plastic wrap or wax paper. Brush lower half of the sheet with the egg-white mixture and fold top half over. Brush the top with the egg-white mixture. Repeat this

step with a second sheet of phyllo and set on top of the first. Spoon one-quarter of the spinach filling along one long edge. Tuck in the side edges and roll up, jelly-roll fashion. Place on the prepared baking sheet. Repeat with the remaining phyllo, egg-white mixture and filling, making 4 rolls in all. Brush tops of the rolls lightly with the egg-white mixture and sprinkle with seeds, if desired.

Bake for 25 to 30 minutes, or until golden. Cool for 5 minutes. With a serrated knife, cut each roll diagonally into 9 pieces and serve hot. *(The rolls may be prepared, baked and sliced up to 2 days in advance. Reheat in a 350 degree F oven for 10 to 12 minutes, or until heated through.)*
Makes 36 appetizers.

39 CALORIES PER PIECE: 2 G PROTEIN, 2 G FAT, 5 G CARBOHYDRATE; 77 MG SODIUM; 1 MG CHOLESTEROL.

Herbed Yogurt Cheese

Remember to start draining the yogurt the day before blending the cheese.

2 cups yogurt cheese made from nonfat yogurt *(see below)*
2 scallions, trimmed and minced
2 Tbsp. chopped fresh parsley plus leaves for garnish

1 Tbsp. chopped fresh basil or ½ tsp. dried
1 clove garlic, minced
½ tsp. salt
¼ tsp. freshly ground black pepper

In a medium-sized bowl, blend together yogurt cheese, scallions, parsley, basil, garlic, salt and pepper with a wooden spoon. *(The cheese may be prepared ahead and stored, covered, in the refrigerator for up to 2 days.)*

Serve with crostini *(page 59)* and garnish with parsley leaves.
Makes about 2 cups.

24 CALORIES PER TABLESPOON: 3 G PROTEIN, 0 G FAT, 3 G CARBOHYDRATE; 66 MG SODIUM; 1 MG CHOLESTEROL.

Making Yogurt Cheese

Cream cheese contains about 60 times more fat per cup than nonfat yogurt cheese— reason enough for the minimal extra effort required to make the nonfat alternative.

To make yogurt cheese, begin with nonfat plain yogurt that does not contain starch, gums or gelatin. Line a colander with a double thickness of cheesecloth. Set the colander over a large bowl. Spoon in yogurt, cover with plastic wrap and refrigerate overnight. Transfer the cheese to a separate container. Discard the liquid. *(The yogurt cheese can be stored, covered, in the refrigerator for up to 1 week.)* Six cups of yogurt makes about 2 cups of yogurt cheese.

Bedeviled Eggs

*By using only half the yolks and extending the filling with breadcrumbs,
we lowered the saturated fat and cholesterol by half from standard deviled eggs, without any
sacrifice of flavor. Below are some colorful and flavorful variations.*

1   dozen eggs
½   cup fresh (not dry) breadcrumbs
    (page 21)
¼   cup reduced-fat sour cream

2   Tbsp. finely chopped chives or scallions
1   Tbsp. Dijon mustard
    salt & freshly ground black pepper to taste
    paprika for garnish

Lightly tap each egg with the back of a spoon to make a hairline crack. Place eggs in a large saucepan and cover with cold water. Bring to a simmer and cook over medium heat for 9 minutes. (Start timing as soon as the water begins to simmer.) Drain immediately and set the pan and eggs under cold running water for 1 minute. Peel eggs and slice in half lengthwise.

Scoop out yolks, reserving 6 for another use. Set aside the whites. In a small bowl, mash the remaining 6 yolks. Mix in the breadcrumbs, sour cream, chives or scallions and mustard. Season with salt and pepper. Spoon the yolk mixture into the hollows in the egg whites and garnish with a sprinkling of paprika. Arrange on a platter. *(The eggs can be prepared ahead and stored, covered, in the refrigerator for up to 2 days.)*

Makes 24 deviled eggs.

35 CALORIES PER PIECE: 3 G PROTEIN, 2 G FAT, 2 G CARBOHYDRATE; 49 MG SODIUM; 54 MG CHOLESTEROL.

Curried Chutney Eggs

Instead of mustard and chives or scallions, season the egg-yolk mixture with 2 Tbsp. chopped fresh parsley, 1½ tsp. curry, 1 tsp. lemon juice, a pinch of cayenne, salt and pepper to taste. Instead of paprika, garnish each deviled egg with about ¼ tsp. chutney.

Watercress & Roquefort Eggs

Instead of mustard and chives, season the egg-yolk mixture with 2 Tbsp. chopped fresh watercress, 1½ Tbsp crumbled Roquefort cheese, 2 tsp. fresh lemon juice, salt and pepper to taste. Instead of paprika, garnish each deviled egg with a watercress sprig. This version is about 1 gram higher in fat, 1 milligram higher in cholesterol.

Mediterranean Eggs

Instead of mustard and scallions, season the egg-yolk mixture with 2 Tbsp. chopped fresh parsley, 1 Tbsp. capers, 1 tsp. fresh lemon juice, ½ tsp anchovy paste, salt and pepper to taste. Instead of paprika, garnish each deviled egg with a slice of pitted black olive.

Crostini

Preheat oven to 350 degrees F. Cut a 16-inch-long loaf of French bread (baguette) into ⅓-inch-thick slices. Arrange bread on a baking sheet. Set another baking sheet over the top of the bread and bake for 15 minutes. Turn bread over, re-cover with the baking sheet and bake for about 15 minutes longer, or until golden. Let cool. (*The crostini can be stored in an airtight container for up to 1 week.*)

Makes about 4 dozen crostini.

11 CALORIES PER SLICE: 0 G PROTEIN, 0 G FAT, 2 G CARBOHYDRATE; 22 MG SODIUM; 0 MG CHOLESTEROL.

Caponata

Spooned on top of crostini, this Sicilian eggplant relish makes a delicious appetite-stimulating snack. Because the eggplant is roasted instead of fried, the recipe uses 2 tablespoons of oil instead of ½ cup.

1 eggplant (1 lb.)
2 tsp. olive oil
1 onion, finely chopped
½ cup canned tomato sauce
¼ cup dry white wine
¼ cup red wine vinegar
1 small stalk celery, finely chopped
6 black olives, such as Kalamata, pitted and finely chopped
1½ Tbsp. sugar
1 Tbsp. drained capers, rinsed and finely chopped
3 Tbsp. chopped fresh parsley
 salt & freshly ground black pepper to taste

Preheat oven to 400 degrees F. Pierce the eggplant with a fork in several places and set on a baking sheet. Bake for 30 to 40 minutes, or until the eggplant is soft when pressed. Cool for 5 minutes. Peel off skin and discard. Chop the pulp fine.

In a large saucepan, heat oil over medium heat. Add onions and sauté until softened and beginning to color, about 5 minutes. Add the eggplant, tomato sauce, wine, vinegar, celery, olives, sugar and capers; simmer, stirring often, until thickened, 10 to 15 minutes. Chill. Stir in parsley and season with salt, pepper and additional vinegar, if desired. (*The caponata may be stored in the refrigerator for up to two days.*)

Makes about 2 cups.

15 CALORIES PER TABLESPOON: 0 G PROTEIN, 1 G FAT, 2 G CARBOHYDRATE; 35 MG SODIUM; 0 MG CHOLESTEROL.

Hummus

Roasted garlic adds a new depth of flavor to this classic Middle Eastern dip.

1 head garlic
1 19-oz. can chickpeas, drained and rinsed, or 2 cups cooked chickpeas
2 Tbsp. fresh lemon juice
1 Tbsp. reduced-sodium soy sauce

1 Tbsp. tahini (sesame paste)
2 Tbsp. chopped fresh parsley plus a sprig for garnish
salt to taste
paprika for garnish

Preheat oven to 425 degrees F. Remove the loose papery outside skin from the garlic head without separating the cloves. Slice off the top ½ inch. Wrap in a small square of foil and roast for about 40 minutes or until the garlic is very soft. Unwrap and cool slightly. Separate the cloves and peel.

In a food processor, puree the garlic, chickpeas, lemon juice, soy sauce, tahini and about 2 Tbsp. water (enough to make a fairly firm dip). Transfer to bowl, stir in parsley and season with salt. *(The hummus may be made ahead and stored, covered, in the refrigerator for up to 2 days.)*

Garnish with a sprig of parsley and a sprinkle of paprika. Serve surrounded by fresh vegetables and Pita Crisps *(see below)*.

Makes about 1⅔ cups.

24 CALORIES PER TABLESPOON: 1 G PROTEIN, 1 G FAT, 4 G CARBOHYDRATE; 103 MG SODIUM; 0 MG CHOLESTEROL.

Pita Crisps

**Pita crisps are the perfect scoop for dips and spreads.
A basket of these is a low-fat snack.**

Preheat oven to 425 degrees F. Cut 4 pita breads (about 6-inch diameter) into 8 triangles. Separate each triangle into 2 halves at the fold and arrange, rough-side up, on a baking sheet. Bake for about 8 minutes or until golden and crisp. *(The pita crisps may be stored in a closed container at room temperature for up to 1 week or in the freezer for up to 2 months.)*

Makes 64 crisps.

10 CALORIES EACH: 0 G PROTEIN, 0 G FAT, 2 G CARBOHYDRATE; 20 MG SODIUM; 0 MG CHOLESTEROL.

Cheese Puffs

We did the classic pâte à choux *one better by swapping egg whites for whole eggs and reducing the amount of butter and oil considerably. These warm, cheesy mouthfuls are slightly crisp on the outside. Cheese Puffs can be made ahead and frozen, then popped into the oven when company arrives unexpectedly.*

1 Tbsp. butter
1 Tbsp. olive oil
½ tsp. salt
½ tsp. cayenne pepper
1 cup all-purpose white flour

2 large eggs
4 large egg whites
¾ cup plus 2 Tbsp. freshly grated Asiago or Parmesan cheese (about 1½ oz.)

Line 2 baking sheets with parchment paper or spray them with nonstick cooking spray. Preheat oven to 425 degrees F.

In a medium-sized saucepan, combine 1 cup water, butter, oil, salt and cayenne; bring just to a boil over medium heat. Remove from heat and add flour all at once. Stir with a wooden spoon until it forms a smooth paste. Return the mixture to low heat and cook, stirring for about 3 minutes. This will slightly dry the paste. Remove from heat and cool for 2 minutes.

Lightly whisk together eggs and 3 of the whites. With a wooden spoon or electric mixer, beat ¼ of the egg mixture into the flour paste until absorbed. Repeat with 3 more additions of the egg mixture, until the mixture is

smooth and glossy. Stir ¾ cup cheese into the paste.

Using a pastry bag or spoon, drop 1-inch mounds 1½ inches apart on the prepared baking sheets. Lightly beat the remaining egg white and brush it over each puff. Sprinkle with 2 Tbsp. cheese. Bake, one sheet at a time, for 20 to 25 minutes, or until the puffs are firm and well browned. Serve warm.

(The puffs may be made ahead, stored at room temperature in a closed container for up to 8 hours and reheated for 5 minutes at 350 degrees F. They may be frozen, well wrapped, for up to 2 months and reheated for 10 minutes at 350 degrees F.)

Makes 4½ dozen puffs.

24 CALORIES PER PUFF: 1 G PROTEIN, 1 G FAT, 2 G CARBOHYDRATE; 59 MG SODIUM; 10 MG CHOLESTEROL.

Parmesan Straws

A nice, crisp nibble to serve with drinks. These appetizers work beautifully for entertaining because they can be prepared in advance and refrigerated or frozen.

1 large egg white
2 Tbsp. olive oil
¼ tsp. salt
⅛ tsp. cayenne (optional)

6 sheets phyllo dough (14x18 inches)
¾ cup freshly grated Parmesan or Asiago cheese (about 1½ oz.)

Preheat oven to 400 degrees F. Lightly coat 2 baking sheets with nonstick cooking spray or line with parchment paper. In a small bowl, whisk together egg white, oil, salt and cayenne, if using.

Lay a sheet of phyllo on a work surface with a short side toward you. Keep remaining phyllo sheets covered with plastic wrap or wax paper. With a pastry brush, lightly coat the lower half of the sheet with the egg-white mixture and sprinkle with 2 tsp. cheese. Fold the upper half over to cover the lower half. Brush the right half of the folded sheet with egg-white mixture, sprinkle with 1 tsp. cheese and fold the left half over the cheese. Brush the bottom half of the folded sheet with the egg-white mixture, sprinkle with ½ tsp. cheese and fold the upper half over the lower half. Finally, brush the top with the egg-white mixture and sprinkle with ½ tsp. cheese. Cut into ten ½-inch strips using a knife or serrated pastry cutter. With a wide spatula, transfer the strips to the baking sheet, placing them about ½ inch apart. Repeat the procedure with the remaining 5 sheets of phyllo, egg-white mixture and cheese. Bake the straws for 8 to 10 minutes, until golden and crisp. Transfer to a rack to cool. *(The straws may be stored in an airtight container at room temperature for 1 week or in the freezer for up to 2 months.)*

Makes about 5 dozen straws.

19 CALORIES PER STRAW: 1 G PROTEIN, 1 G FAT, 3 G CARBOHYDRATE; 38 MG SODIUM; 1 MG CHOLESTEROL.

Wonton Chips

These fun-to-make snacks are a great alternative to potato chips.

1 **1-lb. package wonton skins**
¼ **cup toasted sesame seeds** *(see below)* <u>or</u>

2 tsp. **dried marjoram and** 2 tsp. **dried thyme**
    salt to taste

Preheat oven to 400 degrees F. Spray two baking sheets with nonstick cooking spray. Spread a dish towel on the counter. Fill a medium-sized bowl with cold water. Bring a large pot of water to a boil and add 4 wonton skins, one at a time. After about 20 seconds, or when the wontons look like cooked noodles, remove them with a slotted spoon and immerse in the bowl of cold water. Immediately arrange in a single layer on the towel to drain.

When you have enough wontons to fill a baking sheet, arrange them in a single layer on the sheet. Sprinkle with sesame seeds <u>or</u> herbs and salt. Bake for 12 to 15 minutes, or until golden and crisp. (Watch carefully toward the end to avoid burning.) Remove to a rack to cool. Repeat procedure with remaining wontons. *(The chips may be made ahead and stored in a closed container at room temperature for up to 1 week or in the freezer for up to 2 months.)*

Makes about 40 chips.

12 CALORIES PER CHIP: 1 G PROTEIN, 0 G FAT, 2 G CARBOHYDRATE; 6 MG SODIUM; 0 MG CHOLESTEROL.

To Toast Sesame Seeds:

Toasting seeds and spices brings out their flavors.

Heat a small, heavy, dry skillet over medium-high heat. Add seeds and cook, stirring constantly or shaking the pan, for 2 to 3 minutes, or until lightly browned and fragrant. Let cool.

SOUPS

RECIPES

Curried Seafood Bisque

An exotic mix of spices, herbs, vegetables, apples and chunks of shrimp and scallops, this bright soup earns raves each time we serve it.

2 tsp. vegetable oil, preferably canola oil
2 tart apples, such as Granny Smith, peeled, cored and chopped
1 large onion, chopped
1 small red bell pepper, cored, seeded and chopped
1 carrot, chopped
1 small stalk celery, chopped
1¾ cups defatted reduced-sodium chicken stock
1 large potato, peeled and diced
2 Tbsp. golden raisins
1-1½ Tbsp. curry powder
¼ tsp. ground cardamom
¼ tsp. ground allspice

¼ tsp. dried thyme
1¾ cups defatted beef stock
⅔ cup instant nonfat milk powder
3 Tbsp. tomato sauce
1½ cups skim milk
¾ lb. shrimp, peeled, deveined and coarsely chopped
½ lb. bay or sea scallops, cut into bite-size pieces
½-1 tsp. salt
⅓ cup mango chutney, such as Major Grey's, for garnish (optional)
2 Tbsp. chopped fresh cilantro for garnish (optional)

In a large soup pot, heat oil over medium-high heat. Add apples, onions, red peppers, carrots and celery. Sauté for 7 to 10 minutes, or until vegetables are softened.

Stir in chicken stock, potatoes, raisins, curry, cardamom, allspice, and thyme and bring to a boil. Reduce heat to low, cover, and simmer, stirring frequently, for 12 to 15 minutes, or until the potatoes are tender. Puree the mixture in batches, in a blender or food processor, until smooth. Add a little beef stock if mixture is too thick. Rinse out the pot and return the puree to it. Combine ½ cup beef stock, milk powder and tomato sauce in

a blender or food processor. Puree until smooth. Stir the tomato mixture into the pot, along with the remaining beef stock and milk. *(The soup may be made ahead to this point and refrigerated for up to 24 hours. Reheat over medium heat for about 10 minutes. Do not boil.)*

Add shrimp and scallops and cook over medium-high heat, stirring frequently, for 3 to 5 minutes, or until the seafood is opaque. (Do not boil.) Add salt to taste. Just before serving, garnish with chutney and cilantro, if using, or set out a small bowl of each and allow guests to garnish their own.

Makes about 10 cups.

151 CALORIES PER CUP: 15 G PROTEIN, 2 G FAT, 19 G CARBOHYDRATE; 516 MG SODIUM; 61 MG CHOLESTEROL.

Down East Fish Chowder

Low-fat milk thickened with a bit of cornstarch gives this nourishing chowder body and creaminess—without the cream. A little salt pork rounds out the flavor.

1 oz. lean salt pork, diced	5-6 large potatoes, peeled and diced (4 cups)
1 large onion, chopped	1 Tbsp. chopped fresh thyme or 1 tsp. dried
2 stalks celery, chopped	3 bay leaves
2 cloves garlic, minced	2 Tbsp. cornstarch
3 cups bottled clam juice or fish stock	2 cups low-fat milk
1½ lbs. haddock or cod fillets, skinned and cut into 1-inch cubes	salt & freshly ground black pepper to taste
	2 Tbsp. chopped fresh parsley

Heat a heavy stockpot over medium heat. Add salt pork, and cook until golden, 3 to 5 minutes. Add onions, celery and garlic and sauté until softened, 5 to 10 minutes. Add clam juice or fish stock, fish, potatoes, thyme and bay leaves and simmer until potatoes are tender, about 10 minutes. Discard bay leaves and remove pot from the heat. With a slotted spoon, transfer about 2 cups of solids to a bowl and mash with a potato masher or fork. Return to the soup.

In a small bowl, dissolve cornstarch in ¼ cup water. In a small saucepan, scald milk over low heat. Stir the cornstarch mixture and add to the milk. Cook, whisking constantly, until thickened. Stir into the soup. If necessary, reheat the soup. Season with salt and pepper. Ladle into bowls and garnish with parsley.

Serves 6.

284 CALORIES PER SERVING: 25 G PROTEIN, 6 G FAT, 33 G CARBOHYDRATE; 452 MG SODIUM; 54 MG CHOLESTEROL.

Fish Stock

It is difficult to find a commercial fish stock, although some fish markets may offer a frozen stock. Ask your fishmonger for heads and bones.

3 lbs. white fish heads and bones	2 cloves garlic, crushed
2 cups dry white wine	4 sprigs fresh parsley
2 onions, chopped	3 sprigs fresh thyme or ½ tsp. dried
2 leeks, white parts only, cleaned and chopped	1 bay leaf
2 stalks celery, chopped	

Rinse fish bones in cold water. Place in a nonaluminum stock pot with remaining ingredients and enough cold water to cover, about 3½ qts. Bring just to a boil. Reduce heat to low, skim off any foam and simmer, uncovered, for 30 to 35 minutes, skimming occasionally. Strain stock through a fine sieve. *(The stock can be refrigerated for 2 days or frozen for up to 6 months.)*

Makes about 3 qts.

New Orleans Gumbo

You can capture the depth of flavor of the traditional Creole "brown roux"
with much less fat by toasting the flour first.

¼ cup all-purpose white flour
1 Tbsp. vegetable oil, preferably canola oil
1 onion, chopped
1 large green bell pepper, diced
1 stalk celery, minced
4 cloves garlic, minced
4 cups defatted reduced-sodium chicken stock
1 14-oz. can whole tomatoes, drained and chopped
10 okra pods, trimmed and cut into ½-inch-long pieces (1 cup)
½ tsp. freshly ground black pepper

¼ tsp. dried thyme
¼ tsp. dried oregano
⅛ tsp. cayenne pepper
1 bay leaf
½ cup long-grain white rice
6 oz. medium shrimp, peeled and deveined
¼ lb. boneless, skinless chicken breast or thigh meat, trimmed of fat and membrane and cut into ½-inch pieces
2 oz. andouille or kielbasa sausage, thinly sliced
   salt to taste
   Louisiana hot sauce or Tabasco to taste

Preheat oven to 400 degrees F. Spread flour on a pie plate and toast for 20 minutes, or until it turns deep golden, stirring occasionally. Transfer to a plate; let cool.

In a heavy stockpot, heat oil over medium heat. Add onions, green peppers, celery and garlic; sauté for about 7 minutes, or until the onions are lightly browned. Stir in the toasted flour. Gradually stir in chicken stock and bring to a simmer, stirring. Add tomatoes, okra, pepper,

thyme, oregano, cayenne and bay leaf. Cover and cook for 15 minutes. Stir in rice and cook, covered, for 15 minutes longer. Add shrimp, chicken and sausage; simmer for 5 minutes longer, or until the shrimp is opaque inside, the chicken is no longer pink and the rice is tender. Discard the bay leaf and season with salt. Ladle into bowls and serve with Louisiana hot sauce or Tabasco.

Serves 4.

362 CALORIES PER SERVING: 22 G PROTEIN, 10 G FAT, 39 G CARBOHYDRATE; 411 MG SODIUM; 92 MG CHOLESTEROL.

Chicken Stock

Do not discard chicken backs and necks; store them in the freezer until you have enough to make stock.

7-8 lbs. chicken pieces (backs, necks, wings)
2 carrots, unpeeled
1 large onion, studded with 3 whole cloves
1 head garlic, unpeeled (optional)

5 sprigs fresh parsley
3 sprigs fresh thyme or ½ tsp. dried
1 bay leaf

Place chicken in a large stockpot with 4½ qts. cold water. bring to a boil, skim foam and reduce heat to low. Add remaining ingredients and simmer, uncovered, for 3 hours. Strain stock through a fine sieve. Skim fat, if

using immediately, or refrigerate overnight and remove solidified fat. *(The stock can be refrigerated for up to 2 days or frozen for up to 6 months.)*

Makes about 10 cups.

New Orleans Gumbo, opposite

Smoked Salmon Spread, page 54

Fricassee of Salmon With Cucumbers & Dill, page 167

Breakfast Burrito, page 24

Sour Cream Mushroom Soup

Hard to believe that we were able to slash 28 grams of fat per serving from the lush mushroom soup recipe submitted by Jan Heffington. When we switched from half-and-half, whipping cream and sour cream to low-fat milk and reduced-fat sour cream, we found it was necessary to double the mushrooms for a flavor boost and increase the flour to maintain the velvety consistency.

1½ tsp. vegetable oil, preferably canola oil	3½ cups defatted beef broth
1 large onion, chopped	1 cup reduced-fat sour cream
½ tsp. dried tarragon	1 cup 1% milk
¼ tsp. nutmeg, preferably freshly grated	salt & freshly ground black pepper to taste
1 lb. mushrooms, trimmed and sliced (6 cups)	pinch cayenne pepper or Tabasco (optional)
½ cup all-purpose white flour	

In a large heavy saucepan, heat oil over medium-low heat. Add onions and sauté until soft and translucent, 5 to 7 minutes. Add tarragon and nutmeg and cook for 1 minute more. Stir in mushrooms, cover pot and let vegetable mixture steam for about 5 minutes, until mushrooms exude their moisture.

Sprinkle flour over the vegetable mixture. Increase heat to medium and cook, stirring, for 3 to 4 minutes.

Gradually stir in beef broth, stirring and scraping any flour that may have clung to the pot. Simmer, stirring occasionally, until thickened and smooth, 5 to 7 minutes.

Stir together sour cream and milk until smooth; whisk into the mushroom mixture and return to a simmer. Season with salt and pepper and cayenne or Tabasco, if desired, and serve.

Serves 6.

158 CALORIES PER SERVING: 7 G PROTEIN, 6 G FAT, 19 G CARBOHYDRATE; 521 MG SODIUM; 12 MG CHOLESTEROL.

R$_x$ *Jan Heffington of Morrison, Colorado*

Black Bean Soup

Two·ounces of smoked ham and a smidgen of salt pork add depth and richness to this hearty soup.
Quick Corn Bread (page 43) is a good accompaniment.

½ oz. lean salt pork, minced
1 small onion, finely chopped
1 stalk celery, finely chopped
1 carrot, finely chopped
2 cloves garlic, finely minced
1 tsp. ground cumin
3 16-oz. cans black beans

3 cups defatted reduced-sodium chicken stock
6 Tbsp. chopped fresh cilantro or parsley
2 oz. smoked ham, diced (½ cup)
1 Tbsp. tomato paste
1 Tbsp. fresh lime juice
¼ tsp. cayenne pepper
⅓ cup nonfat plain yogurt

Heat a large heavy saucepan over medium heat. Add salt pork and sauté for 3 to 5 minutes, or until golden. Add onions, celery, carrots, garlic and cumin; sauté until softened, about 5 minutes. Transfer the mixture to a food processor or blender and add 2 cans undrained black beans. Puree until very smooth and return the mixture to the pot.

Drain and rinse the remaining can of black beans and add to the pot, along with chicken stock, 4 Tbsp. cilantro or parsley, ham, tomato paste, lime juice and cayenne. Heat through and ladle into bowls. Garnish with yogurt and the remaining 2 Tbsp. cilantro or parsley.

Serves 4.

474 CALORIES PER SERVING: 41 G PROTEIN, 9 G FAT, 84 G CARBOHYDRATE; 1,337 MG SODIUM; 12 MG CHOLESTEROL.

Calico Corn Chowder

*Red peppers, corn and fresh herbs bring color and texture to this
slightly spicy version of a familiar chowder.*

1½ tsp. vegetable oil, preferably canola oil
2 large onions, chopped
1 stalk celery, chopped
1 red bell pepper, cored, seeded and diced
3 cloves garlic, minced
½ tsp. ground cumin
3½ cups defatted reduced-sodium chicken stock
1 Tbsp. chopped fresh thyme or 1½ tsp. dried

1 bay leaf
2 cups corn kernels, fresh (2 large ears) or
   frozen
1 large potato, peeled and diced
2 Tbsp. cornstarch
1 12-oz. can evaporated skim milk
   salt & freshly ground black pepper to taste
   pinch cayenne pepper

In a large heavy saucepan, heat oil over medium-low heat. Add onions and sauté for 5 minutes. Add celery, red pepper, garlic and cumin and sauté for 2 to 3 minutes. Add chicken stock, thyme and bay leaf and bring to a boil. Reduce heat to low and simmer, uncovered, for 10 minutes. Add corn and potatoes, return to a simmer and cook until all vegetables are tender, 5 to 10 minutes.

Place cornstarch in a small bowl, slowly add evaporated milk, stirring until smooth. Stir into the soup and return to a simmer. Cook, stirring for 2 minutes, until thickened. Discard bay leaf. Season with salt and pepper and cayenne. Serve immediately.

Serves 6.

129 CALORIES PER SERVING: 6 G PROTEIN, 2 G FAT, 23 G CARBOHYDRATE; 73 MG SODIUM; 2 MG CHOLESTEROL.

Lightening Cream Soups & Sauces

The easiest place to begin to trim the fat in a cream sauce is to replace the roux (a mixture of flour, butter or oil) with a slurry (a starch—such as cornstarch or flour dissolved in a liquid). Instead of cream, try skim milk or evaporated skim milk. Evaporated skim milk, from which about half of the water has been removed, contains only ½ percent or less fat, and its rich taste makes it particularly handy as a substitute for cream in soups.

Leek & Potato Soup

A creamy soup with a delicate unexpected tarragon accent. It makes a fine beginning to a meal or try it with salad and bread for lunch or a light supper.

1½ tsp. vegetable oil, preferably canola oil
3 leeks, trimmed, cleaned and thinly sliced (3 cups)
2 cloves garlic, minced
6 cups defatted reduced-sodium chicken stock

1 lb. all-purpose potatoes (about 3 medium), peeled and cut into small chunks
½ cup reduced-fat sour cream
½ tsp. dried tarragon
   salt & freshly ground black pepper to taste

In a large heavy saucepan (at least 3-qt. capacity) or stockpot, heat oil over low heat. Add leeks and sauté until softened, about 10 minutes. Add garlic and sauté for 2 minutes more. Add chicken stock and bring to a boil. Reduce heat to low and simmer, uncovered, for 10 minutes. Pour the mixture through a strainer set over a large bowl. Puree the leeks in a food processor or blender until smooth, adding some of the stock if neces-sary. Return the puree and stock to the saucepan. Add potatoes and simmer, covered, until potatoes are soft, 10 to 15 minutes. Remove from heat and mash potatoes thoroughly with a potato masher.

Stir in sour cream, tarragon, salt and pepper. Return to low heat and heat until hot, but not boiling. Serve hot or chilled.

Serves 6.

134 CALORIES PER SERVING: 3 G PROTEIN, 3 G FAT, 24 G CARBOHYDRATE; 36 MG SODIUM; 5 MG CHOLESTEROL.

Roasted Tomato Soup

Roasting the tomatoes gives this simple soup a nice complexity and depth of flavor with very little fat.

1½ tsp. olive oil
3 lbs. ripe tomatoes, cored, seeded and halved (8 to 10 medium-sized tomatoes)
2 red onions, chopped

1 clove garlic, minced
3 cups defatted reduced-sodium chicken stock
3 Tbsp. chopped fresh basil
   salt & freshly ground black pepper to taste

Preheat broiler. Spray a baking sheet with nonstick cooking spray and place tomatoes on it, cut-side down. Broil for 10 to 12 minutes, or until the skins are blistered and blackened. Let cool, then slip off skins.

In a medium-sized saucepan, heat oil over medium heat. Add onions and cook for 5 minutes. Add garlic and cook for 2 additional minutes, or until onions are softened. In a food processor or blender, combine the tomatoes and onions; process until smooth. Return to the saucepan. Add chicken stock and bring to a boil. Reduce heat to low and simmer for 5 minutes. Remove from heat and stir in basil. Season with salt and pepper. Serve hot or chilled.

Serves 6.

128 CALORIES PER SERVING: 5 G PROTEIN, 3 G FAT, 26 G CARBOHYDRATE; 43 MG SODIUM; 0 MG CHOLESTEROL.

Curried Butternut Squash Bisque

A velvety, spicy first-course soup. Yogurt, swirled into each soup bowl, adds an attractive flourish and provides a refreshing counterpoint to the spices in the soup.

2 tsp. vegetable oil, preferably canola oil *unsalted butter*
3 onions, chopped
2 McIntosh apples, peeled, cored and chopped
3 cloves garlic, minced
~~2 tsp. minced peeled gingerroot~~
1-1½ Tbsp. curry powder *mild*
~~½ tsp. ground cumin~~

4 cups defatted reduced-sodium chicken stock
1 cup apple cider
2 lbs. butternut squash, peeled, seeded and cubed (6 cups)
 salt & freshly ground black pepper to taste
½ cup nonfat plain yogurt
2 Tbsp. skim milk

In a heavy soup pot, heat oil over low heat. Add onions and apples; sauté for 10 minutes, until softened and limp. Stir in garlic, ginger, curry and cumin and cook for 3 minutes. Add chicken stock, cider and squash; bring to a boil. Reduce heat to low and cover the pan; simmer for 30 to 35 minutes, or until the squash is tender.

Pour the mixture through a strainer set over a large bowl. Puree the solids in a food processor or blender until very smooth. Return the puree and liquid to the saucepan.

To serve, heat the soup gently and season with salt and pepper. In a small bowl, stir together yogurt and milk. Ladle the soup into bowls, and add a dollop of the yogurt mixture. Draw the tip of a knife or a toothpick through the yogurt to make decorative swirls.

Serves 8.

107 CALORIES PER SERVING: 4 G PROTEIN, 2 G FAT, 22 G CARBOHYDRATE; 163 MG SODIUM; 1 MG CHOLESTEROL.

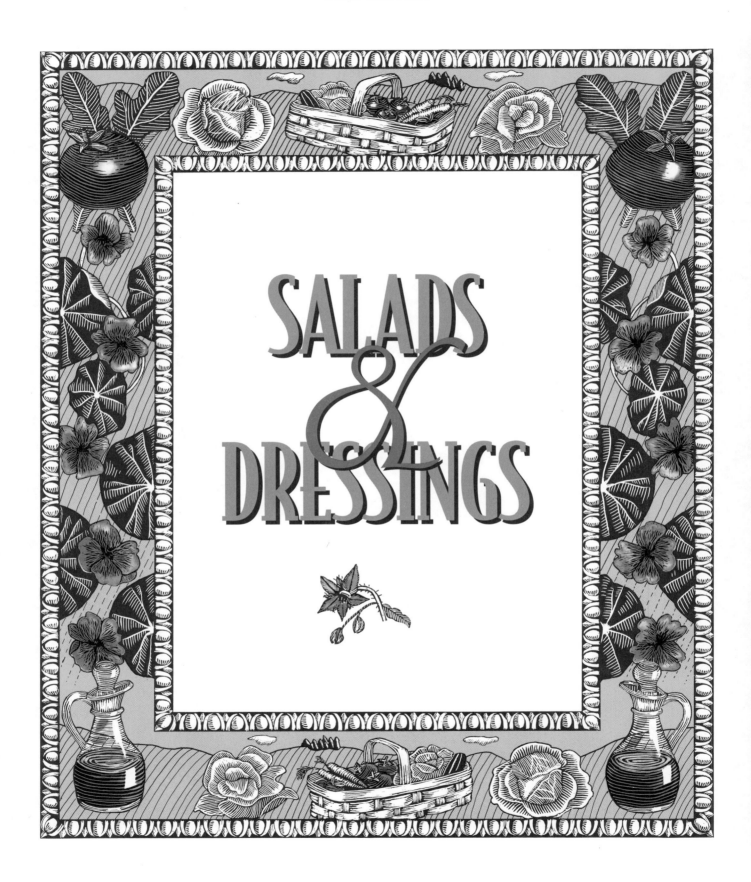

SALADS
&
DRESSINGS

RECIPES

Caesar Salad

*Luxuriously coated romaine, full anchovy flavor and crunchy,
garlicky croutons provide everything you ever wanted in a Caesar Salad.
And this one doesn't give you what you don't want—the classic Caesar's fat and cholesterol.*

2   cups cubed French bread
1   clove garlic, peeled
½   tsp. salt
2   tsp. olive oil, preferably extra-virgin
1   large or 2 small heads romaine lettuce, trimmed, washed and torn into bite-sized pieces (8 cups)

¾   cup Roasted Garlic Dressing *(page 93)*
8   anchovy fillets, rinsed, patted dry and chopped
4   tsp. grated Parmesan cheese
    freshly ground black pepper to taste

Preheat the oven to 400 degrees F. Spread the bread cubes on a baking sheet and toast for 10 to 15 minutes, or until golden and crisp. Chop garlic coarsely, sprinkle with salt and mash with the side of the knife blade. Heat the oil in a nonstick skillet. Add the mashed garlic and cook, stirring until golden brown, about 30 seconds. Remove from heat, add bread cubes and toss until the garlic is well distributed.

In a bowl, combine lettuce, Roasted Garlic Dressing and anchovies; toss well. Divide the salad among four plates and top with the croutons, Parmesan cheese and freshly ground black pepper.

Serves 4.

154 CALORIES PER SERVING: 6 G PROTEIN, 10 G FAT, 12 G CARBOHYDRATE; 742 MG SODIUM; 8 MG CHOLESTEROL.

Salad Pitfalls & Pluses

Many traditional salads like Caesar and Niçoise are higher in fat than most people think. Salad can be either a nutritional gold mine or a minefield of high-fat ingredients. A classic Caesar salad, for instance, can easily contain 25 grams of fat in a serving—as much as a juicy burger with the works. The chef's salad at your local restaurant is likely to be one of the most fatty items on the menu, thanks to the strips of cheese and creamy dressing.

Select salad ingredients with care. Flavor and texture accents are important, so don't eliminate the olives and nuts completely. Just use smaller amounts, finely chopped to spread the delicious flavor around.

Do reach for lots of colorful vegetables. Red peppers, carrots and tomatoes contain vitamins and other compounds that protect living cells. Studies show that plant foods contain an incredible range of these protective substances, and the greater the variety that you eat, the more likely you are to take full advantage of their disease-fighting arsenal.

Greek Revival Salad

This attractive, full-bodied dish celebrates the Greek flavors of feta, black olives and plenty of oregano.

1   clove garlic, peeled
½   tsp. salt
3   Tbsp. tomato juice
2   Tbsp. fresh lemon juice
1   Tbsp. olive oil
1½ tsp. dried oregano, crushed
¼   tsp. freshly ground black pepper
1   medium head romaine, trimmed, washed and torn into bite-sized pieces (6 cups)

1   cucumber, halved lengthwise and sliced
12 cherry tomatoes, sliced and quartered, or 2 larger tomatoes, cored and diced
½   small red onion, thinly sliced
8   black olives, such as Kalamata, pitted and sliced
¼   cup crumbled feta cheese (1 oz.)

Chop garlic coarsely. Sprinkle with salt and mash with the side of the knife blade. Place garlic in a small bowl; whisk in tomato juice, lemon juice, olive oil, oregano and pepper.

Toss lettuce, cucumbers, tomatoes and red onion with the dressing. Scatter olives and feta cheese over the top and serve.
Serves 4.

113 CALORIES PER SERVING: 4 G PROTEIN, 7 G FAT, 13 G CARBOHYDRATE; 526 MG SODIUM; 6 MG CHOLESTEROL.

Salade Niçoise Nouvelle

A colorful summer luncheon entrée with classic flavors dressed in roasted garlic.

1   lb. small red potatoes, scrubbed
    salt to taste
1   cup Roasted Garlic Dressing *(page 93)*
¾   lb. green beans, stem ends trimmed
3   plum tomatoes, cut into eighths
3   hard-boiled eggs, peeled and cut lengthwise into quarters

1   6⅛ oz. can water-packed tuna, drained
8   black olives, such as Kalamata, pitted and sliced
½   small red onion, thinly sliced
2   Tbsp. drained capers, rinsed
2   Tbsp. chopped fresh parsley
8   anchovy fillets, rinsed and patted dry

In a medium saucepan, cover potatoes with cold water, season with salt and bring to a boil. Reduce heat to medium and cook 10 minutes, or until the potatoes are just tender. Drain. Let stand until cool enough to handle. Slice into a large bowl and toss with ¼ cup dressing.

Cook green beans in boiling salted water for 5 minutes, or until just tender. Drain, refresh under cold water and pat dry. Add to potatoes along with another ¼ cup dressing. Toss gently to coat.

Transfer to a platter or individual plates. Arrange tomatoes and eggs around the outside; scatter tuna, olives, onions, capers and parsley over the top. Arrange anchovies decoratively; drizzle with the remaining dressing.
Serves 4.

342 CALORIES PER SERVING: 22 G PROTEIN, 14 G FAT, 37 G CARBOHYDRATE; 603 MG SODIUM; 167 MG CHOLESTEROL.

Grilled Sirloin Salad

As an ingredient surrounded by vegetables—that's the low-fat way to eat steak.
Pepper-coated sirloin and grilled vegetables on a bed of escarole make a lively main-dish salad.

2 Tbsp. reduced-sodium soy sauce
2 Tbsp. balsamic vinegar
2 tsp. sesame oil
2 tsp. brown sugar
1 tsp. minced peeled gingerroot
1 clove garlic, minced
1 tsp. black peppercorns, crushed
1 tsp. Sichuan peppers, crushed

¾ lb. beef sirloin, trimmed of visible fat
    salt to taste
16 scallions, white part only
1 red bell pepper, cored and cut in half
    lengthwise and seeded
12 cups washed, dried and torn escarole leaves
    (about 1½ lbs.)

Prepare a charcoal fire or preheat a gas grill. In a blender or food processor, combine soy sauce, vinegar, oil, sugar, ginger and garlic; blend until smooth and set aside.

In a small bowl, combine black and Sichuan peppers. Press the pepper mixture into both sides of the meat. Season lightly with salt. Place the meat, scallions and red pepper halves on the grill and cook for 4 minutes. Turn the meat and vegetables and cook for 3 to 4 min-

utes longer, until the meat is medium-rare and the vegetables are slightly charred.

Let the meat rest for 5 minutes. Cut the scallions into 1-inch pieces and slice the peppers into long strips. Slice the meat thinly across the grain. Toss escarole with the reserved soy-sauce dressing. Place on a serving platter or 4 plates. Arrange the meat and grilled vegetables over the top and serve.

Serves 4.

218 CALORIES PER SERVING: 23 G PROTEIN, 9 G FAT, 12 G CARBOHYDRATE; 397 MG SODIUM; 57 MG CHOLESTEROL.

How Salty Is Soy Sauce?

Soy sauce comes from the Chinese, who have been making dark and light soy sauce for more than 3,000 years. "Lite" soy sauce is a more recent invention.

Traditional dark soy sauce has a full, rich flavor and a deep brown color. Although it's more flavorful than the light version, dark soy sauce contains less sodium than light. Because of its assertive flavor, it is more suited to foods with strong flavors, such as red meat, while the saltier light soy is best in fish, seafood, vegetables and dipping sauces.

"Lite" is a third kind. On a soy sauce label, "Lite" means *less sodium*. One commonly available version has 100 milligrams of sodium in a half teaspoon, compared to that brand's regular dark sauce with 167 milligrams—a 40 percent reduction. However, new labeling laws in 1994 will not allow the "lite" moniker because that term will only be used to refer to fat-containing products whose fat content is reduced by 50 percent.

Our recipes call for reduced-sodium soy sauce. Check the labels.

Smoked Turkey & Wild Rice Salad

The wild and white rice can be cooked ahead of time,
but the salad should be assembled and tossed shortly before serving.

¾ cup wild rice, rinsed
½ tsp. salt or to taste
½ cup long-grain white rice
½ lb. smoked turkey breast, diced (2 cups)
2 red apples, such as McIntosh, unpeeled,
    cored and diced
5 scallions, trimmed and sliced

1 stalk celery, trimmed and diced
½ cup apple-juice concentrate, thawed
¼ cup cider vinegar
1 tsp. dried tarragon or thyme
    freshly ground black pepper to taste
1 bunch watercress, trimmed and washed
2 Tbsp. toasted pecans *(page 32)*, chopped

In a saucepan, combine 2 cups water, wild rice and ¼ tsp. salt; bring to a boil. Cover and simmer over low heat until the wild rice is tender, 40 to 50 minutes. Meanwhile, in a separate saucepan, bring 1 cup water and ¼ tsp. salt to a boil. Add white rice, cover and simmer over low heat until most of the water has been absorbed, about 20 minutes. Transfer wild and white rice to a sieve and refresh under cold water to cool.

In a large bowl, combine wild rice, white rice, turkey, apples, scallions and celery. In a small bowl, whisk together apple juice concentrate, vinegar and tarragon or thyme. Season with salt and pepper and pour over the salad. Toss well. Taste and adjust seasonings. Mound the salad on a serving platter and garnish with watercress. Sprinkle with pecans and serve.

Serves 4.

395 CALORIES PER SERVING: 24 G PROTEIN, 4 G FAT, 69 G CARBOHYDRATE; 341 MG SODIUM; 47 MG CHOLESTEROL.

Curried Chicken Salad

Chilling the poached chicken breasts in the cooking liquid ensures moist, succulent results.
This salad also works as a sandwich filling with lettuce in pita pockets.

2 cups defatted reduced-sodium chicken stock
6 boneless, skinless chicken breast halves
    (1½ lbs. total), trimmed of fat
½ cup reduced-fat mayonnaise
½ cup nonfat plain yogurt

½ cup mango chutney
2 tsp. curry powder or to taste
1 tart apple, such as Granny Smith, cored and
    chopped
¼ cup currants or raisins

In a large shallow pan, bring chicken stock and 2 cups water to a boil. Add chicken breasts and reduce heat to low. Simmer, partially covered, for 10 to 12 minutes, or until the chicken is no longer pink inside. Transfer chicken to a shallow dish and pour the cooking liquid over the top. Refrigerate until chilled, at least 1 hour or overnight.

Remove the chicken from the cooking liquid and dice.

In a medium-sized bowl stir together mayonnaise, yogurt, chutney and curry powder until well blended. Add the diced chicken, apples and currants or raisins, tossing until thoroughly coated.

Serves 6.

286 CALORIES PER SERVING: 26 G PROTEIN, 9 G FAT, 25 G CARBOHYDRATE; 76 MG SODIUM; 72 MG CHOLESTEROL.

Simple Summer Pasta Salad

Fresh basil perks up this salad featuring the best garden produce, smoked turkey and capers.

6 oz. small pasta shapes, such as penne or rotini
1 Tbsp. salt
1 Tbsp. olive oil
2 cloves garlic, minced
½ cup freshly grated Asiago or Parmesan cheese (1 oz.)
¼ cup reduced-fat mayonnaise
¼ cup defatted reduced-sodium chicken stock
⅓ cup cider vinegar

2 large red bell peppers, cored, seeded and diced
1 head of broccoli, cut into small florets
6 oz. smoked turkey, cut in ¼-by-1-inch strips
1 bunch scallions, trimmed and sliced
3 Tbsp. drained capers, rinsed and chopped
1 Tbsp. chopped fresh basil or 1 tsp. dried
    salt & freshly ground black pepper to taste

In a large pot, bring 4 qts. of water to a boil over high heat. Add pasta and salt and cook for 8 to 10 minutes, or just until tender. Drain in a colander and refresh under cold water; place in a large bowl.

Heat 1 tsp. oil in a large nonstick skillet over medium-high heat and sauté the garlic until light golden. Transfer to a blender, along with cheese, mayonnaise, chicken stock and vinegar; puree until smooth. Set aside.

Heat 1 tsp. of the remaining oil in the skillet over medium-high heat and add red peppers. Sauté for 2 min-utes, or until slightly softened. Add to the pasta. Heat the remaining 1 tsp. of oil in the skillet, add the broccoli florets, and sauté for 2 to 3 minutes, or until bright green and beginning to soften. Add to the pasta.

When the vegetables have cooled, add the turkey, scallions, capers and basil to the pasta mixture. Toss with the dressing. Season with salt, pepper and additional vinegar, if desired. Serve immediately.

Serves 4.

360 CALORIES PER SERVING: 23 G PROTEIN, 11 G FAT, 43 G CARBOHYDRATE; 779 MG SODIUM; 46 MG CHOLESTEROL.

Mama's Potato Salad

Well, it's awfully close to most mothers' potato salads. Here are all the sweet-sour flavors loved by Southerners, but with fat and calories held reasonably in check.

1½ lbs. new potatoes, scrubbed and quartered
    salt to taste
¼   cup skim-milk buttermilk
2   Tbsp. reduced-fat mayonnaise
2   tsp. American-style yellow mustard
1   hard-boiled egg, peeled and chopped

¼   cup finely chopped green bell peppers
2   Tbsp. finely chopped celery
2   Tbsp. finely chopped onions
2   tsp. sweet-pickle relish
    freshly ground black pepper to taste

In a medium-sized saucepan, cover potatoes with 5 cups water, season with salt and bring to a boil. Cook until tender, about 10 minutes. Drain and let cool.

In a large bowl, stir together buttermilk, mayonnaise, mustard, egg, bell peppers, celery, onions and relish; add potatoes and toss gently. Season with salt and pepper. Refrigerate for at least an hour before serving. *(The salad can be made ahead and stored, covered, in the refrigerator for up to 24 hours.)*

Serves 6.

115 CALORIES PER SERVING: 3 G PROTEIN, 2 G FAT, 20 G CARBOHYDRATE; 156 MG SODIUM; 38 MG CHOLESTEROL.

Tricolor Coleslaw

Red and green cabbage and bright orange carrots make a colorful, healthful combination. For an especially nutty flavor, use Savoy instead of regular green cabbage.

3   Tbsp. reduced-fat mayonnaise
3   Tbsp. nonfat plain yogurt
1   Tbsp. Dijon mustard
2   tsp. wine or cider vinegar
1   tsp. sugar
½   tsp. caraway seed (optional)

    salt & freshly ground black pepper to taste
2   cups shredded red cabbage (¼ of a small head)
2   cups shredded green cabbage (¼ of a small head)
1   cup grated carrots (2 medium carrots)

In a large bowl, combine the mayonnaise, yogurt, mustard, vinegar, sugar and caraway seed, if using. Season with salt and pepper. Add cabbage and carrots and toss well. Serve within 2 hours.

Serves 4.

70 CALORIES PER SERVING: 2 G PROTEIN, 3 G FAT, 10 G CARBOHYDRATE; 37 MG SODIUM; 4 MG CHOLESTEROL.

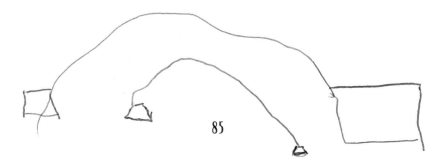

Southwestern Three-Bean Salad

This spiced-up variation on an old standard omits the usual kidney beans and green beans as well as the syrupy dressing. Chipotles give heat and a slightly smoky flavor.

1   16-oz. can black beans, drained and rinsed
1   15-oz. can pinto beans or black-eyed peas, drained and rinsed
1   19-oz. can chickpeas, drained and rinsed
½   small Vidalia, Maui or Walla Walla onion, halved and thinly sliced
¼   cup chopped cilantro

2-3   chipotle peppers packed in adobo sauce, drained and finely chopped
3   Tbsp. wine or cider vinegar
2   Tbsp. olive or canola oil
     salt & freshly ground black pepper to taste
½   head iceberg lettuce, cored and shredded

In a large bowl, combine black beans, pinto beans or black-eyed peas, chickpeas, onions, cilantro, chipotles, vinegar and oil. Toss until well mixed. Season with salt and pepper.

(The salad can be prepared ahead and stored, covered in the refrigerator for up to 2 days.) Arrange lettuce on a serving platter and mound the bean mixture over top.
Serves 6.

298 CALORIES PER SERVING: 15 G PROTEIN, 7 G FAT, 46 G CARBOHYDRATE; 746 MG SODIUM; 0 MG CHOLESTEROL.

Romaine, Red Onion & Orange Salad

Abundant and juicy in winter, sweet oranges brighten up a green salad.
This dressing is based on orange juice and requires only a small amount of olive oil.

1   very small red onion, thinly sliced
⅓   cup fresh orange juice (2 oranges)
2   Tbsp. olive oil, preferably extra-virgin
2   tsp. Dijon mustard
1   small clove garlic, minced

     pinch sugar
     salt & freshly ground black pepper to taste
1   head romaine lettuce or escarole, washed, dried and torn (about 4 cups)
2   navel oranges, peeled and sliced

Soak onions in ice water for 10 minutes; drain.
In a small bowl or a jar, whisk or shake together orange juice, oil, mustard, garlic, sugar, salt and pepper. Put lettuce, orange slices and onions in a large salad bowl. Drizzle the dressing over and toss well. Taste and adjust seasonings and serve.
Serves 4.

120 CALORIES PER SERVING: 2 G PROTEIN, 7 G FAT, 13 G CARBOHYDRATE; 39 MG SODIUM; 0 MG CHOLESTEROL.

Garden Vegetable Salad With Roasted Scallion Dressing

As good as raw greens taste in a salad, a few roasted vegetables lend a heartiness and substance usually supplied by meats and cheeses. To make this into a main dish, add a can of water-packed tuna.

6   scallions
1½ tsp. olive oil
1   Tbsp. fresh lime juice
1   Tbsp. red-wine vinegar
1   tsp. Creole or grainy mustard
¼   cup defatted reduced-sodium chicken stock
    salt & freshly ground black pepper to taste
1   small yellow bell pepper, cored, seeded and cut into ½-inch-wide strips
1   small red bell pepper, cored, seeded and cut into ½-inch-wide strips

1   small zucchini, trimmed and cut into 3-inch-long wedges
1   small yellow squash, trimmed and cut into 3-inch-long wedges
1   red onion, peeled and cut into ¾-inch-thick slices
½   lb. green beans, stem ends trimmed
1   tsp. ground cumin
1   tsp. dried oregano
1   head romaine lettuce, trimmed, washed and torn into bite-sized pieces

Set oven rack at lowest level; preheat to 450 degrees F. Trim off and discard scallion root ends and all but 1 inch of the green tops. Toss the scallions with ½ tsp. oil, arrange them on a baking sheet and roast for 10 minutes, turning once or twice until browned and softened.

Cool and transfer to a blender or food processor. Puree with lime juice, vinegar and mustard. With the motor running, add chicken stock in a slow, steady stream. Season with salt and pepper and set aside.

In a large shallow bowl, toss bell peppers, zucchini, squash, onions and green beans with the remaining 1 tsp. oil, cumin and oregano. Season with salt and pepper. Spread the vegetables out on a baking sheet and roast, turning frequently, until the vegetables are tender and browned, about 15 to 20 minutes.

In a large salad bowl, toss with lettuce and enough of the roasted scallion dressing to coat lightly. Arrange the warm roasted vegetables over the top of the lettuce. Taste and adjust seasonings. Pass the remaining dressing separately.

Serves 6.

52 CALORIES PER SERVING: 2 G PROTEIN, 2 G FAT, 9 G CARBOHYDRATE; 17 MG SODIUM; 0 MG CHOLESTEROL.

Salad Dressing Savvy

Salads are rightly associated with healthy eating. But the wrong dressing can turn salad into a high-fat food. Consider that two popular commercial varieties, blue cheese and Italian, contain 7 to 8 grams of fat and 69 to 77 calories per tablespoon. Light dressings are dramatically lower but may contain a number of chemical preservatives. Why not use garden-fresh herbs and enjoy the simple pleasure of quickly made dressings? Standard homemade dressings can still be high in fat—most vinaigrettes' three-to-one oil-to-vinegar ratio yields 10 grams of fat and 90 calories per tablespoon.

Some low-fat tips:

- Use buttermilk, vegetable purees, flavored vinegars, fruit juice, chicken stock, nonfat yogurt and reduced-fat mayonnaise to enhance fresh flavors without relying on fat as the main ingredient.
- Reduce oil to one-third or one-half the amount called for in traditional recipes.
- Choose olive oil for its high levels of healthful monounsaturates and superior flavor. Use an extra-virgin olive oil or nut oils, such as walnut, in salads, where its taste is most noticeable, and save the less expensive, lighter olive oils or an olive oil-canola blend for cooking.

Basic Vinaigrette

Chicken stock replaces most of the oil in this classic dressing without a loss of flavor or consistency. It is perfect for a simple salad of tender Boston, romaine, red or green leaf lettuce or ripe tomatoes.

2　Tbsp. red-wine vinegar or fresh lemon juice
2　Tbsp. olive oil, preferably extra-virgin
2　Tbsp. defatted reduced-sodium chicken stock
½　tsp. minced garlic
¼　tsp. Dijon mustard
　　salt & freshly ground black pepper to taste
1　Tbsp. chopped fresh parsley, chervil, tarragon, chives or basil (optional)

In a small bowl whisk together vinegar or lemon juice, oil, chicken stock, garlic and mustard until well blended. Season with salt and pepper. Alternatively, combine ingredients in a small jar, secure lid, shake until blended and season. Just before serving, stir in fresh herbs.

Makes about ⅓ cup.

46 CALORIES PER TABLESPOON: 0 G PROTEIN, 5 G FAT, 1 G CARBOHYDRATE; 19 MG SODIUM; 1 MG CHOLESTEROL.

Grilled Sirloin Salad, page 82

89

Garden Vegetable Salad With Roasted Scallion Dressing, page 87

Oven "Fries", page 102, Tricolor Coleslaw, page 85, Barbecued Chicken, page 153

Fusilli With Roasted Tomatoes, Asparagus & Shrimp, page 115

Roasted Garlic Dressing

Made with mellow roasted garlic and chicken stock, this creamy dressing contains very little oil and no egg yolks or mayonnaise. It is perfect with a simple salad of romaine lettuce and red onion rings or with a main-dish salad, such as Salade Niçoise Nouvelle *(page 81).*

2   heads garlic
½   cups defatted reduced-sodium chicken stock
¼   cup wine or cider vinegar

2   Tbsp. olive oil, preferably extra-virgin
2   tsp. Dijon mustard
     salt & freshly ground black pepper to taste

Preheat oven to 400 degrees F. Pull off excess papery outside skin from garlic without separating the cloves. Slice ½ inch off the top of each head. Wrap individually in aluminum foil. Roast for 40 minutes, or until the garlic is very soft. Unwrap the garlic and cool slightly. Separate the cloves and peel.

In a food processor or blender, combine garlic cloves, chicken stock, vinegar, oil and mustard; blend until smooth. Season with salt and pepper. *(The dressing can be stored, covered, in the refrigerator for up to 2 days.)*
Makes about 1 cup.

32 CALORIES PER TABLESPOON: 0 G PROTEIN, 3 G FAT, 1 G CARBOHYDRATE; 28 MG SODIUM; 0 MG CHOLESTEROL.

Parmesan-Pepper Dressing

Toss with crisp greens, such as romaine and curly endive, plus croutons and slivers of red onion.

⅓   cup skim-milk buttermilk
⅓   cup nonfat cottage cheese
⅓   cup freshly grated Parmesan cheese

4   tsp. white-wine vinegar
1   small clove garlic, minced
½   tsp. freshly ground black pepper or to taste

In a food processor or blender, combine buttermilk, cottage cheese, Parmesan, vinegar and garlic; blend until smooth. Stir in pepper.

(The dressing can be stored, covered, in the refrigerator for up to 2 days.)
Makes about 1 cup.

13 CALORIES PER TABLESPOON: 1 G PROTEIN, 1 G FAT, 1 G CARBOHYDRATE; 36 MG SODIUM; 2 MG CHOLESTEROL.

Ginger-Orange Dressing

Spinach, watercress or Belgian endive are good matches for this zesty dressing.

½ cup fresh orange juice
2 Tbsp. vegetable oil, preferably canola oil
2 Tbsp. minced scallions
2 tsp. minced peeled gingerroot

1 tsp. grated orange zest
1 small clove garlic, minced
    salt & freshly ground black pepper to taste

In a small bowl, whisk together all ingredients until well blended. Alternatively, combine ingredients in a small jar, secure lid and shake until blended.

(The dressing can be stored, covered, in the refrigerator for up to 2 days.)
Makes about ⅔ cup.

36 CALORIES PER TABLESPOON: 0 G PROTEIN, 3 G FAT, 1 G CARBOHYDRATE; 1 MG SODIUM; 0 MG CHOLESTEROL.

Buttermilk Dressing

Buttermilk flavor is enhanced by lemon, dill and onion in this thick dressing.

½ cup skim-milk buttermilk
¼ cup nonfat plain yogurt
¼ cup low-fat mayonnaise
1 Tbsp. fresh lemon juice
2 tsp. dried minced onions

½ tsp. dill seed, crushed
½ tsp. salt
½ tsp. sugar
¼ tsp. freshly ground black pepper

In a small bowl, whisk together all the ingredients until well blended.
(The dressing may be stored, covered in the refrigerator for up to 2 days.)
Makes about 1 cup.

16 CALORIES PER TABLESPOON: 1 G PROTEIN, 1 G FAT, 1 G CARBOHYDRATE; 73 MG SODIUM; 1 MG CHOLESTEROL.

French Dressing

A homemade cousin of bottled French Dressing.

¾ cup tomato juice
2 Tbsp. olive oil
1 Tbsp. cider or wine vinegar
1 tsp. Dijon mustard
1 tsp. sugar

1 clove garlic, peeled and crushed
1½ tsp. chopped fresh thyme or ½ tsp. dried
½ tsp. salt
¼ tsp. freshly ground black pepper

Combine all ingredients in a blender or food processor and process until smooth.
(The dressing may be stored in a covered container in the refrigerator for up to 4 days.)
Makes about 1 cup.

19 CALORIES PER TABLESPOON: 0 G PROTEIN, 2 G FAT, 1 G CARBOHYDRATE; 112 MG SODIUM; 0 MG CHOLESTEROL.

CHAPTER SIX

VEGETABLES

RECIPES

Green Bean Casserole Sans the Cans

This is not the no-mess, super-easy recipe of yore, but it is low in fat and high in flavor.
To go one step further, substitute ½ pound fresh green beans for frozen. Simply trim and cut into
1-inch lengths. Then blanch the beans for 1 to 2 minutes in boiling water,
refresh under cold water and spread them in the baking dish.

ONION TOPPING
½ tsp. vegetable oil, preferably canola oil
1 large onion, thinly sliced
½ cup fresh breadcrumbs *(page 21)*

SAUCE & GREEN BEANS
2 cups skim milk
6 black peppercorns
1 bay leaf
  pinch ground nutmeg

½ tsp. vegetable oil, preferably canola oil
1 small onion, minced
½ lb. mushrooms, trimmed and sliced (3 cups)
1 clove garlic, minced
¼ cup all-purpose white flour
¼ cup reduced-fat sour cream
1 tsp. salt
½ tsp. freshly ground black pepper
1 9-oz. package frozen green beans (2 cups)

To make onion topping: In a large nonstick skillet, heat oil over low heat. Add sliced onions and cook, stirring occasionally, for 30 minutes, or until very tender and golden. Set aside.

Meanwhile, preheat oven to 350 degrees F. Spread breadcrumbs on a baking sheet and toast for 5 to 10 minutes, stirring once, or until lightly browned. Set aside.

To make sauce: In a medium-sized heavy saucepan, combine milk, peppercorns, bay leaf and nutmeg and heat over low heat until steaming. Remove from heat, let stand for 5 minutes and strain into a measuring cup. (Discard peppercorns and bay leaf.)

Meanwhile, in a large heavy saucepan, heat oil over medium heat. Add onions and cook, stirring often, for 3 to 4 minutes, or until golden. Add mushrooms and gar-

lic and cook, stirring, for 3 to 4 minutes, or until tender. Sprinkle flour over the vegetables and cook, stirring, for 1 minute. Slowly pour in milk, whisking constantly. Bring to a boil, stirring. Reduce heat to low and cook, stirring for 1 minute, or until thickened. Remove from heat. Whisk in sour cream. Add salt and pepper. (Onions, breadcrumbs and sauce can be prepared ahead and stored in separate containers, covered, in the refrigerator for up to 2 days.)

To assemble and bake casserole: Preheat oven to 425 degrees F. Spread frozen beans evenly over the bottom of a shallow 2-qt. baking dish and pour the sauce over the top. In a small bowl, toss together the reserved onions and breadcrumbs and spread over the beans. Bake for 15 to 25 minutes, or until bubbling.

Serves 6.

131 CALORIES PER SERVING: 6 G PROTEIN, 3 G FAT, 21 G CARBOHYDRATE; 469 MG SODIUM; 3 MG CHOLESTEROL.

R$_x$ *Jenifer Jill Mathers of East Burke, Vermont*

Cream-of-Something Soup Alternatives

Canned cream-of-mushroom soup is little more than old-fashioned white sauce flavored with mushrooms. Fortunately, it is possible to make a creamy sauce without butter and using skim milk instead of whole milk or cream *(page 98)*. To help compensate for the flavor that would have come from fat in the commercial preparations, you can boost the flavor of the skim milk by infusing it with peppercorns, bay leaf and nutmeg. Sautéed fresh mushrooms provide additional rich flavor and a dollop of reduced-fat sour cream gives the sauce a silky texture.

Baked Stuffed Onions

A fine accompaniment to roast meats and poultry,
these onions are easy to make ahead when entertaining.

3   Spanish onions
3   oz. day-old Italian bread, without crust
    (six ½-inch-thick slices)
½   cup skim milk
1   large egg, lightly beaten
3   oz. mushrooms (6 large), cleaned, trimmed
    and chopped

2   Tbsp. drained capers, rinsed and chopped
1   Tbsp. chopped fresh parsley
1   clove garlic, minced
½   tsp. salt
¼   tsp. freshly ground black pepper
¼   cup fine dry unseasoned breadcrumbs
1½ tsp. olive oil, preferably extra-virgin

Preheat oven to 375 degrees F. Keeping the whole onions intact, peel away the outer layer. With a paring knife, carefully, trim root ends so they are flat. In a large pot of boiling water, cook onions for 10 minutes, or until tender. Drain and cool.

Meanwhile, in a small bowl, combine bread with milk; let soak for 10 minutes. Squeeze bread almost dry and, with your fingers break it into a large bowl. Stir in egg, mushrooms, capers, parsley, garlic, salt and pepper. Set aside.

Cut onions in half horizontally. Scoop out some of the center of each onion and chop coarsely. (Reserve the onion halves) Add the chopped onion to the bread mixture and mix well. Fill the onion halves with the bread mixture and sprinkle with dry breadcrumbs. *(The onions can be prepared ahead and stored, covered, in the refrigerator for up to 8 hours.)*

Arrange the onions in a shallow 2-qt. baking dish and drizzle with oil. Bake, uncovered, for about 25 minutes, or until the tops are golden and the onions are heated through.

Serves 6.

115 CALORIES PER SERVING: 4 G PROTEIN, 2 G FAT, 22 G CARBOHYDRATE; 335 MG SODIUM; 1 MG CHOLESTEROL.

Quick Vegetable Ragoût

Cooking this blend of vegetables and herbs in a parchment package results in a fragrant stew that contains no added fat. This makes a lovely first course or vegetable side dish.

¼ cup dry white wine
1 Tbsp. tomato paste
1 Tbsp. chopped fresh basil or parsley
2 cloves garlic, minced

2 cups frozen lima beans
2 cups frozen artichoke hearts
1 pt. cherry tomatoes, quartered
  salt & freshly ground black pepper to taste

Preheat oven to 400 degrees F. Prepare 4 pieces of parchment paper or aluminum foil for *papillotes (page 151)*. In a medium-sized bowl, whisk together wine, tomato paste, basil or parsley and garlic. Add lima beans, artichoke hearts and cherry tomatoes; toss to coat. Season with salt and pepper. Divide the vegetable mixture among the prepared *papillotes*, placing it in the center of one half of each opened paper heart. Seal the packages and place them on a baking sheet; bake for 10 to 12 minutes, or until the packages are puffed. Transfer the packages to small individual plates and serve.

Serves 4.

156 CALORIES PER SERVING: 9 G PROTEIN, 1 G FAT, 30 G CARBOHYDRATE; 164 MG SODIUM; 0 MG CHOLESTEROL.

Roasted Summer Vegetables

Few people think to cook summer vegetables in the oven, yet high-heat roasting keeps them juicy and flavorful. Lightly seasoned with herbs and a touch of olive oil, this dish cooks quickly and is excellent either served hot, at room temperature or cold.

1 red bell pepper, cored, seeded and cut into strips
1 yellow bell pepper, cored, seeded and cut into strips
2 red onions, peeled and cut into wedges
2 small summer squash, ends trimmed, cut into ½-inch-thick strips
2 small zucchini, ends trimmed, cut into ½-inch-thick strips

4 cloves garlic, peeled and thinly sliced
1 Tbsp. olive oil
1 Tbsp. chopped fresh oregano or 1 tsp. dried
  salt & freshly ground black pepper to taste
2 Tbsp. chopped fresh parsley
1 Tbsp. balsamic vinegar

Preheat oven to 425 degrees F. In a large bowl, toss together peppers, onions, squash, zucchini, garlic, olive oil, oregano, salt and pepper. Spread the vegetables on a baking sheet or metal roasting pan and roast for 20 minutes, or until tender, stirring several times. Transfer to a serving bowl and cool slightly. Add parsley and vinegar and toss until mixed. Taste and adjust seasonings.

Serves 6.

58 CALORIES PER SERVING: 2 G PROTEIN, 3 G FAT, 8 G CARBOHYDRATE; 271 MG SODIUM; 0 MG CHOLESTEROL.

Braised Winter Vegetables With Thyme

The inspiration for this recipe comes from Dean Fearing of The Mansion on Turtle Creek in Dallas. It is an easy way to cook some of the less glamorous vegetables that are abundant in cold weather. Cutting each vegetable into a slightly different shape makes for an interesting presentation.

2 tsp. olive oil
4 shallots, peeled and quartered
2 leeks, white part only, cleaned, halved lengthwise and cut into ½-inch pieces
2 carrots, peeled and sliced
2 parsnips, peeled, cut into quarters lengthwise and cut into sticks

1 celery stalk, cut in half lengthwise and sliced diagonally
1 Tbsp. fresh thyme leaves or 1 tsp. dried
¼ cup dry white wine
¼ cup defatted reduced-sodium chicken stock
   salt & freshly ground black pepper to taste

In a large nonstick skillet, heat oil over medium heat. Add shallots and sauté for 2 minutes, or until softened. Add leeks, carrots, parsnips and celery and sauté for 1 minute. Sprinkle with thyme, then stir in wine and stock. Reduce heat to low, cover the pan tightly and simmer until the vegetables are tender, 7 to 10 minutes. Season with salt and pepper and serve immediately.

Serves 4.

31 CALORIES PER SERVING: 1 G PROTEIN, 1 G FAT, 6 G CARBOHYDRATE; 15 MG SODIUM; 1 MG CHOLESTEROL.

Slimmed-Down Scalloped Potatoes

Sliced potatoes are simmered until tender in skim milk, then topped with reduced-fat sour cream and run under the broiler until golden. The results are sensational.

3 cloves garlic, peeled
1 lb. all-purpose potatoes, preferably Yukon Gold (about 3 medium), peeled and sliced
2 cups skim milk
½ onion, finely chopped

½ tsp. salt
   pinch nutmeg, preferably freshly grated
   freshly ground black pepper to taste
½ cup reduced-fat sour cream
2 Tbsp. freshly grated Parmesan cheese

Cut 1 clove garlic in half and rub vigorously over the inside of a shallow 2-qt. baking or gratin dish. Spray the dish with nonstick cooking spray. Mince remaining garlic.

In a medium-sized heavy saucepan, combine potatoes, milk, onions, minced garlic, salt, nutmeg and black pepper. Bring to a simmer over low heat, stirring occasionally. Simmer, uncovered, until potatoes are tender, about 10 minutes. Using a slotted spoon, transfer potatoes to the prepared dish.

Measure out ¼ cup of the milk mixture and pour into a small bowl. Whisk in sour cream. Pour over the potatoes. Top with Parmesan.

Preheat broiler. Spoon the sour cream mixture evenly over the potatoes and broil until golden brown, about 2 to 3 minutes. Serve immediately.

Serves 4.

197 CALORIES PER SERVING: 9 G PROTEIN, 4 G FAT, 31 G CARBOHYDRATE; 423 MG SODIUM; 12 MG CHOLESTEROL.

Oven "Fries"

Much lower in fat than their deep-fried cousins. Serve with grilled chicken or hamburgers.

1½ lbs. all-purpose potatoes, preferably Yukon
  Gold or Russet (about 4 medium), unpeeled,
  scrubbed
2 tsp. olive oil

½ tsp. salt
¼ tsp. paprika
  freshly ground black pepper to taste

Set oven rack on the upper level; preheat to 450 degrees F. Coat a baking sheet lightly with nonstick cooking spray. Cut each potato lengthwise into 8 wedges.

In a large bowl, combine olive oil, salt, paprika and pepper. Add potato wedges and toss to coat. Spread the potatoes on the prepared baking sheet and roast for 20 minutes. Loosen and turn the potatoes; roast for 10 to 15 minutes longer, or until golden brown. Serve immediately.

Serves 4.

129 CALORIES PER SERVING: 2 G PROTEIN, 2 G FAT, 25 G CARBOHYDRATE; 272 MG SODIUM; 0 MG CHOLESTEROL.

Buttermilk Mashed Potatoes

*Garlic cloves, cooked along with the potatoes, give this puree extra body.
Buttermilk gives them a luxurious taste, without the fat.*

2 lbs. all-purpose potatoes, preferably Yukon
  Gold (about 6 medium potatoes), peeled and
  cut into chunks
6 cloves garlic, peeled

  salt to taste
2 tsp. butter
1 cup skim-milk buttermilk
  freshly ground white or black pepper to taste

Place potatoes and garlic in a large heavy saucepan. Add water to cover and season with salt. Bring to a boil. Reduce heat to medium, cover, and cook for 10 to 15 minutes, or until potatoes are very tender.

Meanwhile, in a small saucepan, melt butter over low heat, cook until it begins to turn light brown, about 1 minute. Stir in buttermilk and heat until just warm. (Do not overheat the buttermilk or it will curdle.)

When potatoes are done, drain in a colander and return to the pot. Place pan over low heat and shake for about 1 minute to dry potatoes. Mash potatoes and garlic with a potato masher or an electric hand-held mixer. Add enough of the buttermilk mixture to make a smooth puree. Season with salt and pepper and serve.

Serves 6.

147 CALORIES PER SERVING: 4 G PROTEIN, 2 G FAT, 30 G CARBOHYDRATE; 42 MG SODIUM; 4 MG CHOLESTEROL.

Rutabaga & Potato Puree

Turnips can be substituted for the rutabagas,
but the puree will not have the same creamy yellow color.

1½ lbs. rutabaga, peeled and cut into small
    chunks
1½ lbs. all-purpose potatoes, (about 4 medium)
    peeled and cut into large chunks
 4 cloves garlic, peeled

    salt to taste
⅓   cup skim milk, scalded
 1 tsp. fresh thyme leaves or ½ tsp. dried
    freshly ground white or black pepper to taste

In a large pot, cover rutabagas and potatoes with water. Add garlic and season with salt. Bring to a boil. Reduce heat to medium and cook until the vegetables are very tender, 15 to 20 minutes. Drain thoroughly and return the vegetables to the saucepan. Place the pan over low heat and toss for about 1 minute to dry the vegetables slightly.

Using an electric hand-held mixer or potato masher, mash the rutabagas, potatoes and garlic. Add enough milk to make a smooth puree. Stir in thyme and season with salt and pepper. *(The puree can be prepared ahead and stored, covered, in the refrigerator for up to 2 days. Reheat in a microwave oven at 90 percent power, covered with a lid or wax paper, for 7 to 10 minutes.)*

Serves 8.

108 CALORIES PER SERVING: 3 G PROTEIN, 0 G FAT, 25 G CARBOHYDRATE; 25 MG SODIUM; 0 MG CHOLESTEROL.

Cauliflower With New Mornay Sauce

*"I was given this recipe by a French woman who told me she was taught it by her grandmother,"
wrote Jan Anderson. "Even children like this form of cauliflower." Indeed, a topping of Mornay sauce
is a delicious treatment for numerous vegetables: broccoli, asparagus, fennel, Belgian endive, to name a
few. In our revised version, we have replaced some of the high-fat cheeses and cream with
low-fat cottage cheese, which contributes a rich dairy flavor without the fat.*

1 head cauliflower (about 1¾ lbs.), cut into large florets	¼ tsp. salt
1¼ cups skim milk	¼ tsp. freshly ground black or white pepper
3 Tbsp. all-purpose white flour	3 Tbsp. freshly grated Parmesan cheese
½ cup 1% cottage cheese	1½ Tbsp. unseasoned fine dry breadcrumbs
½ cup shredded Swiss cheese, preferably Gruyère	

Set rack in upper portion of oven; preheat to 375 degrees F. Spray a shallow 2-qt. baking or gratin dish with nonstick cooking spray. Steam cauliflower until tender but not soft, 5 to 7 minutes. Refresh under cool water and set aside.

In a medium-sized heavy saucepan, scald 1 cup milk over medium heat. In a small bowl, stir together flour and the remaining ¼ cup cold milk to make a smooth paste. Stir into the hot milk mixture and cook, stirring constantly, until thickened, about 3 to 4 minutes. Remove from the heat and whisk in cottage cheese, Swiss cheese, salt and pepper. Transfer sauce to a food processor or blender and puree until smooth.

Spread one-third of sauce in prepared baking dish. Arrange cauliflower over it and top with the remaining sauce. Sprinkle cauliflower with Parmesan and breadcrumbs. *(Recipe can be made ahead to this point and stored, covered, in the refrigerator up to 1 day.)* Bake for 30 minutes or until golden brown and bubbly.

Serves 8.

100 CALORIES PER SERVING: 8 G PROTEIN, 3 G FAT, 11 G CARBOHYDRATE; 229 MG SODIUM; 10 MG CHOLESTEROL.

℞ *Jan Anderson of Eugene, Oregon*

Corn Pudding

A number of EATING WELL subscribers lamented the results when they tried to substitute low-fat milk or cut back on the eggs in their family-favorite corn pudding. We found that using evaporated skim milk, rather than regular skim milk, produced a reduced-fat custard with a creamier consistency. For additional creaminess, and to intensify the sweet corn flavor, we pureed half of the corn.

2 cups fresh corn kernels (about 2 large ears)	1 tsp. salt
2 Tbsp. all-purpose white flour	¼ tsp. freshly ground black pepper
3 large eggs	1 tsp. butter
3 large egg whites	2 Tbsp. unseasoned fine dry breadcrumbs
1 cup evaporated skim milk	

Preheat oven to 325 degrees F. Spray a 1½- or 2-qt. soufflé or casserole dish with nonstick cooking spray.

In a food processor or blender, combine 1 cup corn and flour; process until smooth. In a large bowl, whisk together eggs and egg whites. Stir in the pureed corn, the remaining 1 cup corn kernels, milk, salt and pepper.

Pour mixture into the prepared dish and bake for 30 minutes. While the pudding is baking, in a small saucepan melt butter over low heat. Cook until the butter is a light, nutty brown, 30 seconds to 1 minute. Add breadcrumbs and cook, stirring frequently, until crumbs darken slightly, about 1 to 1½ minutes.

When the pudding has baked for 30 minutes, sprinkle the breadcrumb topping over top and continue to bake for 25 to 35 minutes longer, or until a knife inserted near the center comes out clean. Serve immediately.

Serves 8.

98 CALORIES PER SERVING: 7 G PROTEIN, 3 G FAT, 11 G CARBOHYDRATE; 367 MG SODIUM; 82 MG CHOLESTEROL.

R_x *Cindy Hendrick of Bloomington, Minnesota, and Sande Drechsler of Smithtown, New York*

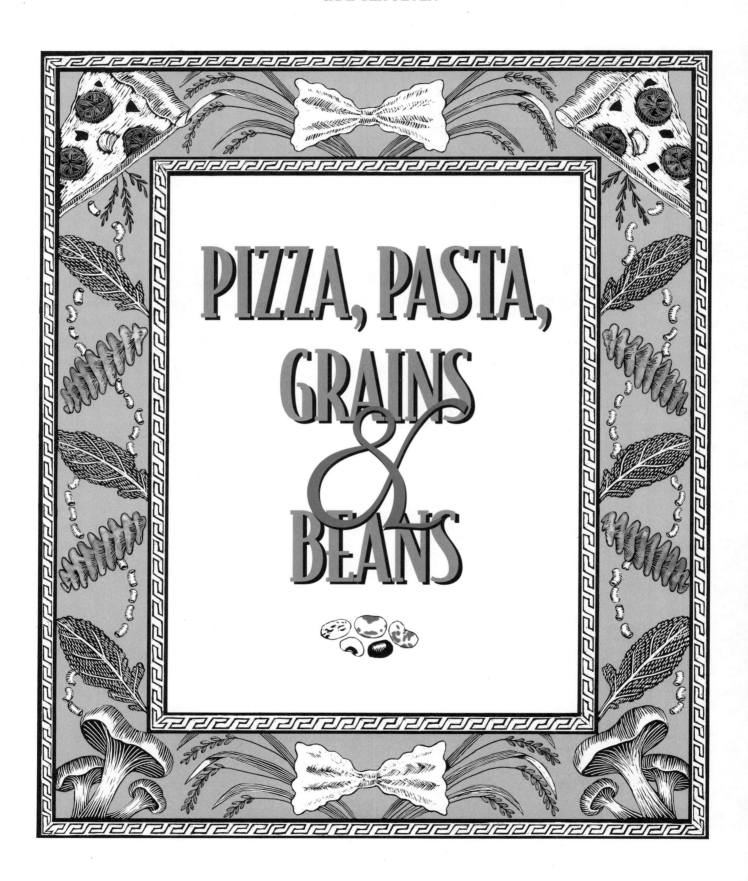

CHAPTER SEVEN

PIZZA, PASTA, GRAINS & BEANS

RECIPES

Quick-Rising Pizza Dough

Here is a versatile foundation for healthful pizzas whose toppings can be as creative as your imagination and palate. A large-capacity food processor will cut down on kneading time.

4-4¼ cups all-purpose white flour
  2 pkg. Rapid-Rise yeast
  2 tsp. salt

  1 tsp. sugar
  2 tsp. olive oil

In a large mixing bowl, stir together 3 cups flour, yeast, salt and sugar. In a small saucepan, combine 1³/₄ cups water and oil. Heat until hot to the touch, 125 to 130 degrees F. With a wooden spoon, gradually stir the oil and water mixture into the flour mixture. Beat until well mixed. Gradually add enough of the remaining flour to make a firm, soft dough. Turn out onto a lightly floured surface and knead for 8 to 10 minutes, or until smooth and elastic. Cover with plastic and let rest for 10 minutes.

Alternatively, in a food processor, combine 4 cups flour, yeast, salt and sugar. Heat 1¹/₂ cups water and oil to 125 to 130 degrees F. With the motor running, gradually add the hot liquid. Process, adding up to 2 Tbsp. cold water until the dough forms a ball, then process for 1 minute to knead. Turn out onto a lightly floured surface, cover with plastic and let rest for 10 minutes. (*The dough can be made ahead, punched down, enclosed in a large plastic bag and stored in the refrigerator overnight. Bring to room temperature before using.*)

Makes eight 6-inch crusts.

244 CALORIES PER PIZZA: 7 G PROTEIN, 2 G FAT, 49 G CARBOHYDRATE; 534 MG SODIUM; 0 MG CHOLESTEROL.

Pesto Pizza

A perfect choice for late August when fresh basil is abundant and tomatoes are sweet and juicy.

1½ cups packed fresh basil leaves
1½ Tbsp. freshly grated Parmesan cheese
1½ Tbsp. olive oil
  1 clove garlic, minced
  3 Tbsp. nonfat plain yogurt

    salt & freshly ground black pepper to taste
  1 recipe Quick-Rising Pizza Dough (*above*)
    cornmeal for dusting pizza peel
  4 cups sliced ripe plum tomatoes (8 tomatoes)

In a food processor or blender, combine basil, cheese, oil and garlic. Process until well blended. Add yogurt and process until smooth. Season with salt and pepper. (*Pesto topping can be prepared ahead and stored, covered, in the refrigerator for up to 2 days.*)

Place a pizza stone, baking tiles or an inverted baking sheet on the lowest rack of the oven; preheat to 500 de-grees F or the highest oven setting. Divide dough into 8 pieces. Using your fists, stretch one piece into a 6-inch round. Alternatively, with a rolling pin, roll out on a lightly floured surface. (Keep remaining dough covered with a towel or plastic wrap.) Place on a cornmeal-dusted pizza peel or inverted baking sheet, using enough cornmeal so that the dough slides easily. Stretch or roll a second round of dough and place beside the first.

Spread 1 Tbsp. pesto on each round of dough. Arrange ½ cup sliced tomatoes over top of each one. Season lightly with salt and pepper.

Carefully slide the pizzas onto the heated pizza stone, baking tiles or baking sheet and bake for 10 to 14 minutes, or until the bottoms are crisp and browned. Working with 2 pizzas at a time, repeat with the remaining dough and toppings.

Makes eight 6-inch pizzas.

291 CALORIES PER PIZZA: 9 G PROTEIN, 5 G FAT, 53 G CARBOHYDRATE; 570 MG SODIUM; 1 MG CHOLESTEROL.

Wild Mushroom & Sage Pizza

The earthy flavor of this pizza is nicely balanced between the rich mushroom and pungent fresh sage. Dried sage will do, but is not as aromatic as fresh. Because the flavors are intense, this pizza is better served as an appetizer than a main dish.

1½ tsp. olive oil
8 cups sliced wild and/or cultivated mushrooms, such as chanterelles, cèpes, shiitake, oyster, button (about 1½ lbs.)
2 cups sliced onions (2 medium) salt & freshly ground black pepper to taste

1 recipe Quick-Rising Pizza Dough *(page 108)* cornmeal for dusting pizza peel
1 cup grated part-skim mozzarella cheese (¼ lb.)
4 tsp. chopped fresh sage or 1 tsp. dried, rubbed

In a small nonstick skillet, heat oil over medium heat. Add mushrooms and onions and sauté for 3 to 5 minutes, or until tender. Season with salt and pepper. Let cool.

Place a pizza stone, baking tiles or an inverted baking sheet on the lowest rack of the oven; preheat to 500 degrees F or the highest oven setting. Divide dough into 8 pieces. Using your fists, stretch one piece into a 6-inch round. Alternatively, with a rolling pin, roll out on a lightly floured surface. (Keep remaining dough covered with a towel or plastic wrap.) Place on a cornmeal-dusted pizza peel or an inverted baking sheet, using enough cornmeal so that the dough slides easily. Stretch or roll a second round of dough and place beside the first.

Sprinkle 2 Tbsp. mozzarella over each round. Arrange ⅓ cup mushroom-onion mixture evenly over the cheese. Sprinkle with ½ tsp. fresh sage or a ⅛ tsp. dried.

Carefully slide the pizzas onto the heated pizza stone, baking tiles or baking sheet and bake for 10 to 14 minutes, or until the bottoms are crisp and browned. Repeat with the remaining dough and toppings.

Makes eight 6-inch pizzas.

321 CALORIES PER PIZZA: 13 G PROTEIN, 5 G FAT, 56 G CARBOHYDRATE; 605 MG SODIUM; 8 MG CHOLESTEROL.

Pizza Primavera

"Primavera" means "springtime" in Italian, which in culinary terms means fresh vegetables.
Inspired by pasta primavera, this vegetable-topped pizza lives up to its name.

1 recipe Quick-Rising Pizza Dough *(page 108)*
  cornmeal for dusting pizza peel
1 cup grated part-skim mozzarella cheese
  (¼ lb.)
4 cups sliced plum tomatoes (8 tomatoes)

2 cups sliced zucchini (1 medium)
8 cups sliced mushrooms (1½ lbs.)
1 cup sliced onions (1 medium)
2 Tbsp. plus 2 tsp. chopped fresh basil
  salt and freshly ground black pepper to taste

Place a pizza stone, baking tiles or an inverted baking sheet on the lowest rack of the oven; preheat to 500 degrees F or the highest oven setting. Divide dough into 8 pieces. Using your fists, stretch one piece into a 6-inch round. Alternatively, with a rolling pin, roll out on a lightly floured surface. (Keep remaining dough covered with a towel or plastic wrap.) Place on a cornmeal-dusted pizza peel or an inverted baking sheet, using enough cornmeal so that the dough slides easily. Stretch or roll a second round of dough and place beside the first.

Sprinkle 2 Tbsp. cheese over each round of dough. Arrange ½ cup tomato, ¼ cup zucchini, 1 cup mushrooms and a few slices onions over the cheese. Sprinkle 1 tsp. basil over the top and season with salt and pepper.

Carefully slide the pizzas onto the heated pizza stone, baking tiles or baking sheet and bake for 10 to 14 minutes, or until the bottoms are crisp and browned. Repeat with the remaining dough and toppings.

Makes eight 6-inch pizzas.

323 CALORIES PER PIZZA: 14 G PROTEIN, 4 G FAT, 58 G CARBOHYDRATE; 610 MG SODIUM; 8 MG CHOLESTEROL.

Caramelized Onion Pizza

Rosemary and black olives added to the dough give this pizza an earthy flavor, and browned
onions add sweetness. For delicious appetizers, cut the pizza into small wedges.

1½ tsp. olive oil
  4 cups sliced onions (4 medium)
    salt & freshly ground black pepper to taste
  1 Tbsp. balsamic vinegar
  ¾ cup Kalamata or Gaeta olives, pitted and
    chopped (about ¼ lb.)

1 Tbsp. chopped fresh or 1 tsp. crumbled dried
  rosemary
1 recipe Quick-Rising Pizza Dough *(page 108)*
  cornmeal for dusting pizza peel
1 cup grated part-skim mozzarella cheese
  (¼ lb.)

In a large nonstick skillet, heat oil over medium-low heat. Add onions, season with salt and pepper; sauté for about 20 minutes, or until lightly browned and very tender. Stir in vinegar, taste and adjust seasonings. Let cool.

Place a pizza stone, baking tiles or inverted baking sheet on the lowest rack of the oven; preheat to 500 degrees F or the highest oven setting. Add olives and rosemary to pizza dough and knead on a lightly floured surface until they are mixed in. Divide dough into 8 pieces. Using your fists, stretch one piece into a 6-inch round.

Alternatively, with a rolling pin, roll out on a lightly floured surface. (Keep remaining dough covered with a towel or plastic wrap.) Place on a cornmeal-dusted pizza peel or an inverted baking sheet, using enough cornmeal so that the dough slides easily. Stretch or roll a second round of dough and place beside the first.

Sprinkle 2 Tbsp. cheese over each pizza round and arrange ¼ cup of the reserved onions over the top.

Carefully slide the pizzas onto the heated pizza stone, baking tiles or baking sheet and bake for 10 to 14 minutes, or until the bottoms are crisp and browned. Working with 2 pizzas at a time, repeat with the remaining dough and toppings.

Makes eight 6-inch pizzas.

327 CALORIES PER PIZZA: 12 G PROTEIN, 8 G FAT, 53 G CARBOHYDRATE; 693 MG SODIUM; 8 MG CHOLESTEROL.

Eggplant Pizza

This layering of tomato, cheese, eggplant and mushrooms is moist and flavorful.
You can roast the eggplant several hours ahead, but keep it covered.

2 eggplants (2 lbs.), cut into ⅛-inch-thick slices
2 tsp. salt
1 recipe Quick-Rising Pizza Dough *(page 108)*
   cornmeal for dusting pizza peel
1½ cups Tomato Sauce *(page 112)*

1 cup grated part-skim mozzarella cheese (¼ lb.)
8 cups sliced mushrooms (1½ lbs.)
4 tsp. chopped fresh oregano or 1 tsp. dried
   freshly ground black pepper to taste

Sprinkle eggplant with salt and let sit in a colander for 30 minutes. Rinse and pat dry. Meanwhile, place a pizza stone, baking tiles or an inverted baking sheet on the lowest rack of the oven; preheat to 400 degrees F.

Arrange the eggplant slices in a single layer on a lightly oiled baking sheet and bake for 3 to 4 minutes on each side, or until the eggplant is tender and lightly browned. Let cool.

Increase temperature to 500 degrees F or the highest oven setting. Divide dough into 8 pieces. Using your fists, stretch one piece into a 6-inch round. Alternatively, with a rolling pin, roll out on a lightly floured surface. (Keep remaining dough covered with a towel or plastic wrap.) Place on a cornmeal-dusted pizza peel or an inverted baking sheet, using enough cornmeal so that the dough slides easily. Stretch or roll a second round of dough and place beside the first.

Spread 3 Tbsp. tomato sauce over each round of dough and sprinkle 2 Tbsp. cheese over the top. Arrange 1 cup mushrooms and several eggplant slices over the cheese and sprinkle with ½ tsp. fresh or ⅛ tsp. dried oregano. Season with salt and pepper.

Carefully slide the pizzas onto the heated pizza stone, baking tiles or baking sheet and bake for 10 to 14 minutes, or until the bottoms are crisp and golden. Repeat with the remaining dough and toppings.

Makes eight 6-inch pizzas

331 CALORIES PER PIZZA: 13 G PROTEIN, 5 G FAT, 59 G CARBOHYDRATE; 1,235 MG SODIUM; 8 MG CHOLESTEROL.

Tomato Sauce

This general-purpose tomato sauce works as well for pasta as for pizza.
It may be frozen for up to two months.

1½ tsp. olive oil
3 cloves garlic, minced
1 28-oz. can tomatoes (with juices), chopped
2 Tbsp. tomato paste

2 tsp. fresh chopped oregano or ½ tsp. dried
1 tsp. fresh thyme or ¼ tsp. dried
salt & freshly ground black pepper to taste

In a large saucepan, heat oil over medium heat. Add garlic and sauté for 2 minutes, or until lightly browned. Add tomatoes, tomato paste, oregano and thyme. Reduce heat to low and simmer, uncovered, stirring occasionally, for 30 minutes, or until thickened. Season with salt and pepper. Cool the sauce to room temperature before spreading it on the pizza dough.

Makes about 2¼ cups.

30 CALORIES PER ¼ CUP: 1 G PROTEIN, 1 G FAT, 5 G CARBOHYDRATE; 173 MG SODIUM; 0 MG CHOLESTEROL.

Tex-Mex Pizza

With the Mexican flavors of cilantro, jalapeño peppers and jack cheese,
this pizza tastes like an open-faced quesadilla.

1 recipe Quick-Rising Pizza Dough *(page 108)*
cornmeal for dusting pizza peel
4 cups sliced plum tomatoes (8 tomatoes)
2 Tbsp. plus 2 tsp. minced, seeded jalapeño pepper, or to taste (about 3 peppers)

salt & freshly ground black pepper to taste
1 cup grated reduced-fat Monterey Jack cheese (¼ lb.)
2 Tbsp. plus 2 tsp. chopped fresh cilantro

Place a pizza stone, baking tiles or inverted baking sheet on the lowest rack of the oven; preheat to 500 degrees F or highest oven setting.

Divide dough into 8 pieces. Using your fists, stretch one piece into a 6-inch round. Alternatively, with a rolling pin, roll out on a lightly floured surface. (Keep remaining dough covered with a towel or plastic wrap.) Place on a cornmeal-dusted pizza peel or an inverted baking sheet, using enough cornmeal so that the dough slides easily. Stretch or roll a second round of dough and place beside the first.

Arrange ½ cup tomatoes over each round of dough. Sprinkle with 1 tsp. jalapeños and season with salt and pepper. Sprinkle 2 Tbsp. cheese over the top.

Carefully slide the pizzas onto the heated pizza stone, baking tiles or baking sheet and bake for 10 to 14 minutes, or until the bottoms are crisp and browned. Repeat with the remaining dough and toppings. Before serving, sprinkle each pizza with 1 tsp. cilantro.

Makes eight 6-inch pizzas.

260 CALORIES PER PIZZA: 8 G PROTEIN, 2 G FAT, 52 G CARBOHYDRATE; 582 MG SODIUM; 1 MG CHOLESTEROL.

Rosemary Focaccia

Straight from the oven, this flatbread (actually a pizza crust with a light savory topping of onions and herbs) is a satisfying snack. Focaccia is equally at home on a party buffet, tucked into the picnic basket or as an accompaniment to soups or salads.

DOUGH

2¾ cups all-purpose white flour (plus a little extra for kneading)
1 pkg. active dry yeast (1 Tbsp.)
1 tsp. salt
1 tsp. chopped fresh rosemary
1 Tbsp. honey
2 tsp. olive oil, preferably extra-virgin
cornmeal for dusting baking sheet

TOPPING

1 tsp. olive oil, preferably extra-virgin
1 red onion, thinly sliced
½ tsp. chopped fresh rosemary
1 large egg white, lightly beaten
½ tsp. kosher salt
freshly ground black pepper to taste

To make dough: In a large mixing bowl, stir together 2½ cups flour, yeast, salt and rosemary. In a small saucepan, combine 1 cup warm water, honey and oil. Heat until warm to the touch (120 to 130 degrees F). With a wooden spoon, gradually stir the liquid into the flour mixture. Stir vigorously until well mixed. Gradually work in the remaining ¼ cup flour to make a firm, soft, smooth dough. Turn out onto a lightly floured surface and knead for 8 to 10 minutes, or until smooth and elastic, adding additional flour as needed to prevent it from sticking.

Alternatively, in a food processor combine all the flour with the yeast, salt and rosemary. With the motor running, add the heated liquid ingredients and process until the dough forms a ball. Process for 1 minute to knead.

Place the dough in a lightly oiled bowl and turn to coat with oil. Cover with plastic wrap and let rise for 1½ hours, or until doubled in bulk.

Preheat oven to 450 degrees F. Lightly spray a large baking sheet with nonstick cooking spray and dust lightly with cornmeal.

To make topping and bake focaccia: In a small nonstick skillet, heat oil over medium heat. Add onions and rosemary; sauté until the onions are light golden, about 5 minutes. Add ¼ cup water and simmer until all the liquid has evaporated, about 2 minutes. Let cool.

Turn dough out onto a lightly floured surface and, with floured hands, form the dough into a rectangular shape. Transfer to the prepared baking sheet and press dough to cover the baking sheet. Brush egg white over the surface of the dough. Sprinkle the reserved onion mixture over the surface. Top with kosher salt and pepper. Bake for 13 to 15 minutes, or until golden brown. Transfer to a cutting board and cut into 8 or 16 pieces.

Serves 8.

193 CALORIES PER SERVING: 5 G PROTEIN, 2 G FAT, 37 G CARBOHYDRATE; 392 MG SODIUM; 0 MG CHOLESTEROL.

Linguine With Roasted Summer Vegetables

*Instead of swimming in a cream sauce, linguine is tossed with roasted vegetables
and garlic puree for a full flavor without much fat.*

1   cup defatted reduced-sodium chicken stock
10 large cloves garlic, peeled and cut in half
2   Tbsp. balsamic vinegar
1   lb. cherry tomatoes, cut in half
1   lb. asparagus, trimmed and cut into 2-inch lengths
2   small zucchini (½ lb. total), quartered lengthwise and cut into 2-inch pieces

1   small summer squash (½ lb.), quartered lengthwise and cut into 2-inch pieces
1   large red bell pepper, cored, seeded and cut into chunks
8   scallions, white and tender green parts only, cut into 2-inch lengths
1   Tbsp. olive oil
    salt & freshly ground black pepper to taste
1   lb. linguine

Preheat oven to 450 degrees F. In a small saucepan, combine stock and garlic. Bring to a boil, reduce heat to low and simmer, covered, for 15 to 20 minutes, or until tender. Place in a blender or food processor along with vinegar and puree until smooth. Return to the saucepan and keep warm over low heat.

Meanwhile, in a large bowl, combine tomatoes, asparagus, zucchini, summer squash, red peppers and scallions. Drizzle oil over the top, season with salt and pepper and toss to coat well. Place on a baking sheet and roast, stirring occasionally, for 15 minutes, or until tender.

Meanwhile, in a large pot of boiling salted water, cook linguine for 6 to 8 minutes, or until tender but firm. Drain and place in a large serving bowl. Toss with the roasted vegetables and garlic puree. Season with salt and pepper and serve immediately.

Serves 4.

538 CALORIES PER SERVING: 21 G PROTEIN, 6 G FAT, 103 G CARBOHYDRATE; 173 MG SODIUM; 1 MG CHOLESTEROL.

Fusilli With Lentils & Kale

*Lentils give this sauce a meaty feel, making it an interesting alternative to
long-simmered old-fashioned sauces. For a vegetarian version, substitute vegetable stock for
chicken stock, omit the prosciutto and add about 8 chopped dried tomatoes to the sauce.*

½   cup green lentils, preferably French lentils from LePuy
1½ tsp. olive oil
1   medium-sized onion, chopped
1   medium-sized carrot, chopped
4   cloves garlic, minced
2   oz. prosciutto, trimmed of fat and chopped (¼ cup)
2   cups defatted reduced-sodium chicken stock

1   tsp. chopped fresh rosemary or a pinch dried
1   tsp. fresh thyme or ½ tsp. dried
1   28-oz. can plum tomatoes, drained and chopped
4   cups coarsely chopped kale leaves (½ bunch)
    salt & freshly ground black pepper to taste
1   lb. rotini or fusilli
¼   cup freshly grated Parmesan cheese

In a medium-sized saucepan, cover lentils with cold water; bring to a boil and cook for 5 minutes. Drain and rinse with cold water. In a nonstick skillet, heat oil over medium heat. Add onions, carrots, garlic and prosciutto, and sauté for 3 to 5 minutes, or until the vegetables are softened. Add stock, lentils, rosemary and thyme and bring to a boil. Reduce heat to low, cover and simmer for 15 minutes. Add tomatoes and kale, return to a simmer,

cover and cook for 15 to 20 minutes longer, or until the lentils and kale are tender. Season with salt and pepper.

Meanwhile, in a large pot of boiling salted water, cook rotini or fusilli for 10 to 12 minutes, or until tender but firm. Drain and place in a large, shallow bowl. Add the lentil sauce and toss well. Taste and adjust seasonings and serve immediately with Parmesan.

Serves 6.

433 CALORIES PER SERVING: 18 G PROTEIN, 5 G FAT, 73 G CARBOHYDRATE; 477 MG SODIUM; 7 MG CHOLESTEROL.

Fusilli With Roasted Tomatoes, Asparagus & Shrimp

This entrée celebrates garden-fresh asparagus with flair.
Combining the cooked pasta with the vegetables in the roasting pan ensures that no flavor is lost.

12 plum tomatoes, quartered lengthwise
 4 tsp. olive oil, preferably extra-virgin
    freshly ground black pepper to taste
 1 small head garlic
 1 lb. thin asparagus, trimmed and cut into
    2-inch lengths (or larger stalks, peeled and
    halved lengthwise before cutting)

 1 lb. large shrimp, peeled and deveined
 ¾ lb. corkscrew pasta, such as fusilli or rotini
 2 tsp. fresh lemon juice
 1 Tbsp. chopped fresh oregano or 1 tsp. dried
 1 Tbsp. chopped fresh thyme or 1 tsp. dried
    salt to taste

Set oven rack in lower third of oven; preheat to 450 degrees F.

In a large roasting pan, toss tomatoes with 2 tsp. olive oil and a generous grinding of pepper. Slice the top ½ inch off the garlic head and discard; pull off any loose papery skin. Wrap in aluminum foil and add to the roasting pan.

Roast for 20 minutes, without stirring, or until the tomatoes are wrinkled and beginning to brown. Scatter the asparagus and shrimp over the tomatoes and roast for 10 minutes longer, or until the shrimp are curled and firm and the asparagus is tender. Remove the garlic from the pan, unwrap and let cool for 5 minutes. Cover the roasting pan to keep warm.

Meanwhile, in a large pot of boiling salted water, cook pasta until tender but firm, about 8 minutes. While the pasta is cooking, separate the garlic cloves and squeeze out the soft pulp. Mash to a paste with the flat side of a knife.

Drain the pasta and return to the pot. Add the remaining 2 tsp. olive oil, mashed garlic, lemon juice, oregano, thyme, salt and pepper, tossing to evenly coat the pasta with the seasonings. Transfer the pasta to the roasting pan and toss gently to combine, making sure to scrape up any bits that have adhered to the bottom of the pan. Serve immediately.

Serves 4.

528 CALORIES PER SERVING: 39 G PROTEIN, 8 G FAT, 76 G CARBOHYDRATE; 276 MG SODIUM; 222 MG CHOLESTEROL.

Bow Ties With Chicken, Red Peppers & Artichokes

This combination of simple ingredients results in a sophisticated warm pasta salad.

¾ lb. bow-tie pasta
2 Tbsp. pine nuts
1 Tbsp. olive oil
¾ lb. boneless, skinless chicken breast, trimmed of fat and membrane and thinly sliced
    salt & freshly ground black pepper to taste
2 small red bell peppers, seeded and thinly sliced

2 shallots, minced
2 cloves garlic, minced
1 cup defatted reduced-sodium chicken stock
¼ cup balsamic vinegar
2 tsp. chopped fresh rosemary or 1 tsp. dried
1 9-oz. package frozen artichoke hearts, thawed, or 13¾-oz. can, drained and rinsed

In a large pot of boiling salted water, cook pasta for about 10 minutes, or until tender but firm. Drain and rinse under cold water until cooled. Set aside.

In a small dry skillet, toast pine nuts, stirring, over medium heat for 3 to 4 minutes, or until golden and fragrant. Set aside.

In a wok or 12-inch nonstick skillet, heat 2 tsp. oil over high heat. Add chicken pieces and sauté for 2 to 3 minutes, or until no longer pink inside. Season with salt and pepper and set aside.

Add the remaining 1 tsp. oil to the pan. Add peppers, shallots and garlic, and sauté for 2 minutes, or until the peppers are tender-crisp. Add to the reserved chicken.

Add stock, vinegar and rosemary to the pan and bring to a boil. Add artichokes and the reserved pasta and cook for about 2 minutes, or until heated through. Return the reserved chicken mixture to the pan and toss with the pasta. Taste and adjust seasoning and sprinkle with pine nuts. Serve warm.

Serves 6.

371 CALORIES PER SERVING: 25 G PROTEIN, 8 G FAT, 51 G CARBOHYDRATE; 176 MG SODIUM; 41 MG CHOLESTEROL.

Spaghetti alla Carbonara

"Can this recipe be saved? The eggs are a double whammy—first, they're whole eggs, and second, they're raw. And I don't suppose the pancetta is good for me, either!" wrote David Klueter. By substituting egg whites for two of the whole eggs, we reduced the fat, and by tossing the eggs with very hot pasta over low heat, we are actually cooking them. Instead of 8 ounces of pancetta, we have used 2 ounces of prosciutto, which is leaner.

1 lb. spaghetti
2 tsp. olive oil
4 cloves garlic, peeled and crushed
2 oz. thinly sliced prosciutto, trimmed of fat and cut into slivers
⅓ cup dry white wine

1 large egg
2 large egg whites
¼ cup freshly grated Parmesan cheese (½ oz.)
¼ cup freshly grated pecorino Romano cheese
¼ cup chopped fresh parsley
    salt & freshly ground black pepper to taste

In a large pot of boiling salted water, cook spaghetti until tender but firm, 8 to 11 minutes.

Meanwhile, in a large nonstick skillet, heat oil over medium heat. Add garlic and cook, stirring, for 2 to 3 minutes, or until it just begins to color. Add prosciutto and cook for 1 to 2 minutes longer. Stir in wine and cook until liquid has reduced by half, 2 to 3 minutes. Remove from heat.

In a small bowl whisk together egg, egg whites, cheeses and parsley. Season with a generous grinding of black pepper.

When pasta is cooked, drain in a colander and add to the prosciutto mixture in the skillet. Add the egg mixture and toss over low heat until the eggs become creamy and thick, 30 to 40 seconds. Do not cook too long or the eggs will scramble. Taste and adjust seasonings and serve at once, passing additional black pepper.

Serves 4.

548 CALORIES PER SERVING: 25 G PROTEIN, 9 G FAT, 87 G CARBOHYDRATE; 374 MG SODIUM; 65 MG CHOLESTEROL.

R_x *David A. Klueter of Fairfax, Virginia*

Indispensable Meat Sauce for Pasta

Prosciutto, wine and mushrooms dress up the all-purpose spaghetti sauce;
keep some handy in your freezer to toss with your favorite pasta, layer into lasagna or
spoon over polenta. We have added bulgur to reduce the amount of ground beef.

½ lb. lean ground beef
1 tsp. vegetable oil, preferably canola oil
1 oz. prosciutto, finely chopped
1 large onion, finely chopped
2 carrots, finely chopped
2 stalks celery, finely chopped
1 green bell pepper, cored, seeded and finely chopped
½ lb. mushrooms, trimmed and thinly sliced (3 cups)

3 cloves garlic, minced
½ cup dry red wine
2 28-oz. cans plum tomatoes (with juices), chopped
1 Tbsp. chopped fresh thyme or 1½ tsp. dried
½ tsp. dried oregano
½ tsp. salt
½ tsp. freshly ground black pepper
¼ tsp. red-pepper flakes
¼ cup bulgur

Heat a large Dutch oven over medium heat. Add ground beef and cook, breaking up meat with a wooden spoon until browned, 3 to 5 minutes. Transfer to a colander to drain fat. Set aside.

Add oil to the Dutch oven and heat over low heat. Add prosciutto, onions, carrots, celery, and green peppers and sauté until softened, 15 to 20 minutes. Add mushrooms and garlic and sauté for 10 minutes more.

Add wine, increase heat to medium-high and cook until wine has evaporated. Stir in tomatoes, thyme, oregano, salt, pepper, red-pepper flakes and the reserved beef. Simmer, uncovered, stirring often, for an hour. Add 2 cups water and bulgur. Simmer, for 15 minutes, or until the bulgur is tender. Taste and adjust seasonings.

Makes about 8 cups.

159 CALORIES PER CUP: 10 G PROTEIN, 5 G FAT, 19 G CARBOHYDRATE; 530 MG SODIUM; 19 MG CHOLESTEROL.

Swiss Chard & Wild Mushroom Lasagna

Precooked lasagna noodles are nice and thin, much more like homemade than regular dried lasagna noodles, and of course they save considerable fuss. To ensure that the lasagna browns nicely, it is baked uncovered; the precooked noodles are first soaked in hot water so they will become tender during baking. If precooked noodles are not available, you can use regular cooked lasagna noodles.

TOMATO-MUSHROOM SAUCE

¼ cup dried porcini mushrooms (½ oz.)
2 tsp. olive oil
1 onion, chopped
1 carrot, peeled and chopped
½ lb. mushrooms, cleaned, trimmed and
   quartered (3 cups)
¼ cup chopped fresh parsley
1 tsp. chopped fresh rosemary or ½ tsp. dried
4 cloves garlic, minced
   salt & freshly ground black pepper to taste
¾ cup dry red wine
1 28-oz. can plum tomatoes, drained and
   crushed

SWISS CHARD-CHEESE FILLING

2 bunches Swiss chard (1½ lbs.), stems
   trimmed, washed
2 16-oz. containers 1% cottage cheese, pressed
   (page 26)
1½ cups skim milk
2 Tbsp. all-purpose white flour
¾ cup freshly grated Parmesan cheese
¼ tsp. freshly grated nutmeg
   salt & freshly ground black pepper to taste

NOODLES & CHEESE

12 precooked lasagna noodles (8 oz.)
1 cup grated part-skim mozzarella cheese
¼ cup freshly grated Parmesan cheese

To make tomato-mushroom sauce: In a small bowl, cover porcini with 1 cup hot tap water and soak for 20 minutes. Lift the porcini from the soaking liquid, transfer to a sieve and rinse thoroughly. Press out excess moisture and chop finely. Strain the soaking liquid through a sieve lined with cheesecloth or filter paper. Reserve the porcini and the soaking liquid.

In a large nonstick skillet, heat oil over medium heat. Add onions and carrots; sauté until softened, 2 to 3 minutes. Add fresh mushrooms and sauté for about 3 minutes. Add parsley, rosemary, garlic, the reserved porcini and cook, stirring, for 1 minute. Season with salt and pepper. Add wine and cook until it has nearly evaporated, about 2 minutes. Add the reserved porcini liquid and cook until it has nearly evaporated, 3 to 5 minutes. Add tomatoes and simmer over medium heat, stirring occasionally, until slightly thickened, about 10 minutes. Taste and adjust seasonings.

To make Swiss chard-cheese filling: Place Swiss chard in a large pot with just the water clinging to the leaves. Season with salt. Cook, covered, over medium heat, stirring occasionally, until wilted, 3 to 5 minutes. Drain and refresh with cold water. Press out excess moisture and chop. Set aside.

Place the pressed cottage cheese in a food processor and puree until very smooth. Scrape the puree into a medium-sized bowl and set aside. In a small saucepan, heat 1¼ cups milk until steaming. In a small bowl, stir flour into the remaining ¼ cup cold milk until smooth. Add to the hot milk and cook, whisking constantly until thickened, 2 to 3 minutes. Add to the pureed cottage cheese, along with Parmesan, nutmeg, salt and pepper; mix well. Set 1½ cups of the cheese sauce aside. Add the Swiss chard to the remaining cheese mixture.

To assemble lasagna: In a large bowl, cover lasagna noodles with hot water; let soak for 10 to 15 minutes, or until pliable. Preheat oven to 375 degrees F. Spray a 9-by-13-inch baking dish with nonstick cooking spray. Spread ½ cup of the reserved cheese sauce over the bottom of the prepared dish. Remove 3 noodles from the water, shaking off excess water, and lay them over the sauce. Spread one-third of the Swiss chard-cheese filling over top. Spoon one-third of the tomato-mushroom sauce over and sprinkle with one-third of the mozzarella. Lay 3 noodles over top, cover with another third of the Swiss chard-cheese filling, tomato-mushroom sauce and mozzarella. Repeat with 3 more noodles and the remaining Swiss chard-cheese filling, tomato-mushroom sauce

and mozzarella. Lay 3 noodles over and spread the remaining 1 cup cheese sauce over top. Sprinkle with Parmesan. Bake, uncovered, for 35 to 40 minutes, or until golden and bubbly. Let stand for 10 minutes before serving.

Serves 6.

516 CALORIES PER SERVING: 48 G PROTEIN, 12 G FAT, 50 G CARBOHYDRATE; 671 MG SODIUM; 35 MG CHOLESTEROL.

One-Step, One-Hour Lasagna

*The lasagna recipe contributed by Pam Miller is perfect for a family supper.
It contains a very quick tomato-meat sauce and successfully bypasses the step of boiling the lasagna
noodles. Our revised version has about one-quarter of the fat of the original because
we reduced the ground beef and opted for lower-fat cheeses.*

¼ lb. lean ground beef
1 16-oz. can tomatoes (with juices), chopped, or 2 cups chopped fresh tomatoes
1 14-oz jar spaghetti sauce
7 oz. lasagna noodles

1 16-oz. container 1% cottage cheese
¾ cup shredded part-skim mozzarella cheese (3 oz.)
2 Tbsp. freshly grated Parmesan cheese
2 Tbsp. chopped fresh parsley

Preheat oven to 375 degrees F. In a nonstick skillet, cook beef over medium heat, stirring, for 3 minutes, or until no longer pink. Transfer to a colander and drain fat. Stir in tomatoes and spaghetti sauce. Spread a third of the meat sauce in the bottom of an 11-by-7-inch baking dish. Arrange half the uncooked noodles over the sauce. Spread half the cottage cheese over the noodles. Top with another third of the meat sauce. Repeat, using

remaining noodles, cottage cheese and sauce.

Cover with aluminum foil and bake for 45 to 55 minutes, or until noodles are tender. Sprinkle mozzarella and Parmesan over top. Bake, uncovered, for about 5 minutes, or until cheese is melted. Let stand for 10 minutes, sprinkle parsley over top and serve.

Serves 6.

358 CALORIES PER SERVING: 25 G PROTEIN, 10 G FAT, 41 G CARBOHYDRATE; 884 MG SODIUM; 32 MG CHOLESTEROL.

R_x *Pam Miller of Fairfax, Virginia*

Macaroni & Cheeses

Skip the stick of butter and the extra cup of cheese most macaroni and cheese recipes call for—this revision of Amy Simon's recipe rescue request cuts the fat a whopping 26 grams.

8 oz. elbow macaroni
1 cup skim milk
1 Tbsp. all-purpose white flour
1 cup grated cheddar cheese (3 oz.)
¼ tsp. nutmeg

salt & freshly ground black pepper to taste
1 generous pinch cayenne pepper
1½ cups 1% cottage cheese
2 Tbsp. freshly grated Parmesan cheese
2 Tbsp. unseasoned fine dry breadcrumbs

Preheat oven to 375 degrees F. Coat an 8-by-8-inch baking dish with nonstick cooking spray.

In a large pot of boiling salted water, cook macaroni until tender but firm, 8 to 10 minutes. Drain and rinse with cold water. Set aside.

In a small bowl, whisk together 2 Tbsp. of the milk and the flour. In a small saucepan, scald the remaining milk over medium heat. Add the milk-flour mixture to the milk. Cook, whisking, until the sauce is smooth and thickened. Remove from heat and stir in grated cheese.

Season with nutmeg, salt, pepper and cayenne. Transfer the sauce to a medium-sized bowl and set aside.

Puree cottage cheese in a food processor or blender until very smooth and then stir it into the sauce. Gently stir the macaroni into the cheese sauce. Spoon it into the prepared baking dish. In a small bowl, stir together the breadcrumbs and Parmesan. Sprinkle over the top of the macaroni and cheese. Bake until lightly browned on top and bubbling, 40 to 45 minutes.

Serves 4.

413 CALORIES PER SERVING: 27 G PROTEIN,10 G FAT, 52 G CARBOHYDRATE; 593 MG SODIUM; 30 MG CHOLESTEROL.

℞ *Amy Simon of Hampstead, New Hampshire*

Risotto With Fennel & Peas

Two methods are included here for this subtly flavored risotto. For the conventional method, chicken stock is added a little at a time and the rice is stirred between additions. The microwave technique does not require constant stirring. It also uses less chicken stock because there is less evaporation during cooking.

2 carrots, peeled and cut into ¼-inch-thick slices
5-6 cups defatted reduced-sodium chicken stock
2 tsp. olive oil
1 fennel bulb, trimmed, cored and chopped (2 cups)
1 onion, chopped

1½ cups arborio rice
½ cup dry white wine
1 cup frozen peas, thawed
1 cup freshly grated Parmesan cheese
2 Tbsp. Pernod (anise-flavored liqueur), optional
salt & freshly ground black pepper to taste

Conventional method: Blanch carrots in boiling water until just tender, 2 to 3 minutes. Drain and set aside. In a saucepan, heat chicken stock until simmering; keep warm.

In a Dutch oven or large wide saucepan, heat oil over low heat. Add fennel and onions; sauté until softened, 7 to 10 minutes. Add rice and stir for 1 minute to coat grains. Add wine and cook, stirring frequently with a wooden spoon, until most of the liquid has evaporated, about 3 minutes. Add ½ cup chicken stock and cook, stirring frequently, until most of the liquid has been absorbed, 3 to 5 minutes. Continue adding stock, about ½ cup at a time, and cooking, stirring frequently, until rice is just tender and the mixture is creamy, about 15 minutes. Add peas and the reserved carrots. Stir in cheese and Pernod, if using. Season with salt and pepper and serve at once.

Microwave method: In a microwave-safe dish, combine carrots with 2 Tbsp. water. Cover with vented plastic wrap and microwave at high (100 percent) power for 2 to 3 minutes, or until just tender. Drain and set aside. In a 4-cup glass measuring cup, microwave 3¾ cups stock and wine at high power for 5 to 6 minutes, or until simmering. Set aside.

In a 3-qt. microwave-safe casserole, stir together oil, fennel and onions. Microwave, uncovered, at high power for 5 to 6 minutes, or until vegetables have softened, stirring once. Add rice; stir to coat the grains. Pour in the chicken-stock mixture, cover with lid or vented plastic wrap, and microwave at high power for 5 to 6 minutes, or until boiling. Microwave at medium (50 percent) power for 15 to 17 minutes, or until the rice is just tender and the mixture is creamy, rotating once if necessary. Add peas and the reserved carrots. Let stand, covered, for 5 minutes. Stir in cheese and Pernod, if using. Season with salt and pepper and serve.

Serves 6.

340 CALORIES PER SERVING: 9 G PROTEIN, 7 G FAT, 50 G CARBOHYDRATE; 198 MG SODIUM; 7 MG CHOLESTEROL.

Paella Rápida

*Smoked mussels replace the pork sausages of old-fashioned paella,
adding depth of flavor without the fat.*

2 cups defatted reduced-sodium chicken stock
¼ tsp. saffron threads, crushed, or pinch
   powdered saffron
1 Tbsp. olive oil
½ lb. medium shrimp, peeled and deveined
½ lb. boneless, skinless chicken breast, trimmed
   of fat and cut into ½-inch-thick strips
   salt & freshly ground black pepper to taste
1 onion, chopped

2 cloves garlic, minced
1 14½-oz. can tomatoes (with juices)
⅛ tsp. red-pepper flakes
1 cup arborio rice
1 cup artichoke hearts, canned in water or
   frozen and thawed
1 cup frozen peas, thawed
⅓ cup bottled roasted red peppers, cut into strips
⅓ cup smoked mussels (2 oz.), not packed in oil

In a small saucepan, combine chicken stock and saffron; bring to a simmer. Remove from the heat and set aside.

In a large nonstick skillet, heat 1 tsp. oil over high heat. When the pan is hot, add shrimp and sauté until pink and curled, 3 to 4 minutes. Remove from the skillet and set aside. Add 1 tsp. oil to the skillet. Add chicken and sauté until lightly browned on the outside and opaque inside, 3 to 4 minutes. Remove from the skillet. Season the shrimp and chicken with salt and pepper and set aside.

Reduce heat to medium and add remaining 1 tsp. oil to the skillet. Stir in onions and garlic; sauté until softened, 3 to 5 minutes. (Add 1 to 2 Tbsp. water if they become too dry.) Stir in tomatoes and red-pepper flakes; simmer, uncovered, for 3 minutes, breaking up tomatoes with a wooden spoon. Add rice and stir to coat well with the tomato mixture. Stir in the reserved chicken stock and bring to a simmer. Cover and cook over low heat for 20 minutes.

Gently stir artichoke hearts, peas, roasted red peppers, smoked mussels and the reserved shrimp and chicken into the rice mixture. Cover and cook for 5 to 10 minutes longer, or until the rice is tender and the shrimp and chicken are heated through. (Stir occasionally to prevent scorching, if necessary.) Taste and season with salt and pepper. Serve immediately.

Serves 4.

450 CALORIES PER SERVING: 35 G PROTEIN, 7 G FAT, 58 G CARBOHYDRATE; 423 MG SODIUM; 128 MG CHOLESTEROL.

Barley-Orzo Pilaf

This welcome new grain combination works as an accompaniment to a meat or poultry entrée.
Stuffed into squash it makes a vegetarian main dish.

1   tsp. vegetable oil, preferably canola oil
1   onion, finely chopped
1   clove garlic, minced
½   cup orzo
3   cups defatted reduced-sodium chicken stock

1   cup quick-cooking barley
1   Tbsp. chopped fresh thyme or 1 tsp. dried
2   Tbsp. chopped scallion greens
    salt & freshly ground black pepper to taste

In a medium-sized saucepan, heat oil over medium heat. Add onions and sauté until softened, about 5 minutes. Add garlic and orzo and sauté until orzo is golden, 3 to 5 minutes. Add chicken stock and bring to a boil. Add barley and thyme. Stir once, reduce heat to low, cover and simmer for 10 minutes. Turn off heat and let pilaf rest for 5 minutes to absorb any remaining liquid. Stir in scallions. Season with salt and pepper, and serve.
  Serves 4.

252 CALORIES PER SERVING: 7 G PROTEIN, 2 G FAT, 53 G CARBOHYDRATE; 7 MG SODIUM; 0 MG CHOLESTEROL.

Bulgur With Celery & Sage

This can be a quick unexpected potluck offering,
a simple side dish or a good-for-you stuffing.

2   tsp. olive oil
1   small onion, chopped
2   stalks celery, chopped
2   cloves garlic, minced
1   cup bulgur
½   tsp. dried rubbed sage

½   tsp. dried thyme
½   tsp. dried marjoram
1¾ cups defatted beef stock or water
1   bay leaf
1   Tbsp. chopped fresh parsley
    salt & freshly ground black pepper to taste

In a heavy medium-sized saucepan, heat oil over medium heat. Add onions, celery and garlic and sauté for about 5 minutes, or until the vegetables are softened. Add bulgur, sage, thyme and marjoram; cook, stirring, for 1 minute. Stir in stock or water and bay leaf. Bring to a boil, reduce heat to low, cover and simmer for about 15 to 20 minutes, or until the liquid is absorbed and the bulgur is tender. Remove bay leaf, stir in parsley and season with salt and pepper.
  Serves 4.

190 CALORIES PER SERVING: 4 G PROTEIN, 3 G FAT, 38 G CARBOHYDRATE; 19 MG SODIUM; 0 MG CHOLESTEROL.

Half-Hour Vegetarian Chili

You will not miss the beef in this hearty chili. Bulgur adds
texture to the spicy mixture of vegetables and beans.

1	Tbsp. vegetable oil, preferably canola oil
3	onions, chopped
1	carrot, chopped
1	Tbsp. minced jalapeño pepper
2	cloves garlic, minced
3-4	tsp. chili powder
1	tsp. ground cumin
1	28-oz. can plus 1 14-oz. can tomatoes (with juices), chopped

1	tsp. brown sugar
2	15-oz. cans red kidney beans, drained and rinsed
⅓	cup bulgur
½	cup low-fat plain yogurt
3	scallions, trimmed and chopped
¼	cup chopped fresh cilantro or parsley

In a Dutch oven or a large saucepan, heat oil over medium heat. Add onions, carrots, jalapeños, garlic, chili powder and cumin. Sauté for 5 to 7 minutes, or until the onions and carrots are softened.

Add tomatoes and sugar; cook for 5 minutes over high heat. Stir in beans and bulgur, and reduce heat to low. Simmer the chili, uncovered, for 15 minutes, or until thickened.

Serve, garnished with yogurt, scallions and cilantro or parsley.

Serves 4.

412 CALORIES PER SERVING: 21 G PROTEIN, 6 G FAT, 75 G CARBOHYDRATE; 810 MG SODIUM; 2 MG CHOLESTEROL.

Pizza Primavera, page 110

125

Paella Rápida, page 122

Hoppin' John, page 132

Black Bean Chili, opposite

Black Bean Chili

The deep, rich flavor of the black beans lends itself to this long-cooking, spicy chili.
A few sun-dried tomatoes add a smoky, meaty flavor. The longer this dish cooks, the better;
it's one to make on a weekend. Fromage blanc *is a virtually fat-free fresh cheese that tastes somewhat*
like a mixture of cream cheese and yogurt. Look for it at specialty cheese shops.

1½ lbs. dried black beans, rinsed and picked over (3 cups)
1 Tbsp. vegetable oil, preferably canola oil
2 large onions, chopped
6 cloves garlic, minced
1 bay leaf
4 tsp. cumin seeds
1 Tbsp. sweet Hungarian paprika
½ tsp. cayenne pepper
2 Tbsp. chili powder
2 tsp. dried oregano
1 green bell pepper, seeded and diced

6-8 sun-dried tomatoes (not oil-packed), chopped (⅓ cup)
1 28-oz. can tomatoes, (with juices), seeded and chopped
½ tsp. sugar
    salt to taste
1 Tbsp. cider vinegar
    freshly ground black pepper to taste
¼ cup chopped fresh cilantro plus sprigs for garnish
6 Tbsp. nonfat plain yogurt or *fromage blanc* for garnish

Soak beans overnight in water. Drain. Heat 1 tsp. oil over medium heat in a large stockpot or Dutch oven. Add 1 cup onions and 2 tsp. garlic and sauté for 5 minutes, or until the onions begin to soften. Add beans, about 8 cups water or enough to cover the beans by an inch, and bay leaf. Bring to a boil. Reduce heat to low, cover and simmer for 1 hour.

Meanwhile, toast cumin seeds in a dry heavy skillet over medium-high heat for 3 to 4 minutes, shaking the skillet or stirring constantly, until they begin to color. Remove from heat and add paprika and cayenne. Stir together for about 30 seconds in the hot pan. Grind the spices together in an electric spice mill or blender. Add chili powder and oregano.

In a second large stockpot or Dutch oven, heat the remaining 2 tsp. oil and sauté the remaining 1 cup onions over medium-low heat until they soften, about 5 minutes. Add 2 tsp. garlic and green peppers and sauté for about 5 minutes. Add the spice mixture and dried toma-

toes and sauté for about 3 to 5 minutes, scraping the bottom of the pot carefully so that the spices don't burn. If they cake on the bottom of the pan, add a little water. Add tomatoes, sugar and about ½ tsp. salt and bring to a simmer. Cover and simmer over low heat for 30 minutes, stirring often.

Add the beans with their liquid to the tomato mixture. Add the remaining 2 tsp. garlic. Stir everything together and simmer, covered, for an hour or two, until the beans are thoroughly tender and the broth is thick and fragrant. If you want a thicker chili, simmer, uncovered or partially covered, for the final hour of cooking. Remove bay leaf and stir in vinegar. Season with salt and pepper. *(The chili can be stored, covered, in the refrigerator for up to 2 days. Reheat before serving.)*

Just before serving, stir in chopped cilantro. Garnish each portion with yogurt or fromage blanc and a sprig of cilantro.

Serves 6.

255 CALORIES PER SERVING: 14 G PROTEIN, 5 G FAT, 45 G CARBOHYDRATE; 269 MG SODIUM; 1 MG CHOLESTEROL.

Chickpea Burgers

Vegetarians can step up to the grill. Serve with fresh garden vegetables.

4   tsp. sesame seeds
1   Tbsp. ground coriander
1   Tbsp. ground cumin
1   15½-oz. can chickpeas, drained and rinsed
    (1½ cups)
1   cup cooked brown rice
⅔   cup wheat germ
2   tsp. vegetable oil, preferably canola oil

4   scallions, trimmed and chopped (½ cup)
3   cloves garlic, minced
3   Tbsp. fresh lemon juice
½   tsp. salt
¼   tsp. freshly ground black pepper
4   ½-inch-thick slices tomato
    fresh spinach leaves
4   6-inch pita breads

Prepare the grill or preheat the broiler.

Heat a small skillet over low heat. Add the sesame seeds and stir with a wooden spoon until deep brown, about 2 minutes. Add the coriander and cumin and stir for 10 to 20 more seconds, or until the spices are aromatic and toasted; turn out onto a plate to cool. Grind lightly with a mortar and pestle or spice mill.

In a medium-sized bowl, coarsely mash the chickpeas with a potato masher. Stir in the rice and ⅓ cup wheat germ.

In a large nonstick skillet, heat oil over medium heat.

Add scallions, garlic and ground spices and sauté for 2 minutes, or until softened. Remove from heat; add to the chickpea mixture along with lemon juice, salt and pepper and mix well with a fork or your hands. Shape into four ³/₄-inch-thick patties.

Put the remaining ⅓ cup wheat germ on a plate and press the patties into it to coat both sides. Grill or broil patties and tomato slices for 3 minutes per side, or until lightly browned. Tuck patties into pitas and top with grilled tomatoes and spinach.

Serves 4.

380 CALORIES PER SERVING: 16 G PROTEIN, 9 G FAT, 63 G CARBOHYDRATE; 527 MG SODIUM; 0 MG CHOLESTEROL.

Black Bean Frijoles

Mexican and Southwestern refried beans are always fried in lard or bacon drippings.
Here, because the beans are mashed before frying, very little fat is needed. The flavor comes from
sautéing cumin and chili with the beans and simmering them with garlic, onion and cilantro.

1 lb. dried black beans (2 cups), rinsed and picked over
1 Tbsp. plus 1 tsp. vegetable oil, preferably canola oil
1 large onion, chopped
4 cloves garlic, minced

3 Tbsp. chopped fresh cilantro
    salt to taste
4 tsp. chili powder
1 Tbsp. ground cumin
6 Tbsp. nonfat plain yogurt for garnish

Soak beans overnight in water. Drain. In a large heavy-bottomed saucepan or Dutch oven, heat 1 tsp. oil over medium heat. Add onions and garlic; sauté until softened, about 8 to 10 minutes. Add beans and 8 cups fresh water and bring to a boil. Reduce the heat, and simmer, uncovered, for 1 hour. Add cilantro and 1 tsp. salt and simmer, adding water as necessary, until the beans are soft and the liquid is thickened and aromatic, about 45 minutes longer. Remove from the heat and cool.

Mash beans coarsely in batches in a food processor or with a potato masher. Make sure not to puree until smooth; you want texture.

Heat the remaining 1 Tbsp. oil in a large nonstick skillet over medium heat. Add chili powder and cumin; sauté for 1 minute. Add the mashed beans and fry, stirring often, until they begin to get crusty and aromatic. If they seem too dry, add some water. Mash and stir as they cook. There should be enough liquid so that they bubble as they cook, while at the same time a thin crust forms on the bottom. Cook for about 10 to 20 minutes and serve immediately topped with a dollop of yogurt.

Serves 6.

255 CALORIES PER SERVING: 15 G PROTEIN, 4 G FAT, 41 G CARBOHYDRATE; 566 MG SODIUM; 0 MG CHOLESTEROL.

Polenta

Polenta is Italian for cornmeal mush. In this version,
the cornmeal is first combined with cold water to prevent lumping and is then stirred
into the boiling water. Serve with Indispensable Meat Sauce (page 117).

2 tsp. salt

1½ cups cornmeal, preferably stone-ground

In a deep heavy saucepan, bring 2½ cups water and salt to boil. Whisk cornmeal into 2 cups cold water. briskly stir cornmeal mixture into the boiling water with a wooden spoon. Return to a boil, stirring, then reduce the heat, so the mixture bubbles slowly. Simmer, stirring

continuously for 20 minutes, or until thickened and smooth. Turn out onto a lightly oiled serving platter. Cool for 5 minutes and serve.

Serves 6.

163 CALORIES PER SERVING: 4 G PROTEIN, 2 G FAT, 34 G CARBOHYDRATE; 267 MG SODIUM; 0 MG CHOLESTEROL.

Hoppin' John ·

This Low Country Carolina dish dates to the 1700s when "Carolina golde" was considered the finest rice in the western world. Dietary fat was not a concern at that time; many early versions of the recipe called for a pound or more of bacon.

4   cups fresh or frozen black-eyed peas
2   tsp. vegetable oil, preferably canola oil
1   onion, chopped
2   red or green bell peppers, cored, seeded and chopped
1   14½-oz. can tomatoes, drained and chopped
6   cloves garlic, minced
1   cup long-grain white rice

2   cups defatted reduced-sodium chicken stock
¼   lb. smoked ham, diced (¾ cup)
1   tsp. salt
    pinch cayenne pepper
3-4 scallions (¾ cup), trimmed and chopped
½   cup chopped fresh parsley
    freshly ground black pepper to taste

If using fresh black-eyed peas, pick over, removing any debris; rinse in a colander. Place peas in a large saucepan and add water to cover by 1 inch. Bring to a boil, reduce heat to low; simmer, uncovered, for 20 minutes. Drain and set aside.

In a Dutch oven or large wide saucepan, heat oil over medium heat. Add onions and peppers; sauté until softened, about 5 minutes. Add tomatoes and garlic and cook, stirring, for 5 minutes. Add rice; stir for 1 minute. Pour in chicken stock and bring to a simmer. Add ham, salt, cayenne and the black-eyed peas. Cover and simmer over low heat for 20 minutes, or until rice and peas are tender and liquid is absorbed. Stir in scallions and parsley. Season with salt and pepper and serve.

Serves 6.

310 CALORIES PER SERVING: 12 G PROTEIN, 4 G FAT, 56 G CARBOHYDRATE; 709 MG SODIUM; 10 MG CHOLESTEROL.

New Year's Black-Eyed Peas

"This traditional New Year's Day dish from southern Virginia is served for good luck in the coming year," wrote Ardath Weaver. This remake uses dried tomatoes instead of salt pork.

1   lb. dried black-eyed peas (2½ cups), rinsed and picked over
1   onion, chopped
1   14-oz. can stewed tomatoes (with juices)

½   cup molasses
6   sun-dried tomatoes (not oil-packed), chopped
2   tsp. salt or to taste
    freshly ground black pepper to taste

In a large bowl, cover peas with cold water; let soak overnight. Drain and rinse the peas; place in a large pot and add onions, stewed tomatoes, molasses, sun-dried tomatoes and 2 cups water. Bring to a boil. Reduce heat to low, cover and simmer until the peas are very tender and the sauce is thick, 2½ to 3 hours. Add more water as needed. Season with salt and pepper and serve.

Serves 6.

279 CALORIES PER SERVING: 7 G PROTEIN, 1 G FAT, 64 G CARBOHYDRATE; 907 MG SODIUM; 0 MG CHOLESTEROL.

R_x *Ardath Weaver of Raleigh, North Carolina*

Stir-Fried Vegetables in Black Bean Sauce

A rich, complex sauce made from fermented black beans adds interest to the tofu and crisp vegetables. Fermented black beans, which are preserved in salt and flavored with ginger, are available in Asian grocery stores, as is premixed five spice powder, a blend of cinnamon, anise seed, coriander, ginger and black pepper.

1½ lbs. firm tofu, cut into 1½-inch-thick slabs
4½ Tbsp. Chinese rice wine or sake
2½ Tbsp. reduced-sodium soy sauce
1 tsp. five spice powder
½ tsp. sesame oil
½ cup defatted reduced-sodium chicken stock or water
1 Tbsp. cornstarch
2 tsp. sugar
¼ tsp. freshly ground black pepper
1 Tbsp. vegetable oil, preferably canola oil

6 garlic cloves, minced
2 Tbsp. fermented black beans, drained and rinsed
1½ Tbsp. minced peeled gingerroot
1 tsp. chili paste
1 red bell pepper, cored, seeded and cut into thin strips
1 yellow bell pepper, cored, seeded and cut into thin strips
2 cups snow peas, strings removed (¼ lb.)
2 cups chopped scallions greens (12 scallions)

Wrap tofu in a cotton towel and place a heavy weight (such as a skillet) on top at room temperature for 30 minutes. Remove weight, unwrap and cut tofu into ¼-inch-thick slices; trim into 1½-by-1-inch rectangles. Set aside. In a medium-sized bowl, stir together 2 Tbsp. of the rice wine or sake, 1 Tbsp. of the soy sauce, five spice powder and sesame oil. Add the tofu and toss to coat evenly. Let stand, covered, at room temperature for 25 minutes.

In a small bowl, stir together chicken stock or water, 1½ Tbsp. rice wine or sake, the remaining 1½ Tbsp. soy sauce, cornstarch, sugar and pepper, and set aside.

Place a rack 4 inches from the heat and preheat the broiler. Place the tofu on a foil-covered baking sheet and broil for 4 minutes per side, or until lightly browned and crisp. Set aside.

In a large nonstick skillet or wok, heat oil over high heat. Add garlic, black beans, ginger and chili paste and stir-fry for 10 to 15 seconds, or until fragrant. Add red and yellow peppers and stir-fry for 1 minute. Add snow peas and the remaining 1 Tbsp. rice wine or sake and stir-fry for 30 seconds. Add scallion greens and the reserved stock mixture and cook for about 45 seconds, stirring, or until thickened. Add the reserved tofu and toss to coat.

Serves 4.

98 CALORIES PER SERVING: 8 G PROTEIN, 5 G FAT, 7 G CARBOHYDRATE; 260 MG SODIUM; 0 MG CHOLESTEROL.

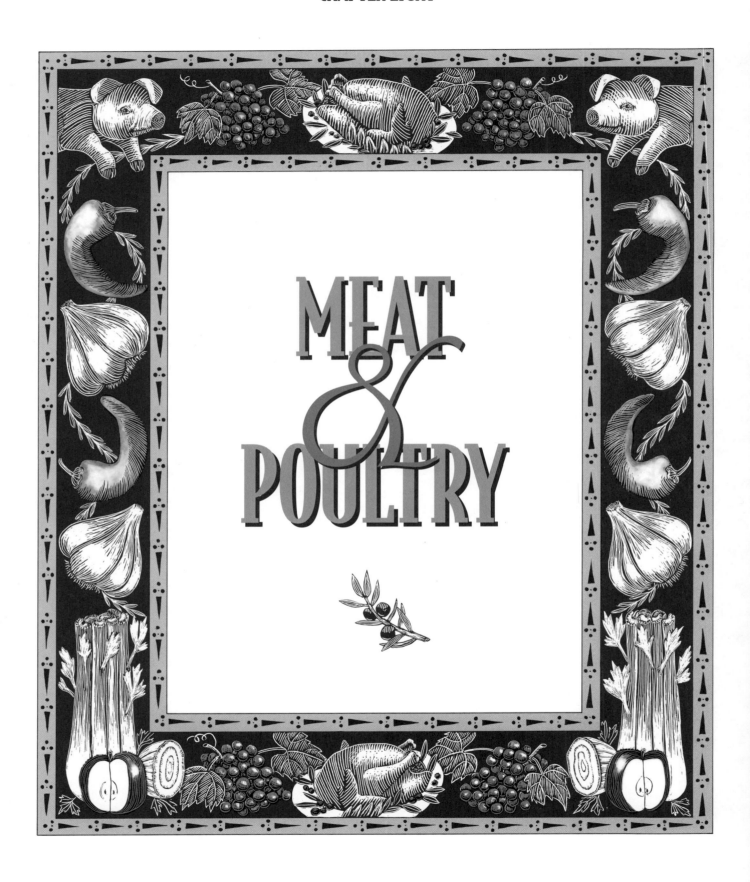

CHAPTER EIGHT

MEAT & POULTRY

RECIPES

Braised Beef With Brandy & Mustard

Sun-dried tomatoes and two kinds of mustard intensify the good beefy flavor of this pot roast. Bottom round is the suggested cut here; eye round, tip and arm pot roast are other lean cuts that will work well.

1 Tbsp. olive oil
1¼ lbs. bottom round steak, trimmed of fat and membrane
½ cup brandy
2 cups defatted beef stock
2 Tbsp. coarse-grained mustard
2 Tbsp. Provence-style or Dijon mustard

4 shallots, peeled and thinly sliced
4 sun-dried tomatoes (not oil-packed), cut into slivers
3 large cloves garlic, peeled and thinly sliced
6 juniper berries
1 bay leaf
 freshly ground black pepper to taste

Preheat oven to 325 degrees F. In a Dutch oven or deep skillet, heat oil over medium heat. Add meat and brown on all sides. Transfer to a plate lined with paper towels and drain off all the fat in the pan. Return the pan to the heat and immediately add brandy, stirring to scrape up any browned bits in the bottom. Cook until the brandy is reduced to a syrupy glaze. Stir in stock, mustards, shallots, sun-dried tomatoes, garlic, juniper berries and bay leaf and bring to a boil. Return the meat to the pan, cover tightly and place in the oven. Bake, turning the meat every 30 minutes, for 1½ to 2 hours, or until very tender. Remove bay leaf and season the sauce with pepper. Cut the meat into thin slices, arrange on a platter and spoon the sauce over.

Serves 4.

350 CALORIES PER SERVING: 38 G PROTEIN, 8 G FAT, 14 G CARBOHYDRATE; 679 MG SODIUM; 90 MG CHOLESTEROL.

Braising Demystified

Braising is nearly idiot-proof. It is hard to cook meat to shoe leather or dry out fish as long as it is *gently* simmering in a broth or tomato sauce. Don't try to rush a recipe by turning up the heat; the meat will be tough and the flavors will fail to develop. Braising is also the ultimate plan-ahead technique. Recipes can be made in advance; the flavor will only improve.

Braising can be done either in the oven or on top of the stove, and both options have advantages. Oven cooking is worry free, but the stovetop method gives you greater control over the cooking and seasoning. You can add more water as needed or turn off the burner when the components are done to your taste rather than by the timer.

The pan for braising is crucial. A Dutch oven or deep skillet works best, both require a tight-fitting cover. If you do not have the right pot, use a flameproof casserole and cover it tightly with aluminum foil. The bottom of the pan should be wide enough to hold all the key ingredients—the meat or fish pieces—in a single layer without crowding. Everything will cook more evenly with room for air and moisture to circulate.

Braiseworthy Lamb Shanks With Roasted Garlic & White Beans

Slow cooking produces meat that is sweet and so tender it almost falls off the bone.

1 cup dried cannellini, great Northern or navy beans
1 large head garlic
1 Tbsp. olive oil
4 1-lb. lamb shanks, trimmed of fat and membrane
2 small carrots, peeled and diced
1 onion, chopped

1 stalk celery, diced
½ cup dry red wine
½ cup defatted beef stock
1 28-oz. can plum tomatoes, drained
2 Tbsp. chopped fresh rosemary or 2 tsp. dried
1 bay leaf
salt & freshly ground black pepper to taste

Sort beans, discarding any debris. Rinse and place in a large bowl. Cover with cold water and let soak for at least 8 hours or overnight. (*Alternatively, in a large pot, cover beans with water and bring to a boil. Boil for 2 minutes. Remove from the heat and let stand for 1 hour.*)

Preheat oven to 300 degrees F. Remove as much of the outer husk of the garlic as possible without separating the cloves. Wrap loosely in aluminum foil and bake for 30 minutes. Unwrap foil and separate the cloves slightly so that they cook evenly. Wrap again and bake for 30 minutes longer, or until the garlic is very soft. Set aside to cool. Increase oven temperature to 325 degrees F.

In a Dutch oven, heat 1½ tsp. oil over medium-high heat. Add lamb shanks and brown on all sides. Remove from the pan and drain on paper towels.

Add the remaining 1½ tsp. oil to the pan, then add carrots, onions and celery; sauté for 2 to 3 minutes, or until softened. Add wine and cook until it has reduced by half, 5 to 7 minutes. Stir in beef stock, tomatoes, rosemary and bay leaf. Peel half the roasted garlic cloves

and add to the pan; bring to a boil. Return the meat to the pan, cover tightly and place in the oven. Bake for 1½ to 2 hours, turning the shanks occasionally, or until the meat is very tender.

Meanwhile, drain beans and place in a large, heavy pot. Add water to cover by about 4 inches and bring to a boil. Reduce heat to low and simmer for 45 minutes to 1 hour, or until the beans are tender. Drain. (*The recipe can be prepared ahead to this point. Cover and refrigerate the stew and beans separately for up to 2 days. Lift off fat that has solidified on the surface of the stew and reheat before proceeding.*)

With tongs, transfer the shanks to a plate, cover and keep warm. Remove bay leaf from the sauce and skim off fat. Boil the sauce for about 5 minutes, or until slightly thickened. Peel the remaining roasted garlic and add to the sauce along with the drained beans. Heat through and season with salt and pepper. Mound the bean mixture on a platter and place the lamb shanks on top.

Serves 4.

445 CALORIES PER SERVING: 40 G PROTEIN, 10 G FAT, 46 G CARBOHYDRATE; 518 MG SODIUM; 89 MG CHOLESTEROL.

Beef Stroganoff

A little tender beef goes a long way when it is
supplemented with flavorful mushrooms and enriched with a robust sauce.

½ lb. beef tenderloin or sirloin
     salt & freshly ground black pepper
2 tsp. olive oil
1 onion, sliced
½ lb. mushrooms, trimmed and sliced (3 cups)
1½ Tbsp. all-purpose white flour

¼ cup dry red wine
¾ cup defatted beef stock
1 tsp. Dijon mustard
3 Tbsp. reduced-fat sour cream
1 Tbsp. chopped fresh parsley
1 lb. egg noodles

Trim all the fat and gristle from the beef; slice across the grain into very thin slices. Season lightly with salt and pepper.

In a large nonstick skillet, heat 1 tsp. oil over high heat. Add the beef strips, half at a time, and sear quickly on both sides; remove to a plate. Turn the heat down to medium and add remaining 1 tsp. oil. Add the onions and sauté for 3 minutes, or until softened and lightly colored. Turn heat down to low, add the mushrooms and sauté for 2 to 3 more minutes, or until they are just beginning to give off moisture. Add flour and cook for 1 minute, stirring. Stir in the wine and let evaporate, about 30 seconds. Stir in the beef stock, bring to a simmer, stirring, and cook until thickened, about 2 minutes. Stir in mustard, sour cream and parsley. Season to taste with salt and pepper. Add the reserved beef strips, and stir just until warmed through. While the stroganoff simmers, cook noodles in boiling salted water. Drain. Serve the stroganoff over noodles.

Serves 4.

564 CALORIES PER SERVING: 28 G PROTEIN, 12 G FAT, 84 G CARBOHYDRATE; 221 MG SODIUM; 131 MG CHOLESTEROL.

Pork Medallions With Port & Dried-Cranberry Sauce

You can substitute pitted prunes or dried cherries for the dried cranberries.
(For a source of dried cranberries see page 240).

½ cup dried cranberries
1 tsp. vegetable oil, preferably canola oil
1 lb. pork tenderloin, trimmed of fat and membrane and cut into 12 medallions ¾ inch thick
     salt & freshly ground black pepper to taste

1 shallot, minced
½ cup port wine
¼ cup balsamic vinegar
1 cup defatted reduced-sodium chicken stock
½ tsp. dried thyme
1 tsp. cornstarch

In a small saucepan, combine dried cranberries and 1 cup water. Bring to a simmer and cook for 3 minutes. Drain, reserving both berries and cooking liquid. Set aside.

In a large nonstick skillet, heat oil over medium heat. Season pork with salt and pepper and add to the skillet; cook for about 3 minutes per side, or until browned on the outside and no longer pink but still juicy inside. Transfer to a platter, cover loosely and keep warm. (Do not wash the skillet.)

Add shallots to the skillet and cook, stirring, for 30 seconds. Pour in port and vinegar and bring to a boil, stirring to scrape up any brown bits. Boil for 3 to 5 minutes, or until reduced by half. Add chicken stock, thyme and reserved cranberry cooking liquid; boil for 5 to 7 minutes, or until reduced again by half.

In a small bowl, dissolve cornstarch in 1 Tbsp. water. Whisk into the sauce and cook, stirring, until slightly thickened and glossy. Stir in the reserved cranberries and season with salt and pepper. Spoon the sauce over the medallions and serve.

Serves 4.

269 CALORIES PER SERVING: 26 G PROTEIN, 6 G FAT, 21 G CARBOHYDRATE; 159 MG SODIUM; 79 MG CHOLESTEROL.

Pork Tenderloin With Braised Red Cabbage

Food writer John Willoughby updated the pork roast that his mother used to serve on Sundays back in Iowa. Like the best of American traditional cooking, it is simple, hearty and delicious.

2 ¾-lb. pork tenderloins, trimmed of fat and membrane
12 fresh sage leaves or ½ tsp. dried
   salt & freshly ground black pepper
1½ tsp. caraway seeds
1 Tbsp. vegetable oil, preferably canola oil
1 red onion, thinly sliced
1 small head red cabbage, cored and shredded (8 cups)

1 Granny Smith apple, cored and grated
½ cup defatted reduced-sodium chicken stock
½ cup dry red wine
3 Tbsp. red-wine vinegar
1 Tbsp. sugar
2 cloves garlic, minced
½ tsp. salt
1 bay leaf

Preheat oven to 425 degrees F. If using fresh sage, make small incisions in pork and insert sage leaves. If using dried sage, rub it over the surface. Rub the pork with salt and pepper and sprinkle with caraway seeds. In a large nonstick skillet, heat 2 tsp. oil over medium-high heat. Brown the pork for about 2 minutes per side and place in a lightly oiled roasting pan. Roast for 10 to 15 minutes, or just until the internal temperature reaches 160 degrees F.

Meanwhile, in the same skillet in which the pork was sautéed, heat the remaining 1 tsp. oil over low heat. Saute onions until soft, about 5 to 7 minutes. Add remaining ingredients and simmer, uncovered, for 10 to 15 minutes, tossing occasionally, until cabbage is tender and most of the liquid has evaporated. Discard bay leaf. Taste and adjust seasonings. Carve the pork into ¾-inch-thick slices and serve with braised cabbage.

Serves 6.

233 CALORIES PER SERVING: 27 G PROTEIN, 7 G FAT, 14 G CARBOHYDRATE; 258 MG SODIUM; 79 MG CHOLESTEROL.

Stir-Fried Pork With Cauliflower & Broccoli

*Stir-frying is an excellent way to emphasize flavor
while using a relatively modest amount of fat.*

¼ cup blanched almonds or cashews, coarsely chopped (optional)
2 Tbsp. reduced-sodium soy sauce
2 Tbsp. defatted reduced sodium chicken stock
4 tsp. cornstarch
1 Tbsp. rice-wine vinegar
2 tsp. sesame oil
2 tsp. sugar
¾ lb. pork tenderloin, trimmed of fat and membrane
1 small bunch broccoli, cut into florets (about 1 lb.)

½ small head cauliflower, cut into bite-sized pieces
1 Tbsp. vegetable oil, preferably canola oil
1 red bell pepper, seeded and thinly sliced
4 scallions, thinly sliced
1 clove garlic, minced
1 hot chili pepper, such as jalapeño or serrano, with seeds, minced
1 Tbsp. minced peeled gingerroot
salt and freshly ground black pepper to taste

If using almonds or cashews, preheat oven to 350 degrees F. Spread nuts on a pie plate or cake pan and toast for 8 to 10 minutes, or until lightly browned and fragrant. In a small bowl, mix together soy sauce, chicken stock, 1 Tbsp. cornstarch, vinegar, sesame oil and sugar and set aside. Cut pork in half lengthwise, then into very thin slices. Sprinkle with the remaining 1 tsp. cornstarch, rubbing it in well.

Blanch broccoli and cauliflower in boiling, salted water for 2 to 3 minutes, or just until tender-crisp. Drain, pat dry and set aside. In a wok or a large nonstick skillet, heat 1 tsp. vegetable oil over high heat until hot but not smoking. Add half the pork and stir-fry for 1 to 2 minutes, or until no longer pink outside. Remove and set aside. Add 1 tsp. oil to the pan and stir-fry the remaining pork. Remove and set aside. Stir-fry bell peppers until just tender, about 30 seconds. Add to the pork.

Add the remaining 1 tsp. oil. Add scallions, garlic, chilies and ginger and stir-fry for about 15 seconds. Return pork and peppers to the pan and add broccoli, cauliflower and soy-sauce mixture. Stir-fry until the sauce has thickened, about 1 minute. Season with salt and pepper to taste. If using nuts, sprinkle them over top and serve with rice.

Serves 4.

226 CALORIES PER SERVING: 23 G PROTEIN, 9 G FAT, 15 G CARBOHYDRATE; 424 MG SODIUM; 59 MG CHOLESTEROL.

Pastitsio

The Greek answer to lasagna, pastitsio can weigh in at a hefty 45 grams of fat per serving. To get the dish to a trimmer form, we cut the amount of meat in half and added bulgur to fill out the meat layer. For an authentic flavor, use Kefalotýri, a goat's milk Greek grating cheese.

MEAT SAUCE

1 tsp. olive or vegetable oil
1 large onion, finely chopped
1½ lbs. lean ground beef or ground turkey
¾ cup dry white wine
1 6-oz. can tomato paste
½ cup bulgur
¾ tsp. ground cinnamon
¾ tsp. ground nutmeg
¾ tsp. ground allspice
1 tsp. salt
½ tsp. freshly ground black pepper

CREAM SAUCE

2 cups 1% cottage cheese (1 lb.)
1½ cups evaporated skim milk (12-oz. can)
1 cup defatted reduced-sodium chicken stock
2 Tbsp. all-purpose white flour
½ cup freshly grated Kefalotýri, Asiago or Parmesan cheese (1 oz.)
salt & freshly ground black pepper to taste

PASTA

1 lb. elbow macaroni or ziti
6 Tbsp. freshly grated Kefalotýri, Asiago or Parmesan cheese (¾ oz.)
1 tsp. vegetable oil, preferably canola oil
½ tsp. salt
2 Tbsp. chopped fresh parsley (optional)

To make meat sauce: In a large nonstick skillet, heat oil over medium heat; add onions and sauté until softened, about 5 minutes. Add meat and cook until no longer pink, about 5 minutes. Drain off fat. Add 1 cup water, wine, tomato paste, bulgur, spices, salt and pepper. Simmer, uncovered, over low heat, stirring occasionally, until bulgur is tender, about 20 minutes. Taste and adjust seasonings.

To make cream sauce: In a food processor or blender, puree cottage cheese until completely smooth. Set aside. In a medium-sized heavy saucepan, combine evaporated skim milk and ³/₄ cup chicken stock. Heat over medium heat until scalding. In a small bowl, stir together flour and the remaining ¹/₄ cup chicken stock until smooth. Stir into the hot milk mixture and cook, stirring constantly, until thickened, about 2 minutes. Remove from the heat and whisk in the pureed cottage cheese and grated cheese. Season with salt and pepper. To prevent a skin from forming, place wax paper or plastic wrap directly over the surface and set aside.

To make pasta: In a large pot of boiling salted water, cook macaroni or ziti until *al dente*, 8 to 10 minutes. Drain and return to the pot. Toss with ¹/₄ cup grated cheese, oil and salt.

To assemble and bake *pastitsio*: Preheat oven to 350 degrees F. Coat a 9-by-13-inch baking dish with nonstick cooking spray. Spread half the pasta mixture over the bottom of the dish. Top with one-third of the cream sauce. Spoon all the meat sauce over, spreading evenly. Cover with another third of the cream sauce. Top with the remaining pasta mixture and cover with the remaining cream sauce. Sprinkle with the remaining 2 Tbsp. grated cheese. (Pastitsio *can be assembled ahead and stored, covered, in the refrigerator for up to 2 days or in the freezer for up to 3 months. If frozen, thaw in the refrigerator before proceeding.*) Bake for 40 to 50 minutes, or until bubbling and golden. Sprinkle with parsley, if using, and serve.

Serves 10.

467 CALORIES PER SERVING: 33 G PROTEIN, 12 G FAT, 52 G CARBOHYDRATE; 929 MG SODIUM; 55 MG CHOLESTEROL.

℞ *Frances Winick of Tucson, Arizona*

Quick Cassoulet

*A far cry from genuine French cassoulet, which is known for
a preponderance of fatty meats and requires hours of cooking; this is nonetheless
a delicious meat-and-bean dish that makes creative use of leftovers.*

2   cups fresh breadcrumbs *(page 21)*
2   tsp. vegetable oil, preferably canola oil
2   onions, chopped plus 1 onion, peeled and left whole
1   carrot, peeled and finely chopped
2   cloves garlic, sliced
½   lb. cooked chicken or turkey meat, cut into ½-inch dice (1½ cups)
¼   lb. smoked cooked ham, cut into ½-inch dice
¼   lb. turkey kielbasa sausage, cut into ⅓-inch-thick slices

1   14.5-oz. can whole tomatoes (with juices), coarsely chopped
½   cup defatted reduced-sodium chicken stock
½   cup dry white wine
½   cup fresh parsley
1½ tsp. chopped fresh thyme or ½ tsp. dried
3   whole cloves
2   19-oz. cans great Northern beans, drained and rinsed
½   tsp. freshly ground black pepper

Preheat oven to 350 degrees F. Spread breadcrumbs on a baking sheet and bake for 6 to 8 minutes, stirring occasionally, or until crisp. Set aside.

In a Dutch oven or flameproof casserole, heat oil over medium heat; add chopped onions, carrots and garlic and sauté for 5 minutes, or until just beginning to color. Add chicken or turkey, ham and kielbasa; sauté for 5 minutes. Add tomatoes, chicken stock, wine, parsley and thyme and bring to a boil. Stud the whole onion with cloves and nestle into the vegetables. Simmer for 5 minutes. Stir in beans and season with pepper. Sprinkle the reserved breadcrumbs over top, transfer to the oven and bake for about 30 minutes or until bubbly.

Serves 8.

398 CALORIES PER SERVING: 28 G PROTEIN, 7 G FAT, 55G CARBOHYDRATE; 482 MG SODIUM; 28 MG CHOLESTEROL.

New "Veau" Veal Stew

*A sophisticated yet simple dish that freezes well. In Nancy Zager's recipe, the meat and onions
were sautéed in ½ cup butter; we used 1 tablespoon of vegetable oil. Sauté the meat in batches so the
pieces are well-browned, and cook the onions long enough to bring out their sweetness.*

1   Tbsp. vegetable oil, preferably canola oil
1½ lbs. veal rump roast or round steak, trimmed of fat and cut into 1-inch cubes
4   large onions, sliced
1   lb. mushrooms, trimmed and halved (6 cups)
3   cloves garlic, minced
1   14-oz. can tomatoes (with juices), chopped or mashed
1   Tbsp. sugar

1   Tbsp. paprika
1   tsp. nutmeg
1   tsp. mace
1   tsp. salt
½   tsp. freshly ground black pepper
1   cup nonfat yogurt
3   Tbsp. cornstarch
1   lb. noodles
2   Tbsp. chopped fresh parsley

In a Dutch oven, heat 1 tsp. oil over medium-high heat. Add half of the veal and brown on all sides. Transfer to a plate and set aside. Add 1 tsp. oil to the pan and brown the remaining veal. Set aside. Add the remaining 1 tsp. oil to the pan and reduce heat to medium-low. Add onions and sauté until very soft, about 10 minutes. Add mushrooms and garlic and sauté for 5 minutes longer.

Stir in tomatoes, sugar, paprika, nutmeg, mace, salt and pepper; bring to a boil. Return the veal to the pan and reduce heat to low. Cover and simmer until the veal is tender, 1 to 1¼ hours. *(The recipe can be prepared ahead to this point. Store, covered, in the refrigerator for up to 2 days. Gently reheat before continuing.)*

In a small bowl, stir together yogurt and cornstarch until smooth. Add to the stew and cook, stirring, until thickened, about 1 minute. While the stew is simmering, cook noodles in boiling salted water. Drain. Serve the stew over noodles. Sprinkle with parsley.

Serves 6.

606 CALORIES PER SERVING: 48 G PROTEIN, 11 G FAT, 79 G CARBOHYDRATE; 573 MG SODIUM; 187 MG CHOLESTEROL.

R_x *Nancy Zager of Stamford, Connecticut*

Cooking With Yogurt

There is no mystery to cooking with yogurt, provided a few simple rules are followed.

- Whenever possible, stir yogurt rather than beat it, or it will separate.
- When substituting yogurt for other dairy products, acid ingredients like wine, lemon juice or vinegar should be reduced to compensate for yogurt's natural tartness.
- When replacing milk with yogurt, counteract the acidity by adding ½ teaspoon baking soda for each cup.
- Heating yogurt too rapidly or at too high a temperature can cause it to separate into unattractive curds and whey. To prevent it from curdling, try to have yogurt at room temperature before heating it. For foolproof results, "temper" it by stirring in a tablespoon of cornstarch per cup of yogurt. Add yogurt near the end of cooking and keep the heat low.

High-Low Meat Loaf

*Higher in healthful carbohydrates and lower in fat than most meat loaf, that is.
This American standard has been tastily rejuvenated with the substitution of bulgur for some of the
beef. Cold leftovers make a mean sandwich; please pass the pickles.* Note: *To release the most
flavor from the dried herbs, crush them between your fingers.*

⅔ cup bulgur
1 tsp. vegetable oil, preferably canola oil
1 onion, chopped
2 cloves garlic, minced
1 large egg
2 large egg whites
1½ lbs. lean ground beef
2 cups fresh whole-wheat breadcrumbs
(page 21)

1 8-oz. can tomato sauce
¼ cup chopped fresh parsley
1½ Tbsp. cider vinegar
1 Tbsp. Dijon mustard
1½ tsp. salt
1 tsp. dried thyme
1 tsp. dried basil
1 tsp. dried oregano
¾ tsp. freshly ground black pepper

In a small bowl, combine bulgur with 1 cup water and let soak for 30 minutes or until the bulgur is tender and the water is absorbed.

Preheat oven to 350 degrees F. Lightly coat a large baking dish or cookie sheet with nonstick cooking spray.

Heat oil in a small skillet over low heat and add onions. Sauté for 3 minutes, or until lightly colored. Add the garlic and sauté for 2 more minutes. Remove from the heat.

In a large bowl, whisk the egg and egg whites until combined. Add the bulgur, onions and garlic, and the remaining ingredients. Use a rubber spatula or your hands to mix thoroughly.

Shape the meat loaf mixture into an oval loaf and place in the prepared pan. Bake for 45 minutes to 1 hour, or until the internal temperature is 160 degrees F. Let stand for 10 minutes before slicing.

Serves 8.

361 CALORIES PER SERVING: 27 G PROTEIN, 14 G FAT, 33 G CARBOHYDRATE; 833 MG SODIUM; 95 MG CHOLESTEROL.

Braised Beef With Brandy & Mustard, page 136

145

Pork Medallions With Port & Dried-Cranberry Sauce, page 138

Chicken With Mustard & Leeks en Papillote, page 151

147

Beef Burger With Caramelized Onions, opposite

148

Beef Burgers With Caramelized Onions

To reduce the amount of fat in these juicy burgers, we've used less meat and plumped them up with bulgur.

⅓ cup bulgur
2 tsp. olive oil
4 cups sliced onions (4 medium)
2 tsp. sugar
2 tsp. balsamic vinegar
    salt to taste

¾ lb. lean ground beef
2 Tbsp. tomato paste
¼ cup chopped fresh parsley
¼ tsp. freshly ground black pepper
4 hamburger buns, split and toasted
    lettuce

In a small bowl, combine bulgur with ½ cup warm water; let stand for 30 minutes, or until bulgur is tender and the water is absorbed.

In a large nonstick skillet, heat oil over low heat. Add onions and sugar; sauté until the onions are tender and dark golden, about 15 minutes. Stir in ¼ cup water and vinegar. Season with salt and keep warm.

Prepare the grill or preheat the broiler. In a medium-sized bowl, combine the plumped bulgur, beef, tomato paste, parsley, ½ tsp. salt and pepper; mix thoroughly but lightly. Shape into four ¾-inch- thick patties. Grill over high heat or broil on a lightly oiled rack until browned and cooked through, about 5 minutes per side. Blot the patties with paper towels. Place each patty on a bun, top with the caramelized onions and garnish with lettuce.

Serves 4.

417 CALORIES PER SERVING: 23 G PROTEIN, 15 G FAT, 47 G CARBOHYDRATE; 359 MG SODIUM; 54 MG CHOLESTEROL.

Jerk Turkey Burgers

Jamaican seasonings and grilling bring new flavors to ground turkey.

⅓ cup couscous
2 tsp. vegetable oil, preferably canola
½ cup chopped red bell pepper
2 cloves garlic, minced
1 tsp. dried thyme
¾ tsp. curry powder
¾ tsp. ground cumin
½ tsp. allspice
½ tsp. ground ginger

½ tsp. salt
¼ tsp. freshly ground black pepper
¼ tsp. Spanish paprika
⅛ tsp. cayenne
¾ lb. lean ground turkey
4 hamburger buns, split and toasted
    lettuce
4 slices tomato

In a small bowl, combine couscous with ½ cup water; let stand for 20 to 30 minutes, or until couscous is tender and the water is absorbed.

In a small nonstick skillet heat oil over low heat. Add red peppers, garlic, thyme, curry, cumin, allspice, ginger, salt, pepper, paprika and cayenne. Sauté for 1 minute, or until peppers are slightly softened. Set aside to cool.

Prepare the grill or preheat the broiler. In a medium-sized bowl, combine the couscous, red-pepper mixture and turkey; mix thoroughly but lightly. Shape into four ¾-inch-thick patties. Grill over high heat or broil on a lightly oiled rack until browned and cooked through, about 5 minutes per side. Serve on a bun with lettuce and tomato.

Serves 4.

318 CALORIES PER SERVING: 21 G PROTEIN, 9 G FAT, 34 G CARBOHYDRATE; 358 MG SODIUM; 56 MG CHOLESTEROL.

Temperance at the Plate

Although prime-rib feasts may be no more than a fond memory for people concerned with their health, we do not have to banish meat entirely to eat well. The National Research Council advises consuming lean meat in smaller and fewer portions than is customary in the United States, which translates to no more than four to six ounces of meat, poultry, fish or equivalent amount of high-protein plant foods each day.

Here's why. A typical steak dinner of 20 years ago derived about 57 percent of its calories from fat; a modified dinner with 15 percent of calories from fat may still include meat, but in today's version the cut is leaner, the portion is smaller and the vegetable and bread accompaniments are far more generous.

The following sample menus illustrate how a meal heavy with meat can be modified to a more healthful version:

	calories	grams fat
8-ounce sirloin steak	723	52
Large baked potato	220	0
1 Tbsp. butter	100	11
2 Tbsp. sour cream	62	6
Mixed green salad, 1 cup	30	0
2 Tbsp. French dressing	134	13
2 Brown n' Serve dinner rolls	170	4
2 tsp. butter	67	8

TOTAL: 1506 CALORIES, 94 GRAMS FAT, 57% CALORIES FROM FAT

	calories	grams fat
3 ounces London broil *(round steak, trimmed)*	163	5
Large baked potato	220	0
2 Tbsp. low-fat yogurt	18	0
1 cup fresh asparagus, steamed	44	1
1/2 fresh tomato, sliced	12	0
2 slices Italian bread	170	0
1 tsp. olive oil, garlic	40	5

TOTAL: 667 CALORIES, 11 GRAMS FAT, 15% of CALORIES FROM FAT

Chicken With Mustard & Leeks en Papillote

A savory mustard coating keeps the chicken moist; threads of carrot and leek add color.

4   boneless skinless chicken breasts (1 lb. total), trimmed of fat

4   tsp. coarse-grained mustard

2   leeks, trimmed, cleaned and cut into 2½-inch-long julienne strips

2   carrots, peeled and cut into 2½-inch-long julienne strips

4   tsp. chopped fresh thyme or 1 tsp. dried salt & freshly ground black pepper to taste

Preheat oven to 400 degrees F. Prepare 4 pieces of parchment paper or aluminum foil for papillotes *(see below)*. Place a chicken breast in the center of one half of each opened paper heart. Spread mustard evenly over chicken. Distribute leeks, carrots and thyme over the chicken. Season with salt and pepper. Seal the packages and place them on a baking sheet. Bake for 10 to 12 minutes, or until the packages are puffed. (You may want to open one package to check that the chicken is no longer pink inside.) Transfer the packages to individual plates; let each diner open his or her own package.

Serves 4.

189 CALORIES PER SERVING: 28 G PROTEIN, 2 G FAT, 14 G CARBOHYDRATE; 168 MG SODIUM; 66 MG CHOLESTEROL.

All Wrapped Up

In a paper packet, or *en papillote*, meats, fish, vegetables and fruits can all be prepared without adding a drop of fat. In the oven, steam rapidly builds up inside the package to cook the contents efficiently, without any loss of nutrients. The flavors mingle to create delicately and distinctly flavored dishes. Meals in a packet can be prepared easily and quickly—most can be assembled and baked in a half hour—and recipes can be easily divided or doubled. They make for surprisingly elegant entertaining any night of the week. *(See also Fillet of Sole With Spinach & Tomatoes en Papillote, page 169.)*

To prepare a papillote: Cut a piece of parchment paper or aluminum foil about 12 inches by 16 inches. Fold in half to form an 8-by-12-inch rectangle, then cut into a half-heart shape as you would a valentine. Open the heart and arrange the food in the center of one side of the heart. Fold the other half of the heart over to cover the food and bring edges together. Seal the package by crimping the cut edges together in a series of small, neat folds. Bake at 400 degrees F for 10 to 12 minutes.

Chicken Paprikash

Yogurt stands in for sour cream in this Hungarian classic. Stirring cornstarch into the yogurt allows you to simmer the sauce without it curdling. Serve over wide egg noodles.

1 3-lb. chicken, cut into serving pieces, skin
   and fat removed
   salt & freshly ground black pepper
1 Tbsp. vegetable oil, preferably canola oil
1 onion, thinly sliced
3 cloves garlic, minced

2 Tbsp. sweet Hungarian paprika
½ cup defatted reduced-sodium chicken stock
1½ cups nonfat plain yogurt
1 Tbsp. cornstarch
2 Tbsp. chopped fresh parsley

Season chicken lightly with salt and pepper. In a heavy, nonstick skillet, heat oil over medium-high heat. Add chicken, and cook for 4 to 5 minutes, or until the underside is golden. Using tongs, turn the chicken and cook for 4 to 5 minutes, or until the second side is golden.

Sprinkle onions and garlic around the chicken and cook for 2 to 3 minutes, stirring, or until the onions are softened. Sprinkle with paprika and cook, turning the chicken and onion over, about 1 minute. Reduce heat to low. Add chicken stock and cover the pan. Simmer, turning the chicken occasionally, for 20 to 25 minutes, or until the chicken is no longer pink inside. Transfer the chicken to a serving platter and keep warm.

In a measuring cup or small bowl, stir together 1 cup yogurt and cornstarch; add to the skillet. Cook, stirring, for 3 to 4 minutes, or until the mixture boils and thickens. Season with salt and pepper. Pour the sauce over chicken and serve hot. Top each serving with a spoonful of the remaining yogurt and a sprinkling of chopped parsley.

Serves 4.

341 CALORIES PER SERVING: 41 G PROTEIN, 13 G FAT, 15 G CARBOHYDRATE; 207 MG SODIUM; 107 MG CHOLESTEROL.

Skin the Bird

Much of the fat in poultry comes from the skin. By removing skin, you save 5 grams of fat per 3-ounce portion on the average. If the poultry will be sautéed, braised or marinated and then grilled or roasted, remove the skin before cooking. If the meat will be roasted straightaway, the skin can be removed after cooking; the meat will not absorb the fat.

Barbecued Chicken

*Precooking the chicken in the microwave or gently poaching it on the stovetop
before grilling ensures that the meat is cooked through but the sauce is not charred.*

1   3-lb. chicken, cut into 8 pieces, skin and fat
    removed
⅓   cup tomato catsup
¼   cup hoisin sauce

1   Tbsp. cider vinegar
1   Tbsp. molasses
1   tsp. reduced-sodium soy sauce
1   tsp. Chinese chili paste with garlic

Arrange chicken pieces in a microwaveable dish with the thickest parts toward the outside of the dish. Cover with vented plastic wrap and microwave at high power for 8 to 10 minutes, turning the pieces twice, or until tender. (*Alternatively, in a wide saucepan, poach chicken until tender, 10 to 12 minutes.*)

Meanwhile, prepare the grill or preheat the broiler. In a small bowl, whisk together remaining ingredients.

With tongs, remove the chicken from the dish or saucepan and brush both sides generously with barbecue sauce. Grill over medium-high heat or broil, basting with the barbecue sauce often, until the chicken is glazed on the outside and no longer pink inside, about 5 minutes on each side.

Serves 4.

376 CALORIES PER SERVING: 50 G PROTEIN, 13 G FAT, 13 G CARBOHYDRATE; 485 MG SODIUM; 152 MG CHOLESTEROL.

Oven-Fried Chicken

*Typical fried chicken contains about 21 grams of fat in a 5-ounce serving.
Our oven-fried chicken contains just 14 grams.*

1   large egg white
½   cup skim-milk buttermilk
1   tsp. Tabasco sauce
½   cup all-purpose white flour
1   Tbsp. baking powder
1   Tbsp. sesame seeds, toasted (*page 63*)
    and crushed
2   tsp. paprika

1   tsp. dried thyme
1   tsp. dried oregano
1   tsp. salt
¼   tsp. freshly ground black pepper
1   whole 3-lb. chicken, cut into serving-size
    pieces or 2½ lbs. bone-in chicken pieces,
    skin and fat removed
1   Tbsp. vegetable oil, preferably canola oil

Preheat oven to 425 degrees F. Set a rack over a baking sheet and spray with nonstick cooking spray. In a medium-sized bowl, whisk together egg white, buttermilk and Tabasco. Put flour, baking powder, sesame seeds, paprika, thyme, oregano salt and pepper in a large paper bag. Shake the bag to mix well. Dip chicken

pieces, one at a time, into the buttermilk mixture, then dredge in the flour mixture by shaking in the bag. Place the chicken on the prepared rack. Brush oil lightly over the chicken. Bake for 35 to 40 minutes, or until browned on the outside and no longer pink inside.

Serves 4.

365 CALORIES PER SERVING: 41 G PROTEIN, 14 G FAT, 16 G CARBOHYDRATE; 925 MG SODIUM; 114 MG CHOLESTEROL.

Chicken Potpie

This hearty, satisfying supper centerpiece is elevated to company status with
a rich-tasting sauce made with shiitake mushrooms, white wine and pearl onions.

1½ tsp. vegetable oil, preferably canola oil
½ lb. shiitake mushrooms, stems trimmed, sliced
1 clove garlic, minced
6 Tbsp. all-purpose white flour
¼ cup dry white wine
1½ cups defatted reduced-sodium canned or homemade chicken or turkey stock
1 12-oz. can evaporated skim milk (1½ cups)
4 cups cooked diced chicken or turkey (1 lb.)

2 Tbsp. fresh lemon juice
1 Tbsp. chopped fresh parsley
1 tsp. chopped fresh thyme or ½ tsp. dried salt & freshly ground black pepper to taste
2 carrots, peeled and cut into ½-inch chunks
1 cup frozen pearl onions, thawed
¾ cup frozen peas, thawed
1 recipe Light & Fluffy Biscuit dough (page 41)
1 Tbsp. skim milk

In a large, heavy saucepan, heat oil over medium-high heat. Add mushrooms and garlic and sauté until the mushrooms are just tender, 3 to 5 minutes. Sprinkle flour over the mushrooms and cook, stirring, for 1 minute. Pour in wine, stirring with a whisk. Gradually whisk in stock and evaporated skim milk and bring to a boil, stirring. Cook, stirring, until thickened and smooth, about 1 minute. Remove from the heat and stir in chicken or turkey, lemon juice, parsley and thyme. Season with salt and pepper.

Blanch carrots in boiling water until tender, about 3 minutes. Stir the carrots, onions and peas into the filling. Spoon the filling into a deep, 3-qt. casserole dish and set aside while preparing biscuit topping. *(The filling can be prepared ahead and stored, covered, in the refrigerator overnight.)* Preheat oven to 400 degrees F.

Make Light & Fluffy Biscuit dough. Pat the biscuit dough into a ½-inch-thick disk. With a 3-inch cutter, cut out rounds. Gather the dough scraps together and repeat. Cover the filling with biscuit-dough rounds and brush with skim milk.

Bake for 20 minutes. Reduce the oven temperature to 350 degrees F and bake an additional 10 to 20 minutes, or until the biscuits are nicely browned and the filling is bubbling. Serve immediately.

Serves 8.

376 CALORIES PER SERVING: 31 G PROTEIN, 8 G FAT, 42 G CARBOHYDRATE; 448 MG SODIUM; 65 MG CHOLESTEROL.

Chicken Fajitas

Often it's the sour cream or guacamole accompaniments that take fajitas well over the fat limit. Here, tender broiled chicken is combined with a spicy, creamy sauce in this rolled sandwich.

½ lb. boneless, skinless chicken breasts, trimmed of fat and membrane
2 Tbsp. fresh lime juice
  salt & freshly ground black pepper to taste
2 Tbsp. nonfat plain yogurt
2 Tbsp. reduced-fat sour cream
1 Tbsp. chopped fresh cilantro

1 tsp. minced jalapeño pepper
⅛ tsp. ground cumin
1 large onion, thinly sliced
4 flour tortillas
1 cup shredded lettuce
1 ripe tomato, thinly sliced

Preheat the broiler. Put chicken breasts in a shallow nonaluminum dish and sprinkle with lime juice, salt and pepper. Let marinate at room temperature for 10 minutes.

In a small bowl, whisk together yogurt, sour cream, cilantro, jalapeño and cumin. Season with salt and set aside.

Place chicken and onions on a lightly oiled baking sheet and broil for 3 to 4 minutes. Turn the chicken breasts over and stir the onions. Broil for 3 to 4 min-utes, or until the chicken is no longer pink inside.

Meanwhile, to warm the tortillas, wrap them in foil and tuck into the oven on the rack below the baking sheet.

To assemble fajitas, cut the chicken into thin slices. Fill each tortilla with chicken, onions, lettuce and several tomato slices. Top with the reserved yogurt mixture and roll up the tortilla and filling. Serve immediately.

Serves 4.

218 CALORIES PER SERVING: 19 G PROTEIN, 5 G FAT, 24 G CARBOHYDRATE; 54 MG SODIUM; 41 MG CHOLESTEROL.

Turkey Piccata

*Using lemon segments pared of all membrane gives this
piquant sauce sweetness and body that lemon juice alone would not deliver.
Serve this quick sauté with Barley-Orzo Pilaf (page 123).*

1   lemon
⅓   cup all-purpose white flour
½   tsp. salt
½   tsp. freshly ground black pepper
1   lb. turkey breast, cut into ¼-inch-thick
    diagonal slices
2   tsp. olive oil

1   clove garlic, minced
½   cup defatted reduced-sodium chicken stock
1   Tbsp. drained capers, rinsed
½   tsp. sugar
2   tsp. butter
1   Tbsp. chopped fresh parsley

With a sharp knife, remove skin and white pith from lemon and discard. Cut the lemon segments away from their surrounding membranes into a bowl (discard seeds). Chop lemon segments coarsely. Combine flour, salt and pepper in a plastic bag. Dredge turkey lightly in the flour mixture, shaking off excess. Heat oil in a large nonstick skillet over medium-high heat. Cook the turkey for 2 to 3 minutes per side, or until the outside is golden brown and the interior is no longer pink. Transfer to plates or a platter and keep warm. Add garlic and chicken stock to the skillet. Bring to a boil and cook, stirring, for 1 minute, scraping up brown bits. Add lemon, capers and sugar, and cook 30 seconds longer; swirl butter into the skillet until the butter has melted. Spoon the sauce over the turkey. Sprinkle with parsley and grind more pepper over top.

Serves 4.

243 CALORIES PER SERVING: 36 G PROTEIN, 5 G FAT, 11 G CARBOHYDRATE; 421 MG SODIUM; 100 MG CHOLESTEROL.

Turkey-Stuffed Cabbage Rolls With Sauerkraut

*Originally made with a combination of ground beef and pork,
these cabbage rolls are filled with ground turkey, and brown rice is used instead
of the traditional white. They are best when made a day ahead.*

⅓ cup brown rice
   salt
1 large head green cabbage (3-3½ lbs.)
1 large egg white
1 lb. ground turkey
1 onion, finely chopped

1 46-oz. can tomato juice
½ tsp. freshly ground black pepper
2 lbs. sauerkraut, rinsed and drained
3 Tbsp. brown sugar or honey
2 Tbsp. chopped fresh parsley

In a small saucepan, bring ⅔ cup water to a boil. Stir in brown rice and a pinch of salt. Reduce heat to low, cover and simmer for about 35 minutes, or until the rice is tender and the water has been absorbed. Fluff with a fork and let cool.

Meanwhile, in a saucepan large enough to hold the cabbage snugly, bring water to a boil and add a pinch of salt. Cut out and discard the core and tough outer leaves of cabbage. Place the cabbage in boiling water; cover partially to keep submerged and boil gently until the leaves are pliable, about 20 minutes. Drain cabbage, refresh under cold water and set aside.

In a large bowl, beat egg white lightly with a fork. Add ground turkey, the cooked rice, onions, ½ cup tomato juice, 1 tsp. salt and pepper; mix with a wooden spoon or your hands.

Preheat oven to 325 degrees F. Carefully peel off 12 to 16 of the larger cabbage leaves. Pat dry and trim away any thick rib or core. Place about 3 Tbsp. of the filling in a cylindrical shape across the center of one leaf.

Fold the sides of the leaf over filling, then, starting at the base of the leaf, roll to enclose the filling, forming a neat package. Set aside, seam-side down, on a tray while you fill cabbage leaves with the remaining filling. Thinly slice any remaining cabbage.

Spread about half of the sauerkraut in a 3½-to-4-qt. roasting pan. Scatter sliced cabbage over the sauerkraut and arrange the stuffed cabbage leaves in a single layer on top. Top with the remaining sauerkraut and sprinkle with brown sugar.

Pour the remaining tomato juice over the cabbage rolls. Cover the pan and bring to a simmer on the stovetop. Transfer to the oven and bake for 1½ hours, or until the cabbage is very tender. *(The cabbage rolls can be prepared ahead and stored, covered, in the refrigerator for up to 2 days. Reheat in a covered roasting pan in a 350 degree F oven for 40 to 45 minutes.)* Garnish with parsley and serve hot.

Serves 8.

275 CALORIES PER SERVING: 20 G PROTEIN, 9 G FAT, 35 G CARBOHYDRATE; 1,148 MG SODIUM; 21 MG CHOLESTEROL.

Turkey With Madeira Gravy

Steam-roasting keeps the bird moist without adding fat.
Once the steaming liquid is defatted, it provides the base for a rich-tasting gravy.

1 16-20 lb. turkey, trimmed of fat
    salt & freshly ground black pepper
1 onion, quartered
2 sprigs fresh thyme or 1 tsp. dried

GRAVY
1 cup thinly sliced mushrooms (¼ lb.)
1 stalk celery, finely chopped
1 small onion, finely chopped
1 medium-sized carrot, finely chopped
3 Tbsp. all-purpose white flour
¼ cup Madeira wine or dry sherry

Preheat oven to 325 degrees F. Rinse turkey and wipe the cavity dry. Season the cavity with salt and pepper and stuff it with onion and thyme. Fasten the neck skin to the back with a skewer. Tuck the wings behind back and tie the legs together. Place the turkey, breast-side up, on a lightly oiled rack in a roasting pan. Pour 3 cups water into the pan and roast for 4 to 5 hours, or until the juices run clear when the thigh is pierced with a skewer and the internal temperature registers 180 degrees F. Baste the turkey often and replenish the water as it evaporates from the pan. Cover the turkey with parchment paper or aluminum foil if it gets too brown. Transfer the turkey to a serving platter and cover while you make the gravy.

To make gravy: Pour pan drippings into a bowl and place it in the freezer. Without washing the roasting pan or adding fat, warm the pan over medium heat. Add mushrooms, celery, onions and carrots and sauté for 5 to 10 minutes, or until lightly browned. Sprinkle flour over the vegetables and cook, stirring, for 1 minute. Remove from heat.

Remove the pan drippings from the freezer and, using a bulb baster, carefully remove 2¼ cups liquid from underneath the layer of fat. (Add more turkey or chicken stock or water if necessary.) Use a paper towel to remove any traces of fat from the surface of the liquid. Add the defatted drippings and Madeira or sherry to the roasting pan and bring to a boil, stirring constantly. Simmer, stirring, for several minutes, or until thickened. Season with pepper.

To serve, remove string and skin from the turkey and carve. Serve with gravy.

Serves 12, with leftovers.

221 CALORIES FOR 4 OZ. TURKEY & ¼ CUP GRAVY: 34 G PROTEIN, 6 G FAT, 5 G CARBOHYDRATE; 88 MG SODIUM; 87 MG CHOLESTEROL.

Roast Chicken With Guava Glaze

Cuba's Chinese immigrants inspired this recipe.
Guava glaze adds an appetizing gloss to the skinless bird.

ROAST CHICKEN

1 4-lb. roasting chicken, skinned and trimmed of fat
1 tsp. ground cumin
   salt & freshly ground black pepper to taste
2 large cloves garlic, minced
1 Tbsp. olive oil
2 Tbsp. fresh lime juice

GUAVA GLAZE

¾ cup guava jelly
¾ cup bottled guava nectar or juice
¼ cup fresh lime juice
3 Tbsp. jalapeño jelly
1½ tsp. Worcestershire sauce
1½ tsp. red wine vinegar
1 tsp. paprika
½ tsp. ground cumin
1 cup diced fresh papaya (½ papaya)

To marinate and roast chicken: Season chicken inside and out with cumin, salt and pepper. Mix together the garlic and oil and rub over the chicken. Tie the legs together and tuck the wing tips under the back. Set the chicken in a shallow glass dish and sprinkle with lime juice. Cover and marinate for 2 to 3 hours in the refrigerator.

Preheat oven to 400 degrees F. Line a roasting pan with aluminum foil, set chicken in the pan, cover loosely with aluminum foil and roast for 45 minutes.

To make guava glaze: Meanwhile, in a small saucepan, combine guava jelly, guava nectar or juice, lime juice, jalapeño jelly, Worcestershire, vinegar, paprika and cumin. Bring to a boil. Reduce heat to low and simmer, stirring often, until the sauce has thickened and reduced to 1 cup, 10 to 15 minutes. Remove from the heat.

To glaze chicken: Once the chicken has roasted for 45 minutes, brush it with hot glaze and return to the oven. Roast, uncovered, brushing with glaze every 10 minutes, for 20 to 30 minutes longer, or until the juices run clear when the thigh is pierced with a fork and a meat thermometer inserted in the thigh registers 180 degrees F. Transfer the chicken to a warmed platter and brush with glaze one last time. Bring the remaining glaze to a simmer. Remove from the heat and stir in papaya. Serve the chicken with the glaze alongside.

Serves 6.

410 CALORIES PER 4-OZ. SERVING: 34 G PROTEIN, 11 G FAT, 44 G CARBOHYDRATE; 121 MG SODIUM; 101 MG CHOLESTEROL.

Sage, Onion & Apple Stuffing

Use fresh sage or rubbed sage in this recipe; the ground version is too bitter.

4 cups cubed whole-wheat bread (6 slices)
4 cups cubed white sandwich bread (6 slices)
giblets from 1 turkey (liver discarded)
1½ tsp. vegetable oil, preferably canola oil
2 stalks celery, chopped
1 large onion, chopped
4 apples, preferably McIntosh, peeled, cored and chopped

4 tsp. chopped fresh sage or 1½ tsp. rubbed dried sage
2 tsp. chopped fresh thyme or 1 tsp. dried
½ cup chopped cranberries
½-1 cup defatted reduced-sodium chicken stock salt & freshly ground black pepper to taste

Preheat oven to 350 degrees F. Spread whole-wheat and white bread on a baking sheet and bake for 15 to 20 minutes, or until lightly toasted.

In a small saucepan, cover giblets with 1 cup water and bring to a boil. Reduce heat to low and simmer, covered, for 10 minutes. Drain, reserving the cooking liquid. Finely chop the giblets and set aside.

In a large nonstick skillet, heat oil over medium heat. Add celery and onions; sauté for 5 to 7 minutes, or until softened. Add apples and sauté for 3 minutes longer.

Add the giblet-cooking liquid, sage and thyme. Reduce heat to low and simmer for 5 to 7 minutes, or until the apples are tender and most of the liquid has evaporated.

Transfer to a large bowl and add the toasted bread, reserved giblets and cranberries. Drizzle ½ cup chicken stock over the bread mixture and toss until evenly moistened. If baking in a casserole dish, add the remaining ½ cup chicken stock. Season with salt and pepper.

Makes 8 cups, enough to stuff one 12-lb. turkey or enough to serve 8 as a side dish.

154 CALORIES PER CUP: 4 G PROTEIN, 3 G FAT, 30 G CARBOHYDRATE; 218 MG SODIUM; 0 MG CHOLESTEROL.

Taking the Stuff Out of Stuffing

A look at traditional stuffing recipes shows that the butter was usually measured in sticks, not tablespoons. By opting for chicken stock, wine, fruit juices or a combination thereof, the fat content is radically reduced.

We wondered if the cooking juices from a roasting turkey that seep into the stuffing would turn a low-fat recipe into a high-fat one. It turns out that although the bird's juices provide the stuffing with plenty of flavor, they add little fat. The fat that accumulates in the pan is primarily from the dark meat, which lies beneath the stuffing during cooking.

Stuffings can be stuffed into the bird cavity or baked alone in a lightly oiled covered casserole dish in a 325-degree F oven for 35 to 45 minutes, or until heated through. If you would like a crisp top for bread stuffing, remove the cover for the last 15 minutes of baking.

Sausage Stuffing

Turkey sausage contains about half the fat of pork sausage.

8   cups cubed whole-wheat bread (12 slices)
½   lb. bulk turkey sausage
1½ tsp. vegetable oil, preferably canola oil
3   stalks celery, chopped
2   onions, chopped
1   clove garlic, minced
3   Golden Delicious or McIntosh apples,
    peeled, cored and chopped

2   Tbsp. chopped fresh sage or
    2 tsp. rubbed dried sage
1   tsp. chopped fresh thyme or ½ tsp. dried
½   tsp. dried basil
1½-2 cups defatted reduced-sodium chicken stock
    salt & freshly ground black pepper to taste

Preheat oven to 350 degrees F. Spread bread on a baking sheet and bake for 15 to 20 minutes, or until lightly toasted.

Heat a large nonstick skillet over medium heat. Add sausage and cook, stirring with a wooden spoon to break up the sausage, for 5 to 10 minutes, or until no longer pink. Drain in a colander to remove excess fat. Set aside.

Add oil to the skillet and heat over medium-low heat. Add celery, onions and garlic; sauté for about 5 min-utes, or until softened. Add apples and sauté for 8 to 10 minutes longer, or until tender. Transfer to a large bowl and add the reserved sausage, toasted bread, sage, thyme and basil. Toss well. Drizzle 1½ cups chicken stock over the bread-sausage mixture and toss until evenly moistened. If baking in a casserole dish, add the remaining ½ cup chicken stock. Season with salt and pepper.

Makes 8 cups, enough for one 12-lb. turkey or to serve 8 as a side dish.

196 CALORIES PER CUP: 9 G PROTEIN, 5 G FAT, 30 G CARBOHYDRATE; 492 MG SODIUM; 18 MG CHOLESTEROL.

Safe at the Plate

Warm, moist stuffing in the closed cavity of a turkey is a nurturing environment for bacteria. To avoid the risk of food poisoning, there are a few precautions you need to take when roasting stuffed poultry.

- Do not premix the stuffing. If you wish to prepare ahead, chop and measure the ingredients and store them separately in the refrigerator.
- Temperature and timing are important. The stuffing must be cool before it is placed in the bird, and the bird must be stuffed just before going into the oven.
- Pack stuffing loosely in the cavity because the stuffing will expand during cooking.
- Use a meat thermometer to check doneness of the stuffing as well as the bird. The temperature of the meat should reach 185 degrees F and the stuffing should reach 165 degrees F.
- Spoon all of the stuffing into a serving bowl as soon as the bird is out of the oven.

Wild Rice & Bulgur Stuffing

A departure from classic bread-based stuffing,
this mixture can be also be served as an accompaniment to game.

1½ tsp. vegetable oil, preferably canola oil
3 stalks celery, chopped
2 onions, chopped
2 cloves garlic, minced
1 cup wild rice
3 cups defatted reduced-sodium chicken stock
½ tsp. salt plus more to taste

1 cup bulgur
½ cup pecans, toasted *(page 32)*, coarsely chopped
1 cup golden raisins
½ cup chopped fresh parsley
   freshly ground black pepper to taste

In a heavy saucepan, heat oil over medium heat. Add celery, onions and garlic; sauté for about 5 minutes, or until softened. Stir in wild rice. Add chicken stock and ½ tsp. salt and bring to a boil. Reduce heat to low, cover and simmer for 40 to 45 minutes, or until the rice is tender and the liquid has been absorbed.

Meanwhile, in a bowl, cover bulgur with 2 cups water. Let soak for 30 minutes. Preheat oven to 350 degrees F.

In a small saucepan, cover raisins with water and bring to a boil. Reduce heat to low and simmer for 5 minutes. Drain and set aside.

Stir the soaked bulgur, pecans, raisins and parsley into the cooked wild rice. Season with salt and pepper. Let cool completely before stuffing.

Makes 8 cups, enough to stuff one 12-lb. turkey or to serve 8 as a side dish.

247 CALORIES PER CUP: 6 G PROTEIN, 7 G FAT, 44 G CARBOHYDRATE; 156 MG SODIUM; 0 MG CHOLESTEROL.

Corn Bread Stuffing

Toasting the walnuts for this recipe brings out their flavor.

1 loaf Quick Corn Bread *(page 43)*
1½ tsp. vegetable oil
2 stalks celery, chopped
1 large onion, chopped
⅓ cup walnuts, toasted *(page 32),*
   coarsely chopped

1 cup dried currants
⅓ cup port wine or medium-dry sherry
2 Tbsp. chopped fresh parsley or sage
2 tsp. chopped fresh thyme or 1 tsp. dried
1½-2 cups defatted reduced-sodium chicken stock
   salt & freshly ground black pepper to taste

Using your fingers, break corn bread into coarse crumbs and spread on a baking sheet. Bake for about 35 minutes, or until golden brown. Spread walnuts on pie plate and bake for about 10 minutes, or until fragrant. Let cool and chop coarsely. Set aside.

In a large nonstick skillet, heat oil over medium heat. Add celery and onions; sauté for about 5 minutes, or until softened. Transfer to a large bowl and add the toasted corn-bread crumbs, walnuts, currants, port or sherry, parsley or sage, and thyme. Toss well. Drizzle 1½ cups chicken stock over the crumb mixture and toss until evenly moistened. If baking in a casserole dish, add the remaining ½ cup chicken stock. Season with salt and pepper.

Makes 8 cups, enough to stuff one 12-lb. turkey or enough to serve 8 as a side dish.

319 CALORIES PER CUP: 8 G PROTEIN, 11 G FAT, 47 G CARBOHYDRATE; 306 MG SODIUM; 27 MG CHOLESTEROL.

CHAPTER NINE

FISH
&
SEAFOOD

RECIPES

Swordfish Steaks With Middle Eastern Flavors

The meaty texture of swordfish has earned it status as classic grilling fare.
Its full flavor stands up to the spices in this dish.

2 8-oz. swordfish steaks, about ¾-inch thick
2 Tbsp. finely chopped fresh parsley
1-2 minced jalapeño or other hot peppers (optional)
4 tsp. vegetable oil, preferably canola oil
3 Tbsp. fresh lemon juice

1 clove garlic, minced
1 tsp. ground turmeric
1 tsp. ground cinnamon
1 tsp. ground cumin
   salt & freshly ground black pepper to taste

Place swordfish steaks in a shallow glass dish. In a small bowl, combine all remaining ingredients. Spread mixture over both sides of fish. Cover and refrigerate for 1 hour.

Prepare a charcoal fire or preheat a gas grill. Once the fire is at medium heat, grill the steaks for 4 to 5 minutes per side. The flesh should be opaque. Remove from the grill. Cut each steak into 2 portions and serve.
Serves 4.

167 CALORIES PER SERVING: 19 G PROTEIN, 9 G FAT, 3 G CARBOHYDRATE; 89 MG SODIUM; 38 MG CHOLESTEROL.

Secrets to Grilling Fish

- Scrub the grill rack with a stiff wire brush to prevent food from sticking.
- Make sure the rack is very hot before placing the fish on it by setting the scrubbed rack over the fire as soon as it is lit.
- Cover the seafood with a very thin film of vegetable oil just before cooking.
- Once the fish is on the grill, leave it in the same place for at least a minute before moving it. This allows a sear to develop between metal and flesh, which helps avoid sticking.
- The American Seafood Institute recommends that fish be cooked for 10 minutes per inch of flesh. Because the intensity of heat varies widely during grilling, begin testing for doneness after the fish has cooked for half of the estimated time.
- It is best to grill fish in pieces weighing about eight ounces each; smaller pieces are too thin to remain moist in the center. Cut each piece in half before serving.

Fricassee of Salmon With Cucumbers & Dill

The firm flesh of salmon makes it an excellent candidate for sautéing.
Serve this dish with steamed new potatoes.

2 cucumbers (1½ lbs. total), preferably seedless, washed and trimmed
2 Tbsp. all-purpose white flour
¼ tsp. salt plus more to taste
¼ tsp. freshly ground black pepper
1½ lbs. skinless salmon fillets, preferably center-cut, cut into 1½-inch cubes

4 tsp. olive oil
⅓ cup defatted reduced-sodium chicken stock
pinch sugar
¼ cup chopped fresh dill or 4 tsp. dried
fresh dill sprigs for garnish (optional)
lemon wedges for garnish

Cut cucumbers in half lengthwise. Using a spoon, scoop out any seeds. Cut cucumber into 1½-inch-by-½-inch sticks and set aside. In a shallow dish, combine flour, salt and pepper. Dredge salmon pieces in the flour mixture, shaking off the excess.

In a large nonstick skillet, heat 2 tsp. oil over high heat. Add half of the salmon and sauté for 4 to 5 minutes, or until lightly browned on the outside but still pink inside. Transfer the salmon to a plate and set aside.

Wipe out the skillet with paper towels and add the remaining 2 tsp. oil. When hot, sauté the remaining salmon in the same manner. Set aside.

Wipe out the skillet again and add the cucumbers, stock and sugar. Season with salt and pepper and bring to a simmer. Cover and simmer for 3 to 4 minutes, or until the cucumbers are tender-crisp.

Remove the cover, increase heat to high and boil for several minutes, or until the pan juices are reduced to 2 Tbsp. Add the reserved salmon and chopped or dried dill to the skillet and simmer over medium heat, covered, for 2 to 3 minutes, or just until heated through and the salmon flesh is opaque.

Taste and adjust seasonings. Garnish with dill sprigs and lemon wedges before serving.

Serves 6.

216 CALORIES PER SERVING: 24 G PROTEIN, 10 G FAT, 6 G CARBOHYDRATE; 164 MG SODIUM; 63 MG CHOLESTEROL.

How Fish Take the Heat

Various types of fish respond best to certain cooking techniques using moist heat or dry heat.

Moist-Heat Cooking

These fish taste best when cooked by steaming, poaching, braising and baking *en papillote*:

catfish	flounder	pike	snapper	whitefish
cod	fluke	pollack	sole	whiting
dab	ocean perch	sea bass	walleye	

Dry-Heat Cooking

These fish can be baked, broiled, grilled or pan seared:

bluefish	mackerel	sea trout	striped mullet
butterfish	pompano	shark	tilefish
haddock	porgy	smelt	yellowtail

Moist or Dry Heat

These fish are versatile enough to take a wide range of techniques:

grouper	monkfish	red mullet	striped bass	tuna
halibut	orange roughy	salmon	swordfish	
mahi-mahi	redfish	sea robin	trout	

Lemony Stuffed Fillet of Sole

Why drown the delicate flavors of sole in a sea of butter?
This revised stuffed sole recipe remains a simple yet elegant entrée with about half the
calories and a fraction of the fat in the original recipe from reader Bonnie Cady.

2 cups fresh whole-wheat breadcrumbs
  (page 21)
2 tsp. vegetable oil
⅓ cup chopped celery
2 Tbsp. chopped onion
2 Tbsp. chopped fresh dill
1 Tbsp. chopped fresh parsley

1 tsp. fresh lemon juice
1 tsp. grated lemon zest
¼ tsp. salt
¼ tsp. freshly ground black pepper
1 lb. sole fillets
¼ cup dry white wine

Preheat oven to 350 degrees F. Spread breadcrumbs on a baking sheet and bake for 6 to 8 minutes, stirring occasionally, or until crisp. Transfer to a bowl and set aside.

In a small nonstick skillet, heat oil over medium heat. Add celery and onion and sauté for 3 to 5 minutes, or until softened. Add to the breadcrumbs, along with 1 Tbsp. dill, parsley, lemon juice, lemon zest, salt and pepper. Mix well.

Arrange half of the sole fillets in a single layer in an ungreased 8-by-8-inch baking dish. Sprinkle the breadcrumb mixture evenly over the fillets and place the remaining fillets over top. Pour wine over the fillets and cover the dish with foil. Bake for 15 to 20 minutes, or until the fish flesh is opaque. Garnish with the remaining 1 Tbsp. dill.

Serves 4.

203 CALORIES PER SERVING: 23 G PROTEIN, 5 G FAT, 14 G CARBOHYDRATE; 420 MG SODIUM; 58 MG CHOLESTEROL.

R$_x$ *Bonnie Cady of Harpers Ferry, West Virginia*

Fillet of Sole With Spinach & Tomatoes en Papillote

Designed to be assembled and cooked in about half an hour, this simple yet satisfying recipe can also be doubled or divided without a problem.

1¼ lbs. spinach, trimmed and washed thoroughly
2 cloves garlic, minced
   salt & freshly ground black pepper to taste

4 4-oz. sole fillets
4 small plum tomatoes, cored and sliced

Preheat oven to 400 degrees F. Prepare 4 pieces of parchment paper or aluminum foil for *papillotes (page 151 and photo page 147)*. Put spinach, with water still clinging to its leaves, into a large pot. Cover and steam the spinach over medium-high heat, stirring occasionally, until just wilted, about 5 minutes. Drain; when cool enough to handle, press out excess liquid. Chop and place in a small bowl. Stir in garlic. Season with salt and pepper.

Place one quarter of the spinach mixture in the center of one half of each opened paper heart. Lay a sole fillet over the spinach and arrange tomato slices over the sole. Season with salt and pepper. Seal the packages and place them on a baking sheet. Bake for 10 to 12 minutes, or until the packages are puffed. (You may want to open one package to check that the fish is opaque.) Transfer the packages to individual plates; let each diner open his or her own package.

Serves 4.

156 CALORIES PER SERVING: 27 G PROTEIN, 2 G FAT, 9 G CARBOHYDRATE; 231 MG SODIUM; 55 MG CHOLESTEROL.

Fillet of Sole Florentine

Rolling fish fillets around a spinach filling and topping them with Mornay sauce makes an easy, elegant dinner. By lightening the Mornay sauce, we updated a classic.

1   10-oz. pkg. frozen chopped spinach
3   Tbsp. finely chopped onion
    salt & freshly ground black pepper to taste
    pinch nutmeg, preferably freshly grated
4   5-oz. sole fillets (1¼ lbs. total)

1   tsp. vegetable oil, preferably canola oil
1½ cups skim milk
2   Tbsp. cornstarch
2   Tbsp. freshly grated Parmesan cheese
2   Tbsp. chopped fresh parsley for garnish

Spray a shallow baking dish with nonstick cooking spray. In a medium-sized saucepan, bring ½ cup water to a boil. Add frozen spinach, cover and cook for 2 to 3 minutes or until thawed. Drain in colander and squeeze out as much water as possible. Chop fine. In a small bowl, combine spinach and 1 Tbsp. onion. Season with salt, pepper and nutmeg.

Place sole fillets skinned-side up on a cutting board. Divide the spinach mixture into 4 equal portions and place on the wide end of each fillet. Roll up jellyroll-style to enclose the filling. Place seam-side down in the prepared baking dish. Set aside in refrigerator. Meanwhile preheat oven to 400 degrees F.

In a small saucepan, heat oil over low heat. Add 2 Tbsp. onion and sauté until light golden, 2 to 3 minutes. Pour in 1 cup milk and bring to a simmer. Dissolve cornstarch in remaining ½ cup milk, whisking well to eliminate any lumps. Whisk the cornstarch mixture into the hot milk and cook, whisking constantly, over low heat until thickened. Season with salt, pepper and nutmeg.

Pour sauce over the fish rollups and sprinkle with Parmesan cheese. Bake, uncovered, for 20 minutes, or until top is golden brown and the fish flesh is opaque. Garnish with a little chopped parsley and serve immediately.

Serves 4.

218 CALORIES PER SERVING: 32 G PROTEIN, 4 G FAT, 13 G CARBOHYDRATE; 278 MG SODIUM; 76 MG CHOLESTEROL.

Braised Monkfish

Monkfish and mahi-mahi are well suited to braising; their flesh is firm and absorbs the aromatic seasonings in an intriguing way. This is a simple dish to make for a large group. Serve with rice to soak up the delicious juices.

2 tsp. olive oil
2 heads garlic, cloves separated and peeled
2 oz. sliced prosciutto, trimmed of fat and
   roughly chopped
2½ lbs. monkfish or mahi-mahi fillet

1 cup dry white wine
1 28-oz. can whole tomatoes, drained
2 tsp. chopped fresh thyme or 1 tsp. dried
   freshly ground black pepper to taste

Preheat oven to 425 degrees F. In a large nonstick skillet, heat oil over medium heat. Add garlic cloves and cook, stirring, for about 5 minutes, or until the garlic is golden. Add prosciutto and cook for 1 minute longer. Move the garlic and prosciutto to the side of the pan. Add fish to the pan and cook for 3 minutes per side, or until browned.

Transfer the fish into a shallow 3-qt. baking dish. Pour wine into the skillet and bring to a boil, stirring to scrape up any brown bits. Add tomatoes and thyme. Simmer the sauce, stirring to break up the tomatoes, for about 5 minutes. Season with a generous grinding of pepper; pour sauce over the fish. Cover with a tent of aluminum foil and bake for 20 to 30 minutes, or until the fish is opaque in the center.

Serves 10.

144 CALORIES PER SERVING: 19 G PROTEIN, 3 G FAT, 4 G CARBOHYDRATE; 253 MG SODIUM; 30 MG CHOLESTEROL.

Is It Done Yet?

There is an easy, effective way to figure out when a fish fillet or steak is perfectly cooked. Do what most professional chefs do: take a peek inside. Fish is generally quite pliable; pick it up with tongs and bend or twist it to get a good view of the interior. Alternatively, slip a knife blade into the center of the fish and lift slightly. Properly cooked fish has opaque flesh, while undercooked fish will appear slightly translucent.

Oven-Steamed Flounder With Cantonese Flavors

A dramatic, flavorful dish that can be prepared in about 45 minutes, including marinating time. Black sea bass, red snapper, walleye (yellow pike) and sole are also delicious prepared this way.

4   scallions, trimmed and cut into 2-inch julienne strips
1   2-inch piece gingerroot, peeled and cut into julienne strips
4   4-oz. flounder fillets
2   Tbsp. reduced-sodium soy sauce

2   Tbsp. dry sherry
1   tsp. sesame oil
½   tsp. sugar
    dash hot chili oil or large pinch white pepper
    cilantro leaves for garnish (optional)

Scatter about ⅓ of the scallions and ginger into a 9-by-13-inch baking dish. Place fillets in the dish, skinned side facing down, folding any thin tail ends under to create a uniform thickness. Scatter on remaining ginger and most of the remaining scallions, reserving a few for the garnish. In a small bowl, combine soy sauce, sherry, sesame oil, sugar and chili oil or pepper and pour the mixture evenly over the fish. Let marinate in refrigerator for 15 minutes to 1 hour. Meanwhile, preheat oven to 375 degrees F.

Cover the baking dish with foil and place it in the oven. Bake for 15 minutes, or until the fish flesh is opaque. Garnish with remaining scallions and cilantro (if using).

Serves 4.

137 CALORIES PER SERVING: 23 G PROTEIN, 3 G FAT, 2 G CARBOHYDRATE; 393 MG SODIUM; 40 MG CHOLESTEROL.

Shucking the Myth that Shellfish Are High in Cholesterol

Until recently, some shellfish were considered on the "avoid" list for healthful diets. Luckily for seafood lovers, however, new studies have shown that eating shellfish regularly does not cause blood cholesterol to rise, provided, of course, that saturated fats are avoided or reduced in preparation.

Shellfish gained their undeserved notoriety back in the days when scientific methods for measuring cholesterol in foods were less precise than they are today. Early cholesterol readings were often too high, because techniques did not discriminate between the various sterols (the group of molecules to which cholesterol belongs). And in those days even the experts thought it was mostly dietary cholesterol that caused blood cholesterol to rise.

Now we know that eating too much saturated fat and too much fat in general are far more powerful causes of high blood cholesterol. Shellfish are extremely low in all fats, ranging from less than one gram for a three-ounce serving of scallops or lobster, to a little more than two grams of fat for a similar helping of oysters. The small amount of fat they do contain is ideal; it is mostly monounsaturated and polyunsaturated and includes beneficial omega-3 fatty acids.

Sauté of Shrimp With Fragrant Indian Spices

What could be simpler than a one-pan skillet dinner? For extra flavor, toasting the cumin and coriander seeds before crushing them releases their fragrance. Serve the sauté over basmati rice.

½ tsp. cumin seed
¼ tsp. coriander seed
1 Tbsp. olive oil
1½ lbs. large shrimp, peeled, deveined and patted dry
⅛ tsp. red-pepper flakes
salt & freshly ground black pepper to taste
2 Tbsp. minced shallots
5 large cloves garlic, minced
1½ Tbsp. minced peeled gingerroot
2 tsp. curry powder

1 28-oz. can plum tomatoes (with juices), chopped
1 red bell pepper, cored, seeded and thinly sliced
1 green bell pepper, cored, seeded and thinly sliced
1 small zucchini, scrubbed, cut into 2½-inch-by-½-inch sticks
½ cup chopped fresh cilantro or parsley
1 Tbsp. fresh lemon juice

In a small, dry skillet over medium-high heat, toast cumin and coriander seeds, shaking the pan, for 30 to 40 seconds, or until fragrant. Let cool and crush with the bottom of a heavy pan.

In a large heavy skillet, heat oil over medium-high heat. Add shrimp and red-pepper flakes and sauté for 2 to 3 minutes, or until the shrimp turn bright pink. With a slotted spoon, transfer to a plate. Season with salt and pepper and set aside.

Add shallots, garlic, ginger, curry powder and crushed cumin and coriander seeds to the skillet. Cook, stirring, for 1 minute, or until the shallots are lightly browned. Stir in tomatoes, peppers and zucchini. Cook the mixture, stirring often, over medium heat, for 8 to 10 minutes, or until the sauce is slightly thickened. Add the reserved shrimp, cilantro or parsley, and lemon juice to the skillet and heat through.

Serves 6.

187 CALORIES PER SERVING: 25 G PROTEIN, 5 G FAT, 11 G CARBOHYDRATE; 389 MG SODIUM; 173 MG CHOLESTEROL.

Outer Banks Crab Gratin

Most delicious gratins begin with a cream sauce thickened with a butter-flour roux and hard-boiled eggs and mayonnaise. This low-fat sauce uses flour and skim milk instead of a roux for thickening. The new gratin, which contains only 149 calories and 3 grams of fat per serving, as compared to 366 calories and 29 grams of fat in the original, masks neither the flavor of the crab nor its nutritional virtues.

2 Tbsp. fresh breadcrumbs *(page 21)*	3 Tbsp. reduced-fat mayonnaise
⅔ cup skim milk	1 tsp. minced jalapeño pepper (optional)
2 Tbsp. all-purpose white flour	1½ tsp. dry mustard
⅔ cup evaporated skim milk	⅛ tsp. cayenne pepper or less to taste
1 lb. lump crabmeat, fresh or frozen and thawed, picked over and patted dry	salt & freshly ground black pepper to taste
2 hard-boiled eggs, white part only, finely chopped	

Preheat oven to 350 degrees F. Spread breadcrumbs evenly on a baking sheet and bake for 5 to 8 minutes, or until golden brown. In a small bowl, combine ⅓ cup skim milk with flour and stir until smooth. In a small saucepan, heat remaining ⅓ cup skim milk and evaporated skim milk over medium heat until steaming. Whisk in the flour mixture and cook, whisking constantly until thickened, for 30 to 60 seconds. In a medium bowl, combine crabmeat, hard-boiled egg whites, mayonnaise, jalapeños (if using), mustard, cayenne and salt and pepper. Combine milk mixture with crab mixture and spoon into a shallow 2-qt. baking dish. Sprinkle the top with breadcrumbs and bake for 25 minutes, or until heated through.

Serves 6.

149 CALORIES PER SERVING: 20 G PROTEIN, 3 G FAT, 9 G CARBOHYDRATE; 891 MG SODIUM; 44 MG CHOLESTEROL.

℞ *Sybil Basnight of Manteo, North Carolina*

Crab Cakes

Crabmeat is the star in these delicately seasoned cakes.
In traditional recipes, the crab cakes are fried in a generous amount of butter.
To avoid the added fat needed for frying, we broiled the cakes.

1 large egg white
1 lb. lump crabmeat, fresh or frozen and thawed, picked over and patted dry
¾ cup fresh breadcrumbs *(page 21)*
2 Tbsp. reduced-fat mayonnaise
2 Tbsp. fresh lemon juice
1 scallion, trimmed and minced
3 Tbsp. finely diced red bell pepper
3 Tbsp. finely diced green bell pepper
1 Tbsp. chopped fresh parsley
1 tsp. Old Bay seasoning
⅛ tsp. freshly ground black pepper
½ cup. fine dry breadcrumbs
    lemon wedges for garnish

In a large bowl, stir egg white briskly with a fork. Add the crabmeat, breadcrumbs, mayonnaise, lemon juice, scallions, red and green peppers, parsley, Old Bay seasoning and pepper; mix well.

Spray a baking sheet with nonstick cooking spray. Put the dry breadcrumbs in a shallow dish. Form the crab mixture into six ½-inch-thick patties. Lay each patty in the dry breadcrumbs, and then turn each to coat them well on all sides. Pat the crab cakes firmly into rounds and then place them on the prepared baking sheet.

Preheat the broiler. Broil the crab cakes for 4 to 5 minutes, until nicely browned. Turn them gently and broil until heated through and browned, 4 to 5 minutes longer. Serve hot, with lemon wedges.

Serves 6.

181 CALORIES PER SERVING: 18 G PROTEIN, 3 G FAT, 20 G CARBOHYDRATE; 1,003 MG SODIUM; 33 MG CHOLESTEROL.

DESSERTS

RECIPES

Lemon Soufflé

*Light, spirited and not too sweet, this soufflé has a touch of orange juice
and Grand Marnier to mellow the sharpness of the lemon. For a contrast that is both
pleasing to the eye and palate, serve with Raspberry Coulis (page 198).*

¾ cup sugar plus extra for preparing soufflé
   dish(es)
2 Tbsp. cornstarch
⅓ cup fresh lemon juice
2 Tbsp. fresh orange juice
1½ tsp. grated lemon zest

2 Tbsp. orange liqueur, such as Grand Marnier
   or Cointreau
5 large egg whites, at room temperature
¼ tsp. cream of tartar
   pinch salt
   confectioners' sugar for dusting over top

In a small, heavy saucepan whisk together ¼ cup sugar and cornstarch. Gradually whisk in ¼ cup water, lemon juice, orange juice and lemon zest; bring to a boil over medium heat, stirring constantly. Cook, stirring, for 30 to 45 seconds, or until slightly thickened and no longer cloudy. Remove from the heat, stir in orange liqueur and let cool to room temperature. *(The recipe can be prepared ahead to this point. Store, covered, in the refrigerator for up to 2 days. Bring to room temperature before proceeding.)*

Position rack in the lower third of the oven and preheat oven to 350 degrees F. Lightly coat the inside(s) of a 1½-qt. soufflé dish or six 1½-cup individual soufflé dishes with vegetable oil or nonstick cooking spray. Sprinkle with sugar and tap out excess.

In a large, grease-free mixing bowl, beat egg whites with an electric mixer on medium speed until foamy and opaque. Add cream of tartar and salt; gradually increase speed to high and beat until soft peaks form. Gradually add the remaining ½ cup sugar and beat until stiff (but not dry) peaks form.

Stir the lemon mixture well. Whisk about one quarter of the beaten egg whites into the lemon mixture until smooth. Using a rubber spatula, fold the lemon mixture back into the remaining whites. Turn into the prepared dish(es) and smooth the tops with the spatula.

Place the dish(es) in a roasting pan. Fill the pan with hot water to come about one-third of the way up the side(s) of the dish(es). Bake until puffed and the top feels firm to the touch, about 25 minutes for individual soufflés or about 35 minutes for a large soufflé. Dust with confectioners' sugar and serve immediately.

Serves 6.

130 CALORIES PER SERVING: 3 G PROTEIN, 0 G FAT, 29 G CARBOHYDRATE; 91 MG SODIUM; 0 MG CHOLESTEROL.

Eight Steps to a Perfect Dessert Soufflé

1. Much of the work—making the soufflé base and preparing the sauce—can be done in advance. Make sure to allow enough time for the base to come to room temperature before assembling the soufflé.
2. Preheat the oven at least 15 minutes before baking. Position the rack in the lower third of the oven.
3. Prepare a straight-sided mold by lightly brushing it with vegetable oil or spraying it with non-stick cooking spray. Sprinkle granulated sugar inside the mold, tilting it to evenly distribute the sugar. Tap out excess sugar. The sugar coating gives the soufflé a delightful crisp crust.
4. Make certain that the mixing bowl and beaters are spotless, without a trace of fat.
5. Eggs are easiest to separate when they are cold, but egg whites whip to a greater volume when they are at room temperature. To warm, set the bowl of whites in a larger bowl of very warm water and stir gently for a few minutes or until they are at room temperature.
6. For speediest assembly, measure sugar, salt and cream of tartar and set beside the whites.
7. Beat the egg whites until they form stiff—but not dry—peaks: overbeaten egg whites may cause the soufflé to collapse.
8. As soon as whites are ready, whisk about one quarter of the beaten whites into the soufflé base to lighten it. Then gently fold this mixture back into the remaining whites.

Whipping Evaporated Skim Milk

When thoroughly chilled, canned evaporated skim milk whips up into a light frothy topping that can be used as a substitute for whipped cream. Before beating, place it in a mixing bowl in the freezer for 30 minutes, or until ice crystals form around edge of bowl. Chill beater also. Whipped cream will usually double in volume, but evaporated skim milk will triple. The air bubbles dissipate quickly, so it works best in mousses that are bound with gelatin or frozen. Evaporated skim milk has a distinctive flavor, which can overpower delicate dishes. It works best when combined with vibrant flavors.

Reformed Chocolate Mousse

The quintessential chocolate mousse sent to us by Susan Niemczyk carries two-thirds of the recommended daily fat allotment for an average-sized woman in every serving. Our mousse reformation, with only 288 calories and 6 grams of fat per serving, as compared to 486 calories and 40 grams of fat in the original recipe, doesn't require a warning from the Surgeon General.

2   Tbsp. coffee liqueur, dark rum or strong
    brewed coffee
1   envelope unflavored gelatin (2½ tsp.)
1   large egg
¾   cup unsweetened cocoa powder
½   cup corn syrup

1½ cups skim milk
3   oz. semisweet chocolate, chopped
1   tsp. pure vanilla extract
5   large egg whites
1   cup sugar
    pinch salt

Pour liqueur, rum or coffee into a small bowl, sprinkle gelatin over the surface and let stand to soften. In a medium-sized bowl, whisk whole egg, cocoa, corn syrup and ½ cup milk together until smooth. In a heavy saucepan, heat the remaining 1 cup milk until steaming. Gradually whisk the hot milk into the egg mixture.

Return to the saucepan and cook over low heat, stirring constantly with a wooden spoon, for about 5 minutes, or until slightly thickened. Remove from the heat and add the gelatin mixture, stirring until the gelatin has dissolved. Add chocolate and stir until chocolate has melted. Stir in vanilla, transfer to a large bowl and set aside to cool to room temperature.

Place egg whites in a large mixing bowl. Set it over a larger pan of hot water and stir for a few minutes until warmed slightly.

In a small saucepan, combine sugar with ½ cup water.

Bring to a boil, stirring occasionally. Cook over medium-high heat, without stirring, until the syrup registers 240 degrees F and is at the soft-ball stage (when a bit of syrup dropped into ice water forms a pliable ball), about 5 minutes. Remove syrup from heat. Set aside.

Beat egg whites with an electric mixer just until soft peaks form. Return the syrup to the heat until it boils. Gradually pour hot syrup into egg whites but not directly onto the beaters, beating constantly. Continue beating until egg whites are cool and very stiff, about 5 minutes.

Whisk ¼ of the egg whites into the chocolate mixture. Fold in the remaining whites. Spoon into a serving bowl or individual glasses, cover and refrigerate until set, at least 4 hours or overnight.

Serves 8.

288 CALORIES PER SERVING: 8 G PROTEIN, 6 G FAT, 51 G CARBOHYDRATE; 99 MG SODIUM; 27 MG CHOLESTEROL.

R̲x̲ *Susan J. Niemczyk of Washington, D.C.*

Peach Melba Shortcake, page 192

Roast Chicken With Guava Glaze, page 159

Sauté of Shrimp With Fragrant Indian Spices, page 173

183

Cherry & Nectarine Cobbler, page 193

Frozen Lemon Mousse

Lightened with Italian meringue and whipped evaporated skim milk, this is a fat-free dessert.
Serve with Blackberry Sauce (page 199) or Raspberry Coulis (page 198).

3 large egg whites
¾ cup sugar
¼ cup light corn syrup
½ cup fresh orange juice, chilled

⅓ cup fresh lemon juice, chilled
2 tsp. grated lemon zest
¼ cup evaporated skim milk

Lightly coat a 6-to-8-cup ring mold or other decorative mold with nonstick cooking spray. Place egg whites in a large mixing bowl. Set it over a larger bowl of hot water and stir for a few minutes until warmed slightly.

In a small saucepan, combine sugar with corn syrup and ¼ cup water. Bring to a boil, stirring occasionally. Cook over medium-high heat, without stirring, until the syrup registers 240 degrees F and is at the soft-ball stage (when a bit of syrup dropped into ice water forms a pliable ball), about 3 to 5 minutes. Remove syrup from heat. Set aside.

In a large mixing bowl, beat egg whites with an electric mixer just until soft peaks form. Return the syrup to the heat until it boils. Gradually pour hot syrup into egg whites but not directly onto the beaters, beating constantly. Continue beating until egg whites are cool and very stiff, about 5 minutes.

Gently whisk in orange and lemon juices and lemon zest.

In a separate, chilled mixing bowl with chilled beaters, beat evaporated skim milk until it forms firm, but not stiff, peaks. Using a whisk, fold it into the beaten egg-white mixture until smooth. Turn the mousse into the prepared mold. Cover and freeze for at least 8 hours or preferably overnight.

To unmold and serve: Dip the mold in hot water for about 8 to 10 seconds. Run a knife around the edges to loosen the mousse and invert it onto a platter. Return it to the freezer briefly to firm.

Serves 8.

170 CALORIES PER SERVING: 2 G PROTEIN, 0 G FAT, 42 G CARBOHYDRATE; 38 MG SODIUM; 0 MG CHOLESTEROL.

Making Italian Meringue

Because of concerns of salmonella contamination in eggs, raw meringues are no longer recommended. Even though Italian meringue is a little more complicated to make than basic raw meringue, there is the additional advantage of greater stability. Italian meringues will hold in the refrigerator for several days, making them perfect for low-fat fillings and mousses. For all these reasons, we use Italian meringue frequently in desserts.

To ensure that the temperature of the meringue reaches 160 degrees F, several important steps must be followed. First, the whites must be warmed over hot water, bringing their temperature to about 100 degrees F. Then a 240-degree F sugar syrup is beaten into the whites in a quick, steady stream. The meringue is then beaten until it cools.

Plum Pudding

Save your suet for the birds; this scrumptious holiday dish uses prune puree,
a little vegetable oil and extra spices to produce a pudding with only 4 grams of fat per serving,
compared to 27 grams in the original sent to us by Mary Wood. Accompany this dessert
with Grand Marnier Light "Whipped Cream" or Lemon Sauce (page 200).

3 cups all-purpose white flour	¼ cup brandy
1 Tbsp. ground cinnamon	2 Tbsp. vegetable oil, preferably canola oil
1½ tsp. ground cloves	½ cup dark raisins
1 tsp. salt	½ cup golden raisins
1 tsp. baking soda	½ cup dried currants
1½ cups skim milk	½ cup diced candied orange rind
¾ cup molasses	1 tsp. grated lemon zest
⅓ cup prune puree *(page 187)*	2 Tbsp. orange liqueur, such as Grand Marnier

Coat a 2-qt. pudding mold, soufflé dish or bowl with nonstick cooking spray. If the mold has a flat bottom, line it with wax or parchment paper. Sift flour, cinnamon, cloves, salt and baking soda together into a large bowl. In a small bowl, whisk together milk, molasses, prune puree, brandy and oil. Make a well in the center of the flour mixture, add the milk mixture and stir with a wooden spoon until well combined. Add raisins, currants, orange rind and lemon zest. Spoon the batter into the prepared mold or dish. Cover with a circle of wax or parchment paper. Cover again with an oiled lid, or an oiled circle of aluminum foil, pleated to allow for expansion, and secured with string.

Place the mold on a rack or a trivet in a large pot.

Add boiling water to come halfway up the sides of the mold. Cover the pot and steam the pudding in simmering water for 3 hours, or until a cake tester inserted in the center comes out clean. (Add more water as needed.) Run a knife around the edge of the dish and unmold the pudding immediately. Brush top and sides with Grand Marnier. Serve warm. *(The pudding can be prepared up to 2 weeks ahead and stored, well wrapped, in the refrigerator. To reheat, steam it in the mold for 45 minutes to 1 hour or unmold and microwave it on a plate, covered loosely with wax paper, at 50 percent power for 10 minutes, or until heated through.)*

Serves 8.

457 CALORIES PER SERVING: 8 G PROTEIN, 4 G FAT, 94 G CARBOHYDRATE; 425 MG SODIUM; 1 MG CHOLESTEROL.

R$_x$ *Mary Wood of New York, New York*

Louisiana Bread Pudding

Serve this classic, homey dessert with Lemon Sauce and Light "Whipped Cream" (page 200).

4 cups cubed French bread (⅓ lb.)
¼ cup pecans or walnuts
2 large eggs
¾ cup plus 2 Tbsp. packed dark brown sugar
2 cups evaporated skim milk
1 Tbsp. pure vanilla extract

1½ tsp. ground cinnamon
1 tsp. nutmeg, preferably freshly grated
½ cup raisins
1 Tbsp. granulated sugar
1 Tbsp. butter

Preheat oven to 325 degrees F. Spread bread cubes on a baking sheet and bake for about 10 minutes, stirring twice, or until firm and lightly toasted. Meanwhile, spread nuts in a pie plate and bake for 8 to 10 minutes, or until fragrant. Let nuts cool and chop coarsely.

In a large mixing bowl, whisk together eggs and brown sugar. Blend in evaporated skim milk, vanilla, cinnamon and nutmeg. Stir in the toasted bread, nuts and raisins. Cover and refrigerate for at least ½ hour or up to 1 hour.

Meanwhile, lightly coat a shallow 2-qt. baking dish with vegetable oil or nonstick cooking spray. Sprinkle with ½ Tbsp. granulated sugar. In a small saucepan, melt butter over low heat. Skim off froth and cook until it begins to turn light nutty brown, 1½ to 2 minutes. (Be careful not to burn the butter.) Transfer to a small bowl and let cool.

Pour the bread mixture into the prepared baking dish. Drizzle browned butter over top and sprinkle with the remaining ½ Tbsp. granulated sugar. Bake the pudding in a 325 degree F oven for 40 minutes, or until firm in the center. Increase the oven temperature to 425 degrees F. and bake for 10 to 15 minutes longer, or until the top is brown and puffed. Let cool for 10 minutes before serving hot or warm.

Serves 8.

288 CALORIES PER SERVING: 9 G PROTEIN, 6 G FAT, 50 G CARBOHYDRATE; 215 MG SODIUM; 60 MG CHOLESTEROL.

Making Prune Puree

From our experiments using fruit puree as a fat substitute in baked goods, we've concluded that replacing about 75 percent of the fat with puree and leaving in 25 percent of the fat gives the best results.

Match the fruit puree to your recipe. Prune puree works well with spicy recipes, such as carrot cake or gingerbread. For recipes with more delicate seasonings, such as zucchini muffins, apple butter works best.

One cup of prune puree contains 407 calories and 1 gram of fat; a cup of butter contains 1,600 calories and 182 grams of fat; and a cup of oil contains 1,944 calories and 218 grams of fat.

In a food processor, combine 6 oz. (1 cup) pitted prunes with 6 Tbsp. hot water; process until smooth. Makes 1 cup.

Indian Pudding

This simple recipe is adapted from the recipe that has been served at
Boston's Durgin Park restaurant for more than a century. Accompany with nonfat frozen
vanilla yogurt or Extraordinary Low-Fat Vanilla "Ice Cream" (page 197).

3   cups 1% milk
½   cup yellow cornmeal, preferably stone-ground
¼   cup molasses
2   Tbsp. sugar
1   Tbsp. unsalted butter

1   tsp. ground cinnamon
1   tsp. ground ginger
½   tsp. nutmeg, preferably freshly grated
¼   tsp. salt
⅛   tsp. baking soda
1   large egg

Preheat oven to 275 degrees F. Coat six 1-cup ramekins with nonstick cooking spray and set aside. Scald 2½ cups milk in a heavy saucepan. Meanwhile, place remaining ½ cup milk in a small bowl and gradually whisk in cornmeal. Whisk the cornmeal mixture into the hot milk. Bring to a boil and boil gently over low heat, whisking frequently, for 15 minutes, or until thickened.

Remove from heat and stir in molasses, sugar, butter, cinnamon, ginger, nutmeg, salt and baking soda. Beat egg in a small bowl, stir in a little of the hot cornmeal mixture and whisk the mixture back into the saucepan. Pour the mixture into the ramekins, place on a baking sheet and bake for 1 to 1½ hours, or until the centers are set. Cool the puddings slightly and serve warm.
Serves 6.

166 CALORIES PER SERVING: 6 G PROTEIN, 5 G FAT, 25 G CARBOHYDRATE; 191 MG SODIUM; 46 MG CHOLESTEROL.

Rice Pudding

Made with skim milk, this comforting dessert (delicious for breakfast too)
has a lovely creamy consistency because Italian arborio rice is used.

3   cups skim milk
½   cup arborio rice
⅓   cup raisins
¼   cup sugar
2-3   tsp. grated lemon zest

1   tsp. pure vanilla extract
    pinch salt
    ground cinnamon for dusting over top
    (optional)

In a heavy medium-sized saucepan, combine milk, rice, raisins and sugar. Bring to a boil, stirring. Reduce heat to low and simmer, uncovered, stirring often, until the rice is tender and the pudding is creamy, 20 to 25 minutes. (Stir almost constantly towards the end to pre-

vent scorching.) Stir in lemon zest, vanilla and salt and pour the pudding into a serving bowl or individual bowls. Let cool slightly. Serve warm or chilled, dusted with cinnamon, if desired.
Serves 4.

234 CALORIES PER SERVING: 8 G PROTEIN, 1 G FAT, 49 G CARBOHYDRATE; 97 MG SODIUM; 3 MG CHOLESTEROL.

English Trifle

Fresh fruit and angel food cake lighten this classic.
A light custard, made with Italian meringue and skim milk, drops the calories by half.
Store-bought angel food cake works fine here.

1   small angel food cake (10 oz.)
⅓   cup raspberry preserves
⅓   cup medium-dry sherry
4   cups fresh fruit (sliced oranges; halved
    seedless grapes; hulled, halved strawberries;
    raspberries; sliced peeled kiwis)

4   cups Light Custard *(page 205)*
¼   cup toasted slivered almonds
    additional fresh fruit for garnish

Cut cake into 2-inch-thick slices and cut slices into 1-by-4-inch strips. Spread preserves over one side of each strip. Arrange half the cake, jam-side up, in the bottom of a 12-cup serving bowl. Sprinkle with half the sherry. Arrange half the fruit over the cake layer and spoon half the custard over the fruit. Re-peat with remaining cake, sherry, fruit and custard. Cover and refrigerate for at least 1 hour or up to 8 hours. Just before serving, sprinkle almonds over the top and arrange fresh fruit decoratively in the center.

Serves 10.

237 CALORIES PER SERVING: 8 G PROTEIN, 3 G FAT, 43 G CARBOHYDRATE; 148 MG SODIUM; 65 MG CHOLESTEROL.

℞ *Elizabeth Truden of Cleveland Heights, Ohio*

Crème Caramel

This is a far cry from the usual four-yolk custard, yet it is rich and golden with a full caramel flavor. The milk for the custard is heated in the saucepan used to make the caramel; this flavors the custard subtly. For a lovely vanilla flavor, you can use a split vanilla bean instead of extract. Add the vanilla bean to the hot milk and let steep for 10 minutes before removing vanilla bean.

½   cup plus ⅓ cup sugar
1   cup skim milk
1   cup evaporated skim milk

2   large eggs
4   large egg whites
1   Tbsp. pure vanilla extract

Preheat oven to 325 degrees F. In a small heavy saucepan, combine ½ cup sugar with ⅓ cup water. Bring to a simmer over low heat, stirring occasionally. Increase heat to medium-high and cook, without stirring, until the syrup turns a deep amber color, 5 to 7 minutes. (Watch it carefully at this point so that it does not burn.) Carefully pour caramel into six ¾-cup ramekins and tilt the ramekins to coat the bottom and sides evenly.

Let saucepan cool for a minute or so, then add the milk and evaporated skim milk to the caramel coating the saucepan. Bring to a simmer, stirring to dissolve the caramel. Remove from heat.

In a medium-sized bowl, lightly whisk eggs, egg whites, ⅓ cup sugar and vanilla. Gradually whisk the milk mixture into the egg mixture. Divide the custard mixture into the caramel-lined ramekins. Skim off any bubbles. Place the ramekins in a roasting or baking pan. Pour hot water two-thirds of the way up the sides of the ramekins. Bake for 25 to 30 minutes, or until a knife inserted in the center of the custard comes out clean. Transfer the ramekins to a rack and cool. Cover and refrigerate until chilled, at least 1 hour or for up to 2 days.

To serve, run the tip of a small knife around the edge of the mold and invert onto a plate.

Serves 6.

190 CALORIES PER SERVING: 9 G PROTEIN, 2 G FAT, 34 G CARBOHYDRATE; 128 MG SODIUM; 73 MG CHOLESTEROL.

Oeufs à la Neige

Meringue "snow eggs" floating in a bowl of custard make a light, sweet way to end a meal.

CUSTARD SAUCE

1½ cups 1% milk
½ vanilla bean, split lengthwise
1 strip orange zest
1 large egg
3 Tbsp. sugar

MERINGUES

1 cup 1% milk
4 large egg whites
1 cup sugar, preferably superfine
½ tsp. pure vanilla extract

CARAMEL & FRUIT GARNISH

½ cup sugar
1 cup strawberries or raspberries

To make custard sauce: Pour milk into a heavy saucepan, add vanilla bean and orange zest. Scald the milk and remove from the heat. Cover and set aside to steep for 10 minutes.

Scald the milk once again. In a mixing bowl, whisk egg and sugar until smooth but not frothy; gradually whisk a little of the hot milk into the egg mixture. Pour all of the egg mixture into the hot milk. Cook over low heat, stirring constantly with a wooden spoon for 15 to 20 minutes, or until the custard thickens slightly. (When you run your finger across the back of the spoon, you should leave a clean trail.) Do not boil. Immediately strain the custard into a clean bowl. Scrape seeds from the vanilla bean and stir them into the custard. Refrigerate for about 1 hour, or until chilled.

To make meringues: Pour milk into a deep wide skillet. Add enough water to come to a depth of about 2 inches and bring to a simmer. In a mixing bowl, beat egg whites with an electric mixer until they form soft peaks; gradually beat in sugar and continue beating until the meringue is stiff and glossy. Blend in vanilla. With 2 soup spoons that have been dipped in cold water, form half of the meringue into 3 large puffs and gently drop them into the simmering liquid. Poach for 8 minutes, gently turn them over with 2 slotted spoons and poach the second sides for about 4 minutes, or until firm. With a slotted spoon, lift the meringues from the liquid and drain briefly on a kitchen towel. Repeat with the remaining meringue. Pour the custard sauce into a shallow serving dish. Arrange meringues over top. *(The meringues can be prepared ahead and stored, covered, in the refrigerator for up to 8 hours.)*

To make caramel: In a small heavy saucepan, combine sugar and ¼ cup water. Bring to a boil, stirring occasionally. Cook over medium-high heat, without stirring, for 3 to 5 minutes, or until the syrup turns amber. Remove the pan from the heat and let cool for 2 to 3 minutes. Drizzle the caramel over the meringues and custard. Garnish with berries.

Serves 6.

278 CALORIES PER SERVING: 7 G PROTEIN, 2 G FAT, 61 G CARBOHYDRATE; 99 MG SODIUM; 40 MG CHOLESTEROL.

Peach Melba Shortcake

Celebrate summer with this updated American standard. The tender buttermilk biscuits are topped with almonds and sugar, forming a crunchy glaze as they bake.

ALMOND-BUTTERMILK BISCUITS

2¼ cups all-purpose white flour
⅓ cup sugar plus 1 Tbsp. for sprinkling over biscuits
1½ tsp. baking powder
¾ tsp. baking soda
¼ tsp. salt
2 Tbsp. cold unsalted butter, cut into small pieces
¾-1 cup skim-milk buttermilk
1 Tbsp. vegetable oil, preferably canola oil

½ tsp. pure vanilla extract
⅛ tsp. pure almond extract
1 Tbsp. skim milk
¼ cup sliced almonds

FILLING

1 pt. fresh raspberries
⅓ cup sugar, preferably superfine
4 ripe peaches
3 cups nonfat vanilla frozen yogurt

To make biscuits: Coat a baking sheet lightly with nonstick cooking spray or line it with parchment paper. Set aside.

In a mixing bowl, stir together flour, ⅓ cup sugar, baking powder, baking soda and salt. Using a pastry cutter or your fingertips, cut butter into the flour mixture until crumbly. In a small bowl, combine ¾ cup buttermilk, oil, vanilla and almond extracts. Make a well in the center of the flour mixture and add the buttermilk mixture. With a fork, stir just until combined, adding additional buttermilk, as necessary, to form a slightly sticky dough. Do not overmix.

Place the dough on a lightly floured surface and sprinkle with a little flour. With your fingertips, gently pat dough to an even 1-inch thickness. Using a 3- or 3½-inch round cookie cutter, cut out biscuits and transfer them to the prepared baking sheet. Gather together scraps of dough and cut remaining biscuits. You should have 6 biscuits. Brush milk over the biscuits. Scatter almonds over the tops and sprinkle lightly with the re-

maining 1 Tbsp. sugar. *(The biscuits can be made ahead and stored, covered, in the refrigerator for up to 1 hour.)*

To prepare filling: In a large bowl, toss berries with sugar. With the back of a wooden spoon, crush a few of the berries. Let stand at room temperature for at least ½ hour, stirring occasionally, until berries have formed a light syrup.

Using a slotted spoon, dip peaches into boiling water for about 20 seconds and refresh under cold water. Peel the peaches, halve, remove pits and slice. Add to the berry mixture and stir gently.

To bake and assemble shortcakes: Preheat oven to 425 degrees F. Bake the biscuits for 10 to 15 minutes, or until golden. Transfer them to a rack and let cool slightly. Using a serrated knife, split the biscuits. Set bottoms on dessert plates; spoon on the fruit mixture and frozen yogurt, and crown with the biscuit lids. Serve immediately.

Serves 6.

452 CALORIES PER SERVING: 14 G PROTEIN, 10 G FAT, 79 G CARBOHYDRATE; 382 MG SODIUM; 14 MG CHOLESTEROL.

Cherry & Nectarine Cobbler

Ruby fruits shine in this summer dessert. Instead of a biscuit topping,
a low-fat, cream-cheese pastry is an unexpected pleasure.

CREAM-CHEESE PASTRY DOUGH

1	cup sifted cake flour
1	tsp. sugar plus 1 Tbsp. for sprinkling over top
	pinch salt
¼	cup well-chilled reduced-fat cream cheese
4	tsp. unsalted butter or margarine
2½-3	Tbsp. skim milk plus 1 Tbsp. for glaze

FRUIT FILLING

2	pts. cherries, pitted
4	large, ripe but firm nectarines, pitted and thickly sliced
2	Tbsp. fresh lemon juice
2	Tbsp. kirsch or Grand Marnier (optional)
½	cup packed brown sugar
2	Tbsp. cornstarch
¾	tsp. ground cinnamon
	pinch salt
3	cups nonfat vanilla frozen yogurt (optional)

To make pastry: In a bowl, stir together flour, 1 tsp. sugar and salt. With a pastry cutter or your fingertips, cut cream cheese and butter or margarine into the flour mixture until crumbly. With a fork, gradually stir in enough milk so the mixture just clumps together. Press the dough into a disk, wrap in plastic and refrigerate for at least ¹/₂ hour. *(The pastry can be prepared ahead and stored in the refrigerator for up to 2 days.)*

To prepare fruit and bake cobbler: Preheat oven to 400 degrees F. In a large bowl, combine cherries, nectarines, lemon juice and kirsch or Grand Marnier, if using. In a small bowl, stir together brown sugar, corn-starch, cinnamon and salt. Sprinkle over the cherry mixture and toss well. Transfer to a shallow 2-qt. baking dish.

On a lightly floured surface, roll pastry to a ¹/₈-inch thickness. Carefully place over the fruit mixture, allowing about ³/₄-inch pastry to hang over the edges. Tuck the overhang under and flute the edges. Brush the top with milk and sprinkle with sugar. Cut several slashes in the pastry as steam vents. Bake for about 45 minutes, or until the pastry is golden and the filling is bubbly. Cool briefly, then serve warm, with frozen yogurt, if desired.

Serves 6 to 8.

257 CALORIES PER SERVING: 4 G PROTEIN, 5 G FAT, 52 G CARBOHYDRATE; 132 MG SODIUM; 11 MG CHOLESTEROL.

Plum-Berry Crisp

Traditional crisp toppings contain a great deal of butter. In this tasty adaptation, apple juice helps bind the topping, allowing us to greatly reduce the amount of butter.

TOPPING

¾	cup packed brown sugar
¾	cup rolled oats
¾	cup all-purpose white flour
2	Tbsp. vegetable oil, preferably canola oil
2	tsp. butter
2	Tbsp. apple juice

FRUIT FILLING

3	ripe but firm peaches or nectarines
1½	lbs. ripe purple plums
1½	cups fresh blueberries
¼	cup maple syrup
3	Tbsp. brown sugar
2	Tbsp. cornstarch
2	Tbsp. fresh lemon juice
¼	tsp. ground nutmeg
	pinch ground ginger
1	qt. nonfat vanilla frozen yogurt (optional)

To make topping: In a large bowl, combine brown sugar, oats and flour. With a pastry cutter or your fingertips, blend in oil and butter until crumbly. Pour in apple juice and stir with a fork until the mixture is evenly moistened. Set aside.

To prepare fruit and bake crisp: Preheat oven to 400 degrees F. If using peaches, dip them into boiling water for about 20 seconds. Remove using a slotted spoon and refresh under cold water; peel. Halve and pit the peeled peaches or nectarines. Cut into thick wedges and place in a large bowl. Pit and slice plums; combine with the peaches. Add blueberries, maple syrup, brown sugar, cornstarch, lemon juice, nutmeg and ginger; toss gently to combine.

Transfer the fruit mixture to a shallow 2-qt. baking dish. Sprinkle the topping evenly over fruit and bake for about 40 minutes, or until the topping is golden and the filling is bubbling.

Let cool for about 10 minutes and serve hot or warm, with frozen yogurt, if desired.

Serves 8.

314 CALORIES PER SERVING: 3 G PROTEIN, 6 G FAT, 66 G CARBOHYDRATE; 20 MG SODIUM; 3 MG CHOLESTEROL.

Simple Noodle Kugel

*Several readers, among them Marlene Kohlenberg, challenged our test kitchen
to come up with a tasty, but healthful, revival of a Jewish dish that usually flaunts a pint of
sour cream, a pint of cottage cheese, half a stick of butter, 4 eggs and a cup of milk.
We took the challenge—lightly.*

10 oz. wide egg noodles (8 cups)	⅔ cup sugar
2 Tbsp. butter	1 Tbsp. pure vanilla extract
2 large eggs	1 tsp. salt
2 large egg whites	½ cup golden raisins
¼ cup cornstarch	1½ cups crushed cornflakes
2 cups nonfat cottage cheese	½ cup packed brown sugar
2 cups nonfat plain yogurt	1 tsp. ground cinnamon
1 cup skim milk	

Preheat oven to 350 degrees F. Coat a 9-by-13-inch glass baking dish with nonstick cooking spray.

In a large pot of boiling water, cook noodles until tender but firm, 5 to 7 minutes. Drain and refresh with cold water. Set aside.

In a small skillet, melt butter over low heat. Skim off froth and cook until it begins to turn light, nutty brown, 1½ to 2 minutes. (Be careful not to burn the butter.) Pour into a small bowl and let cool.

In a large bowl, whisk together eggs, egg whites and cornstarch. Mix in cottage cheese, yogurt, milk, sugar, raisins, vanilla, salt and browned butter. Stir in noodles and turn into the prepared pan. In a small bowl, stir together cornflakes, brown sugar and cinnamon. Sprinkle evenly over the noodle mixture.

Bake for about 1 hour, or until browned and set. (If topping starts to burn, cover with aluminum foil.) Let cool for at least 20 minutes. Cut into squares and serve warm or cold.

Serves 12.

295 CALORIES PER SERVING: 13 G PROTEIN, 4 G FAT, 52 G CARBOHYDRATE; 298 MG SODIUM; 67 MG CHOLESTEROL.

℞ *Marlene Kohlenberg of Oak Park, Michigan*

Out-with-the-Cream Puffs

Traditional recipes use ½ cup butter and 4 to 5 whole eggs. We've reduced the fat to 2 tablespoons and cut out 3 egg yolks. Filled with Light Custard (page 205) or Light "Whipped Cream" (page 200) and fresh berries, these add an elegant flourish to a company dinner.

1 Tbsp. butter
1 Tbsp. vegetable oil, preferably canola oil
¼ tsp. salt
1 Tbsp. sugar

1 cup all-purpose flour
2 large eggs
5 large egg whites

Line 2 baking sheets with parchment paper or spray them with nonstick cooking oil. Set rack in the center of the oven; preheat oven to 425 degrees F.

In a medium-sized saucepan, combine 1 cup water, butter, oil, salt and sugar; bring just to a boil over medium heat. Remove from the heat and add flour all at once. Stir with a wooden spoon until it forms a smooth paste. Return the mixture to low heat and cook, stirring, for about 3 minutes. This will slightly dry the paste. Remove from heat and cool for 2 minutes.

Lightly whisk together the eggs and egg whites. With an electric mixer, beat one quarter of the egg mixture into the flour paste until it is absorbed. Repeat with three more additions of the egg mixture, until the mix-ture is smooth and glossy. *Note:* The unbaked cream puff paste will be much less firm than that of a tradi-tional cream puff.

Drop heaping tablespoons of the mixture, 2 inches apart, on the prepared baking sheets. Bake one sheet at a time for 25 to 30 minutes, or until puffed and well browned. (Cover unbaked cream puffs with plastic wrap.) Poke each puff in two places with the tip of a par-ing knife to allow steam to escape, and cool on a rack.

To serve, cut each cream puff in half with a serrated knife, removing any excess uncooked dough from the center. Fill and serve immediately. *(Cream puffs can be stored in an airtight container in the freezer for up to 1 month.)*
Makes 16 cream puffs.

60 CALORIES PER CREAM PUFF: 3 G PROTEIN, 2 G FAT, 7 G CARBOHYDRATE; 66 MG SODIUM; 29 MG CHOLESTEROL.

Profiteroles

A French version of a hot fudge sundae.

Fill each cream puff with ½ cup Extraordinary Low-Fat Vanilla "Ice Cream" *(page 197)* or nonfat frozen vanilla yogurt and top with 2 Tbsp. Chocolate Sauce *(page 199)* or Orange-Caramel Sauce *(page 205)*.

Extraordinary Low-Fat Vanilla "Ice Cream"

*When one of our testers tasted the homemade ice cream recipe submitted for a
"recipe rescue" by Eleanor Henderson, she lamented that to change it one iota would be
a crime. But, with a whopping 59 grams of fat in each ¾-cup serving,
it would be at least a misdemeanor to ignore the challenge. This version made with—
believe it or not—Marshmallow Fluff cuts fat-per-serving by 57 grams.*

4 cups skim milk	2 Tbsp. pure vanilla extract,
¼ cup corn syrup	preferably Madagascar
3 large egg yolks	2½ cups Marshmallow Fluff
¼ cup cornstarch	

In a large heavy saucepan, combine $3\frac{3}{4}$ cups milk and corn syrup. Heat over medium heat, stirring to dissolve the corn syrup, until steaming. Meanwhile, in a medium-sized bowl, whisk together egg yolks, cornstarch and the remaining $\frac{1}{4}$ cup cold milk until smooth. Gradually whisk 1 cup hot milk into the egg yolk mixture; then pour the egg yolk mixture into the hot milk in the pan. Cook over medium heat, whisking constantly until the mixture boils and thickens, 3 to 5 minutes. (Because the custard is thickened with cornstarch, it will not curdle when it boils.)

Transfer the custard to a large clean bowl and place a piece of wax paper directly over the surface to prevent a skin from forming. Cool completely. Whisk in Fluff and vanilla until as smooth as possible. (The mixture will be a little lumpy; lumps will break down during stir-freezing.) Pour into the canister of an ice cream maker and freeze following the manufacturer's instructions.

Makes about $1\frac{1}{2}$ qts.; serves 8.

341 CALORIES PER 3/4-CUP SERVING: 6 G PROTEIN, 2 G FAT, 75 G CARBOHYDRATE; 106 MG SODIUM; 82 MG CHOLESTEROL.

R_x *Eleanor Henderson of Brick, New Jersey*

Peach-Melon Frozen Yogurt

*Start with frozen fruit and you'll have a delicious, fresh-tasting frozen yogurt
15 minutes later. For convenience, we have used commercially packaged mixed frozen fruit;
strawberries, bananas and blueberries (alone or as a combination) are delicious, but avoid seedy fruits,
such as raspberries. If you would like to double this recipe, process it in two batches.*

3 cups frozen mixed fruit (peaches, melon, grapes)
⅓ cup superfine (instant-dissolving) sugar

½ cup nonfat plain yogurt
1 Tbsp. fresh lemon juice

In a food processor, combine frozen fruit and sugar. Using an on/off motion, process until coarsely chopped. Stir together yogurt and lemon juice. With the machine running, gradually pour the yogurt mixture through the feed tube. Process until smooth and creamy, scraping down the sides of the work bowl once or twice. Scoop the frozen yogurt into serving dishes, cover and freeze for 15 to 30 minutes to firm up slightly before serving.
Makes about 2½ cups; serves 4.

119 CALORIES PER SERVING: 3 G PROTEIN, 0 G FAT, 29 G CARBOHYDRATE; 62 MG SODIUM; 1 MG CHOLESTEROL.

Raspberry Coulis

*Because it is an uncooked sauce, the taste is fresh and flavorful —
delicious with fresh fruits, soufflés, ice cream and chocolate desserts.*

3 cups fresh or unsweetened frozen raspberries, thawed (12-oz. pkg.)

⅓ cup sugar
3 Tbsp. Chambord (optional)

Place the raspberries and sugar in a food processor or blender and puree until smooth. Strain through a fine-meshed sieve into a bowl. Stir in Chambord, if using. Serve at room temperature or chilled.

(The sauce can be prepared ahead and stored, covered, in the refrigerator for 2 days.)
Makes about 1⅓ cups.

20 CALORIES PER TABLESPOON: 0 G PROTEIN, 0 G FAT, 5 G CARBOHYDRATE; 0 MG SODIUM; 0 MG CHOLESTEROL.

Chocolate Sauce

A dark, delicious sauce with merely 1 gram of fat per tablespoon.
For best results, use Dutch-processed cocoa.

⅓ cup unsweetened cocoa powder
1 Tbsp. cornstarch
2 Tbsp. sugar
½ cup corn syrup

⅓ cup evaporated skim milk
1 tsp. vegetable oil, preferably canola oil
2 tsp. pure vanilla extract or 1 Tbsp. Kahlúa (coffee liqueur)

In a small, heavy saucepan, whisk together cocoa, cornstarch and sugar. Gradually whisk in corn syrup and milk. Bring to a boil, stirring, over medium heat. Cook, stirring, for 30 seconds to 1 minute, or until thickened. Remove from the heat and whisk in oil and vanilla or Kahlúa. Let cool and serve at room temperature or chilled. *(The sauce can be prepared ahead and stored, covered, in the refrigerator for up to 1 week.)*

Makes about 1 cup.

63 CALORIES PER TABLESPOON: 1 G PROTEIN, 1 G FAT, 13 G CARBOHYDRATE; 14 MG SODIUM; 0 MG CHOLESTEROL.

Blackberry Sauce

Blackberry sauce is an unexpected accompaniment to
lemon soufflé or low-fat frozen vanilla yogurt.

3 cups fresh or frozen blackberries
¼-⅓ cup sugar

pinch grated lemon zest

In a medium-sized saucepan, stir together blackberries, sugar and lemon zest. Bring to a simmer over medium heat, stirring until the sugar dissolves. Cover and simmer for about 5 minutes, or until the berries are soft and the juices released. Press the berries through a fine sieve, forcing through as much juice and pulp as possible. Discard the seeds.

Makes about 1½ cups.

17 CALORIES PER TABLESPOON: 0 G PROTEIN, 0 G FAT, 4 G CARBOHYDRATE; 0 MG SODIUM; 0 MG CHOLESTEROL.

Lemon Sauce

A fresh light sauce to serve with bread pudding,
gingerbread, plum pudding or waffles.

3 Tbsp. sugar
2 tsp. grated lemon zest
1 tsp. cornstarch

2 Tbsp. fresh lemon juice
1 tsp. butter

In a small saucepan, combine sugar, lemon zest and cornstarch. Gradually whisk in lemon juice and ¹/₂ cup water. Bring to a boil, whisking constantly. Simmer for about 30 seconds, or until slightly thickened. Remove from heat and whisk in butter until melted.

Makes about ¹/₂ cup.

23 CALORIES PER TABLESPOON: 0 G PROTEIN, 0 G FAT, 5 G CARBOHYDRATE; 5 MG SODIUM; 0 MG CHOLESTEROL.

Light "Whipped Cream"

An extremely versatile surrogate whipped cream.
It provides the finishing touch for bread pudding, crisps, cobblers, angel food cake—
anything that you would normally slather with whipped cream.

¹/₃ cup evaporated skim milk, chilled *(page 179)*
¹/₄ cup sugar
2 Tbsp. nonfat plain yogurt

1 Tbsp. orange liqueur, such as **Grand Marnier** or **Cointreau**

In a chilled deep mixing bowl, beat evaporated skim milk with electric beaters for 1 to 2 minutes, or until it is the consistency of whipped cream. Gradually add sugar, yogurt and liqueur and beat for several minutes longer, or until thickened. Serve within ¹/₂ hour.

Makes about 1 cup.

20 CALORIES PER TABLESPOON: 0 G PROTEIN, 0 G FAT, 4 G CARBOHYDRATE; 7 MG SODIUM; 0 MG CHOLESTEROL.

Glazed Cheesecake With Fruit, page 213

Pumpkin-Wheat Bread, page 42

Patty's Cake, page 217

203

Cranberry-Raisin Tart, page 230

Light Custard

Italian meringue lightens and enriches a delicate custard to serve with fruits and trifles.

3   cups skim milk
2   large eggs, separated
⅓   cup cornstarch

1   Tbsp. pure vanilla extract
⅔   cup sugar

Whisk together ¼ cup milk, egg yolks and cornstarch. In a heavy saucepan, heat remaining milk until steaming. Gradually whisk milk into the egg mixture. Return to the saucepan; cook over medium heat, whisking constantly, until custard boils and thickens, about 4 to 6 minutes. Remove from heat, stir in vanilla and transfer to a clean bowl. Place a piece of wax paper or plastic wrap directly on the surface of the custard to prevent a skin from forming and let cool.

Place egg whites in a large mixing bowl. Set it over a larger pan of hot water and stir for a few minutes until warmed slightly.

In a small saucepan, combine sugar with ⅓ cup water. Bring to a boil, stirring occasionally. Continue cooking over medium-high heat, without stirring, for about 5 minutes, or until syrup registers 240 degrees F and is at the soft-ball stage (when a bit of syrup dropped into ice water forms a pliable ball). Remove syrup from heat. Set aside.

Beat egg whites with electric mixer until soft peaks form. Return the syrup to the heat until it boils. Gradually pour syrup into egg whites but not directly onto the beaters, beating constantly. Continue beating until egg whites are cool and very stiff, about 5 minutes. Whisk one quarter of the egg whites into the custard. Fold in remaining egg whites. *(The custard can be stored, covered, in the refrigerator for up to 8 hours.)*

Makes about 4 cups.

275 CALORIES PER CUP: 9 G PROTEIN, 3 G FAT, 53 G CARBOHYDRATE; 127 MG SODIUM; 110 MG CHOLESTEROL.

Orange-Caramel Sauce

This unexpected combination gracefully finishes poached pears, Profiteroles (page 196) or simple frozen yogurt.

1   cup sugar
⅛   tsp. salt

½   cup evaporated skim milk
1   Tbsp. frozen orange-juice concentrate

Combine sugar with ½ cup water in a heavy saucepan. Bring to a boil over medium-high heat, stirring to dissolve the sugar. Cook, without stirring, until it turns a deep amber color, about 8 to 10 minutes. Do not burn. Remove from heat and carefully swirl in 1 Tbsp. water to stop the cooking; be careful, it will spatter. Cool 2 minutes, then gradually stir in evaporated milk. Return pan to very low heat and stir to dissolve the caramel; the mixture must not boil. Remove from the heat and stir in orange-juice concentrate. *(The sauce can be prepared up to a week ahead and stored, covered, in the refrigerator. Let it come to room temperature before serving.)*

Makes about 1 cup.

105 CALORIES PER TABLESPOON: 1 G PROTEIN, 0 G FAT, 26 G CARBOHYDRATE; 52 MG SODIUM; 1 MG CHOLESTEROL.

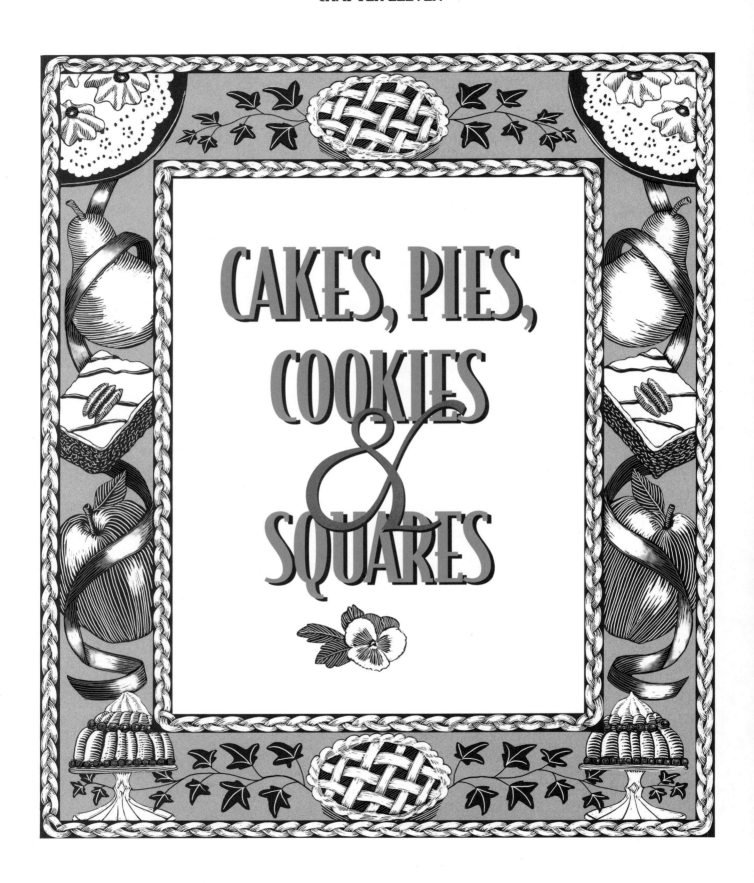

CHAPTER ELEVEN

CAKES, PIES, COOKIES & SQUARES

RECIPES

Devil's Food Layer Cake

*Known for its striking dark color, devil's food is a hallmark American cake.
Its taste is distinctive, due to the combining of baking soda and nonalkalized American-style
cocoa powder. The soda neutralizes the cocoa's natural acidity, lending not only the characteristic
devil's food aroma and taste, but reddish-black color. (Because the reaction of the baking soda with
acid in the cocoa is essential in this cake, be sure not to substitute Dutch processed or
"European-style" cocoa. It is alkalized during manufacture and won't yield satisfactory results.)*

CAKE

- ¾ cup unsweetened American-style cocoa powder, plus more for dusting pans
- 1½ tsp. baking soda
- 2¼ cups sifted cake flour
- ½ tsp. baking powder
- ¼ tsp. salt
- 2½ Tbsp. unsalted butter, slightly softened
- 2 Tbsp. vegetable oil, preferably canola oil
- 2¼ cups sugar
- 1 large egg
- 2 large egg whites
- 1 oz. unsweetened chocolate, melted
- 1 cup nonfat "sour cream"
- 1 Tbsp. pure vanilla extract
- 4 large egg whites, at room temperature

MOCHA FROSTING

- 2½ Tbsp. instant coffee granules
- 2 tsp. pure vanilla extract
- 2 large egg whites
- 1½ cups sugar
- ¼ tsp. cream of tartar
- ¼ tsp. salt
- ½ cup unsweetened American-style cocoa powder
- ½ cup confectioners' sugar

GLAZE

- ½ oz. bittersweet (not unsweetened) or semi-sweet chocolate
- ½ tsp. vegetable oil, preferably canola oil

To make cake: Preheat oven to 350 degrees F. Generously coat three 9-inch round layer cake pans with nonstick cooking spray. Line bottoms with wax paper. Lightly spray paper with nonstick cooking spray. Dust pans with cocoa, tapping out excess.

In a medium-sized bowl, whisk ³/₄ cup very hot tap water into cocoa until smooth. Stir in baking soda and set aside.

Sift together flour, baking powder and salt onto a piece of wax paper. In a large mixing bowl, beat butter and oil with an electric mixer until blended. Add 2 cups sugar, the whole egg and 2 egg whites; beat until very light and well blended, about 2 minutes. Beat in the cocoa mixture until very smooth. Beat in the melted chocolate until evenly incorporated. With the mixer on low speed, beat in half of the dry ingredients, then sour cream and vanilla, then the remaining half of the dry ingredients just until evenly incorporated; do not overbeat.

In a large mixing bowl, beat 4 egg whites with an electric mixer at medium speed until opaque. Raise speed to high and beat until soft peaks form. Gradually beat in the remaining ¹/₄ cup sugar. Continue beating until firm but not dry peaks form. Using a rubber spatula or whisk, fold about 1 cup whites into the chocolate mixture. Then fold this mixture into the remaining beaten whites.

Divide the batter among the prepared pans, spreading to the edges. Bake for 20 to 30 minutes, or until a cake tester inserted in the center comes out clean and the top springs back slightly when pressed lightly. Let cool completely in the pans on racks. Carefully run a knife around pan edges to loosen cakes from the pans. Invert cakes onto racks and peel off paper.

To make frosting: In a small bowl, stir together ¹/₄ cup lukewarm water, instant coffee and vanilla. Set aside. Place egg whites in a large mixing bowl. Set it over a larger pan of hot water and stir for a few minutes until warmed slightly. In a medium-sized saucepan, combine sugar with $1/3$ cup water. Bring to a simmer over medium-high heat. Cover and cook for 2 minutes to allow the steam to wash sugar from pan sides. Uncover and cook, without stirring, for about 2 minutes longer, or until the syrup registers 240 degrees F and is at soft-ball stage (a bit of syrup dropped into ice water will form a soft, pliable ball). Immediately remove the pan from the heat and set aside.

Beat the egg whites with the electric mixer at medium speed until frothy and opaque. Add cream of tartar and salt. Raise speed to high and beat until whites stand in soft peaks. Immediately, return the syrup to the burner and reheat to boiling. Beating whites at high speed, pour boiling syrup in a stream down bowl sides (avoid beaters or syrup will be thrown onto bowl sides). Add the re-served coffee mixture and continue beating at high speed until the mixture is very stiff and has cooled completely, about 5 minutes. Sift cocoa and confectioners' sugar and together onto a sheet of wax paper. Add to the meringue and beat at low speed until completely incorporated.

To assemble cake: Center a layer on a serving platter. Spread a scant $1/4$ of the frosting over top. Repeat with the second layer and another $1/4$ of frosting. Add the third layer and complete decorating by swirling the remaining frosting attractively over cake top and sides.

To make glaze: In a small bowl, set over almost simmering water, melt chocolate with oil, stirring occasionally. With a fork, drizzle the chocolate glaze decoratively over the cake. *(The cake can be held in the refrigerator for up to 1 day.)*

Serves 16.

323 CALORIES PER SERVING: 5 G PROTEIN, 8 G FAT, 61 G CARBOHYDRATE; 220 MG SODIUM; 18 MG CHOLESTEROL.

Enlightened Black Forest Cherry Torte

*One of the most famous and festive of all chocolate cakes, this classic German torte
features cherries and chocolate layers spiked with kirsch (cherry brandy) and topped with
mountains of whipped cream. Well almost. Instead of lathering the torte with whipped cream,
this recipe features an Italian meringue-whipped cream combination. The whipped cream is
stabilized with gelatin so the torte can be made ahead and the flavors allowed to blend.*

CAKE

1½   cups sifted white cake flour
1   tsp. baking powder
¼   tsp. salt
3   large egg yolks
1¼   cups sugar
½   cup Dutch processed (European-style) cocoa
     powder
1¼   tsp. pure vanilla extract
4   large egg whites, at room temperature

CHERRIES & SOAKING SYRUP

2   16-oz. cans unsweetened sour (pie) cherries
½   cup frozen cranberry-juice concentrate,
     thawed
⅓   cup sugar
3   Tbsp. kirsch
1   oz. unsweetened chocolate, coarsely chopped
2   tsp. unsweetened cocoa powder

MERINGUE CREAM & GARNISH

¼   tsp. unflavored gelatin
1   tsp. kirsch or water
⅓   cup whipping cream
3   large egg whites
¾   cup plus 1 Tbsp. sugar
1½   Tbsp. light corn syrup
½   tsp. cream of tartar
1   tsp. pure vanilla extract
1½-2 ounces semisweet chocolate shavings for
     garnish
6-8 red candied cherries for garnish (optional)

To make cake: Preheat oven to 350 degrees F. Line
the bottom of a 9-inch springform pan with a round of
wax paper. Sift flour, baking powder and salt onto a
sheet of wax paper or into a large bowl. In a large mixing bowl, combine egg yolks, ³/₄ cup sugar and 1 Tbsp.
hot tap water. Beat on medium speed until foamy. Raise
speed to high; beat until mixture is light, thick and falls
in ribbons from beaters, about 5 minutes.

In a small bowl, whisk together ¹/₂ cup hot water
and cocoa until smooth. Lower mixer speed and spoon
cocoa mixture in a little at a time. Add vanilla. Gradually raise mixer speed to as high as possible without
causing splattering; continue beating until mixture is
very foamy and increased in volume, about 5 to 10
minutes longer. Sprinkle flour mixture over beaten
mixture. Lightly fold with a rubber spatula just until

thoroughly incorporated.

In a large mixing bowl, beat egg whites until frothy
with mixer on medium speed. Raise speed to high; beat
until soft peaks just begin to form. Gradually add remaining ¹/₂ cup sugar and continue beating until whites
stand in almost firm peaks. Using a whisk, mix about ¹/₃
of whites into yolk mixture. Add yolk mixture back to
whites and continue mixing until ingredients are evenly
incorporated but not overmixed. Immediately turn out
batter into pan, spreading to edges.

Bake for 35 to 45 minutes, or until the cake springs
back when lightly pressed in center. Let cool completely
in the pan on a rack, at least 1 hour. Remove cake from
pan and peel off paper. *(The cake may be prepared ahead
and stored, well wrapped, for up to 36 hours or frozen for up
to 1 week. Thaw before proceeding.)*

To prepare cherries and soaking syrup: Drain cherries, reserving juice. Combine 1 cup drained cherry juice, cranberry juice concentrate, sugar and 1 Tbsp. kirsch in a 4-quart or larger saucepan. Bring mixture to a rolling boil over high heat. Boil syrup 10 minutes, or until slightly thicker and reduced to ³/₄ cup; as mixture boils down, watch carefully and adjust heat to avoid scorching. Immediately remove from heat. Combine chocolate and cocoa in a small deep bowl. Add ¹/₄ cup hot cherry-cranberry syrup, stirring until chocolate partially melts and mixture is blended. Add 2 more tablespoons syrup and stir until mixture is completely smooth. Stir remaining kirsch into chocolate mixture. Cover the chocolate soaking syrup and set aside. Stir cherries into remaining cherry-cranberry syrup. Refrigerate, covered, for at least 2 hours and up to 48 hours, stirring occasionally.

To make meringue cream: In a small saucepan, sprinkle gelatin over kirsch. Let soften for about 5 minutes. Heat over medium heat, stirring, just until gelatin is dissolved. Remove from the heat. Stir cream into gelatin mixture until well blended. Cover and refrigerate until well chilled.

Place whites in a large mixing bowl. Set it over a larger bowl of hot water and stir for a few minutes until warmed slightly.

In a small saucepan, combine sugar, corn syrup and ¹/₄ cup water. Bring to a boil, stirring occasionally. Cook over medium-high heat, without stirring, until the syrup registers 240 degrees F and is at the soft-ball stage (when a bit of syrup dropped into ice water forms a pliable ball), about 5 minutes. Remove syrup from heat. Set aside.

Beat egg whites with an electric mixer just until frothy. Add cream of tartar and beat until soft peaks form. Re-turn the syrup to the heat until it boils. Gradually pour hot syrup into egg whites but not directly onto the beaters, beating constantly. Add vanilla. Continue beating until egg whites are cool and very stiff, about 5 minutes.

With mixer on high speed, whip cream just until firm peaks form. Whisk cream into meringue mixture until evenly incorporated. Refrigerate until mixture is chilled and slightly stiffened, about 35 to 45 minutes.

To assemble torte: Drain the reserved cherries well. If not using candied cherries for garnish, reserve 10 to 12 attractive sour cherries. Using a large serrated knife, slice cake horizontally into 3 equal layers. (If desired, add cutting guides around cake by measuring and marking sides into thirds with toothpicks.) Reserve smooth bottom layer to serve as torte top. Center a remaining layer on serving plate. Using long-bladed spatula or table knife, spread a third of chocolate soaking syrup over cake surface. Spread generous fourth of meringue whipped cream over the layer. Sprinkle half of drained cherries over cream. Top cherries with second cake layer, pressing down lightly. Spread cake surface with another third of the chocolate soaking syrup. Cover with another fourth of cream. Top with remaining cherries. Spread remaining chocolate soaking syrup on cut side of last layer. Place layer, cut side down, over cherries. Using a palette knife or long-bladed spatula, spread remaining cream over top. Pile chocolate shavings in center of torte. Tuck reserved cherries or candied cherries among chocolate pieces.

Refrigerate torte, covered, at least 6 hours and up to 24 hours before serving; longer storage allows flavors to blend. *(Torte may also be frozen, tightly wrapped, for up to a week; thaw completely before serving.)* Let cake warm up a few minutes before serving.

Makes 12 servings.

346 CALORIES PER SERVING: 6 G PROTEIN, 6 G FAT, 70 G CARBOHYDRATE; 132 MG SODIUM; 61 MG CHOLESTEROL.

Angel Food Cake With Eggnog Spices

Eggnog spices highlight a heavenly cake that is light, moist and fat-free.

1 cup sifted cake flour
1½ cups sugar
1 tsp. freshly grated nutmeg
½ tsp. ground cinnamon
¼ tsp. ground mace
¼ tsp. ground allspice

⅛ tsp. ground cloves
⅛ tsp. salt
12 large egg whites, at room temperature
1 tsp. cream of tartar
1 tsp. pure vanilla extract
confectioners' sugar for dusting

Preheat oven to 350 degrees F. Combine flour with ½ cup sugar, nutmeg, cinnamon, mace, allspice, cloves and salt; set aside. Place egg whites in a large bowl and beat with an electric mixer until frothy. Add cream of tartar and continue beating until soft peaks form. Gradually add the remaining 1 cup sugar and the vanilla: beat just until stiff peaks form. Do not overbeat.

Sift the flour mixture over the beaten egg whites in 3 parts, folding in gently after each sifting. Pour batter into an ungreased 10-inch tube pan. Smooth the top and run a small knife or spatula through the batter to remove any air pockets.

Bake for 45 minutes, or until a cake tester comes out clean and the top springs back when touched lightly. Invert the pan over the neck of a bottle and let cool completely.

With a knife, loosen the edges of the cake and invert onto a cake plate. Dust with confectioners' sugar and slice.

Serves 12.

143 CALORIES PER SERVING: 4 G PROTEIN, 0 G FAT, 32 G CARBOHYDRATE; 78 MG SODIUM; 0 MG CHOLESTEROL.

Egg Safety

Experts stress that eggs should be handled and cooked with particular care, necessitating revisions of some traditional meringue-making methods and salad dressings. While the risk of encountering a contaminated egg is low, both raw and cooked eggs should be refrigerated, work areas, utensils and storage containers kept scrupulously clean and leaking or cracked eggs discarded.

It is best to cook all eggs, especially the yolks, to at least 160 degrees F—the temperature at which microorganisms are destroyed.

Glazed Cheesecake With Fruit

A favorite dessert sheds almost an ounce of fat (26 grams) per serving as yogurt cheese again comes to the rescue in place of sour cream. Cereal stands in for nuts. Amy Simon, who submitted the original recipe, said everyone in her household feels the new recipe is every bit as tasty.

CRUST
- ½ cup graham cracker crumbs (8 crackers)
- ½ cup Grape-Nuts cereal
- 2 Tbsp. vegetable oil, preferably canola oil

FILLING
- 2 cups nonfat cottage cheese, pressed to yield 1 cup *(page 26)*
- 2 cups yogurt cheese *(page 57)*
- 1 8-oz. pkg. reduced-fat cream cheese, softened
- 1¼ cups sugar
- 2 large eggs
- 2 large egg whites
- 1 Tbsp. cornstarch
- 1 Tbsp. pure vanilla extract
- 2 tsp. grated lemon zest
- 1 tsp. lemon juice

TOPPING
- 2 cups yogurt cheese *(page 57)*
- ⅓ cup sugar
- 2 tsp. pure vanilla extract

FRUIT & GLAZE
- 4 navel oranges
- ¼ cup apricot preserves
- 2 Tbsp. orange liqueur, such as Grand Marnier
- 4 kiwi fruit, peeled and sliced
- 2 cups hulled strawberries

To make crust: Preheat oven to 350 degrees F. Coat a 9- or 10-inch springform pan with nonstick cooking spray. In a medium-sized bowl, stir together crumbs, cereal and oil. Press into the bottom of the prepared pan and set aside.

To make filling: Put the pressed cottage cheese in a food processor and process until smooth. Add yogurt cheese, cream cheese, sugar, eggs, egg whites, cornstarch, vanilla, lemon zest and lemon juice and process until smooth. Spoon the mixture over the crust. Set the pan on a baking sheet and bake until just set, 40 to 45 minutes for a 10-inch cake or 50 to 55 minutes for a 9-inch cake. Remove from the oven and cool for 15 minutes. Retain oven temperature at 350 degrees F.

To make topping: In a small bowl, stir together yogurt cheese, sugar and vanilla. Spoon over the baked cheesecake, starting at the center and extending to within ½ inch of the edge. Return the cheesecake to the oven and bake for 5 minutes longer. Cool on a rack. Cover and refrigerate for at least 12 hours or for up to 3 days.

To glaze cheesecake: Using a sharp knife, remove skin and white pith from oranges and discard. Cut segments away from their surrounding membranes and reserve. In a small saucepan, melt apricot preserves over low heat. Remove from the heat and stir in orange liqueur. With a pastry brush, brush about half of the apricot preserves mixture over top of the chilled cheesecake. Arrange kiwi fruit, orange segments and strawberries decoratively over top. Brush the remaining apricot preserves mixture over the fruit.

Serves 16.

322 CALORIES PER SERVING: 17 G PROTEIN, 6 G FAT, 52 G CARBOHYDRATE; 271 MG SODIUM; 36 MG CHOLESTEROL.

℞ *Amy Simon of Hampstead, New Hampshire*

Chocolate Cheesecake Renewal

Nancy Zager asked us to reconcile a chocoholic's dream and a fat-conscious cook's nightmare. We did. With a light crumb crust, a pressed nonfat cottage cheese filling and reduced-fat sour cream, our cheesecake weighs in at almost one-third the fat and nearly half the calories. Cocoa adds a deep bittersweet chocolate note, enhanced with a bit of semisweet chocolate and a subtle coffee accent.

CRUST

- 4 oz. chocolate wafers (18 wafers)
- 1 cup Grape-Nuts cereal
- 2 Tbsp. unsweetened cocoa powder
- 2 Tbsp. sugar
- 3 Tbsp. vegetable oil, preferably canola oil

FILLING

- 2 oz. semisweet chocolate
- 2 Tbsp. instant coffee granules
- 4 cups nonfat cottage cheese, pressed to yield 2 cups *(page 26)*
- 1 8-oz. pkg. reduced-fat cream cheese, softened
- 1½ cups sugar
- 1 large egg
- 2 large egg whites
- 1 cup reduced-fat sour cream
- ¾ cup unsweetened cocoa powder
- 2 Tbsp. cornstarch
- ⅛ tsp. salt
- 1 tsp. pure vanilla extract

To make crust: preheat oven to 325 degrees F. Coat a 9-inch springform pan with nonstick cooking spray. Place chocolate wafers, Grape-Nuts, cocoa and sugar in a food processor; process until crumbs form. Add oil and 3 Tbsp. water; process until the crumbs are moistened. Press the crumb mixture into the bottom and about 1½ inches up the sides of the prepared pan. Set aside.

To make filling: Melt chocolate in the top of a double boiler over hot, not boiling, water. Let cool slightly. Dissolve instant coffee in 1 Tbsp. boiling water and set aside. In a blender or food processor, puree the pressed cottage cheese until smooth. Add cream cheese, sugar, egg, egg whites, sour cream, cocoa, cornstarch, salt, vanilla, the melted chocolate and the dissolved coffee; process until smooth. Pour into the crust-lined pan.

Bake for about 1 hour, or until firm around the edge but still shiny and slightly soft in the center. Run a knife around the pan to loosen edges. Let cool in the pan on a rack. Cover and refrigerate until well chilled, at least 8 hours or for up to 2 days. Remove sides. To facilitate cutting, dip a sharp knife in hot water and wipe dry before cutting each slice.

Serves 16.

266 CALORIES PER SERVING: 11 G PROTEIN, 9 G FAT, 37 G CARBOHYDRATE; 231 MG SODIUM; 25 MG CHOLESTEROL.

Rₓ Nancy Zager of Stamford, Connecticut

Carrot Cake

*Contributors of the original carrot cake recipe, Angelo and Sue Bologna
raved about the revised version when they tasted it on CNN's "On the Menu." Since they are both
on very strict diets, they now reduce the fat even further by frosting the cake with fruit butter
rather than cream cheese frosting, saving an additional 3 grams of fat per serving.*

CAKE

2½ cups sifted cake flour
2 tsp. ground cinnamon
2 tsp. baking powder
1½ tsp. baking soda
1 tsp. salt
2 large eggs
2 large egg whites
2 cups sugar
1 cup prune puree *(page 187)*
⅓ cup vegetable oil, preferably canola oil
2 cups grated carrots (5-6 small carrots)
1 8-oz. can crushed pineapple, thoroughly drained
¼ cup walnuts, toasted *(page 32)* and chopped

FROSTING

12 oz. reduced-fat cream cheese, softened
½ cup confectioners' sugar
1½ tsp. pure vanilla extract

To make cake: Coat the inside of three 9-inch round layer-cake pans with nonstick cooking spray. Line the bottoms with wax paper; set aside. Preheat oven to 350 degrees F.

In a medium-sized bowl, stir together flour, cinnamon, baking powder, baking soda and salt. In a large bowl, whisk together eggs and egg whites. Add sugar, prune puree and oil and whisk until smooth. Add the flour mixture to the egg mixture and stir with a wooden spoon until blended. Stir in carrots, pineapple and the toasted walnuts.

Divide the batter among the prepared pans and bake for 30 to 35 minutes, or until a cake tester inserted in the center comes out clean. Cool for 5 minutes in the pan on a rack. Loosen edges and invert cakes onto racks. Peel off paper and cool completely.

To make frosting: In a mixing bowl, combine cream cheese, sugar and vanilla; beat with an electric mixer until smooth and creamy.

To assemble cake: Place 1 cake layer on a serving plate. Spread a scant ¹/₂ cup of the frosting over it. Top with another cake layer and spread another scant ¹/₂ cup frosting. Place the third layer on top and spread with the remaining frosting.

Serves 16.

310 CALORIES PER SERVING: 6 G PROTEIN, 10 G FAT, 52 G CARBOHYDRATE; 392 MG SODIUM; 34 MG CHOLESTEROL.

℞ *Angelo and Sue Bologna of Santa Monica, California*

Marbled Pound Cake

Laden with butter and whole eggs (and often sour cream as well), traditional pound cakes are among America's richest. Our earliest versions resulted in batters with well over 50 percent of their calories from fat. Surprisingly, it is possible to alter the classic proportions to pare fat rather dramatically and still produce a marbled pound cake that is moist and flavorful.

⅓ cup unsalted butter
3 Tbsp. vegetable oil, preferably canola oil
3½ cups sifted cake flour
1½ tsp. baking powder
½ tsp. salt
2 cups plus 2 Tbsp. sugar
1 large egg

2 large egg whites
¾ cup nonfat plain yogurt
¼ cup skim milk
1 Tbsp. pure vanilla extract
2 drops pure almond extract
2½ Tbsp. unsweetened cocoa powder, preferably Dutch-processed

Preheat oven to 350 degrees F. Coat a 12-cup tube pan or Bundt pan with nonstick cooking spray. Dust pan with flour, tapping out excess.

In a small heavy saucepan, melt butter over low heat. Cook, swirling the pan, for 5 minutes, until butter is nutty brown. Immediately remove from heat and pour into a metal bowl or cup. Add oil. Freeze butter mixture until firm but not hard, about 15 minutes.

Sift together flour, baking powder and salt onto wax paper. In a large mixing bowl, combine butter mixture, sugar, egg and egg whites; beat with an electric mixer on medium speed until very light and well blended, about 4 minutes. Beat in vanilla and almond extracts. With mixer on low speed, beat in half of dry ingredients just until incorporated. Beat in yogurt and milk, then remaining dry ingredients just until smoothly incorporated; do not overbeat.

Place cocoa in a medium-sized bowl. Pour 3 Tbsp. very hot tap water over cocoa, stirring until completely smooth. Measure out 1¼ cups batter. Slowly stir batter into cocoa mixture. Pour half of vanilla batter into pan.

Spoon cocoa batter over vanilla batter, forming pools on surface. Top with pools of remaining vanilla batter. Using a table knife held vertically, swirl it deeply through batters to create marbling, as desired. Rap pan sharply on counter several times to eliminate air pockets.

Bake for 50 to 65 minutes, or until a toothpick inserted in the thickest part comes out clean and top springs back when lightly pressed. Transfer pan to wire rack and let stand until cake is completely cooled, at least 2 hours.

Run a knife around pan sides, under edge of cake and around center tube to loosen cake. Rap pan sharply against counter several times to loosen completely. Then invert cake to remove from pan, turning the cake over to show its most attractive marbled side. Place on a platter. It is best if allowed to mellow at least 8 hours before serving. *(The cake can be made ahead and stored in an airtight container, for about 3 days. It may also be frozen, wrapped tightly, for up to 3 weeks.)*

Serves 16.

237 CALORIES PER SERVING: 3 G PROTEIN, 7 G FAT, 42 G CARBOHYDRATE; 157 MG SODIUM; 24 MG CHOLESTEROL.

Patty's Cake

A moist and lemony, cornbread-like cake; best when served with a dollop of nonfat vanilla yogurt. This is an adaptation of Pat Tillinghast's recipe, served at her Providence, Rhode Island restaurant, New Rivers.

1 cup yellow or white cornmeal, preferably stone-ground, plus more for preparing pan
½ cup all-purpose white flour
1½ tsp. baking powder
¼ tsp. salt
1 cup sugar
¼ cup vegetable oil, preferably canola oil
2 Tbsp. butter, softened
2 large eggs

2 large egg whites
½ cup nonfat plain yogurt
1½ Tbsp. grated lemon zest
1 Tbsp. fresh lemon juice
½ tsp. pure lemon extract
1 cup assorted fresh or frozen, thawed berries (strawberries, blueberries or raspberries)
¼ cup black-currant liqueur (such as crème de cassis)

Preheat oven to 350 degrees F. Line the bottom of a 10-inch round cake pan with parchment or wax paper. Spray the pan with nonstick cooking spray and dust with cornmeal, shaking out the excess.

In a medium-sized mixing bowl, sift together cornmeal, flour, baking powder and salt. In a large mixing bowl, whisk together sugar, oil and butter until well combined. Add eggs and egg whites, one at a time, stirring until just combined. In a small bowl, stir together yogurt, lemon zest, juice and extract. Fold into the sugar mixture until just combined. Fold in the dry ingredients until just combined. Do not overmix.

Place the batter in the prepared pan and smooth the top with a rubber spatula. Bake for about 40 minutes, or until the cake is golden and a toothpick inserted into the center comes out clean. Cool for 10 minutes on a rack, invert the cake, peel off the paper and cool completely. *(The cake can be made ahead to this point and refrigerated, wrapped in plastic, for up to 3 days.)*

Toss berries with black-currant liqueur. Cut the cake into wedges and serve, topped with the berries.

Serves 12.

219 CALORIES PER SERVING: 4 G PROTEIN, 8 G FAT, 32 G CARBOHYDRATE; 134 MG SODIUM; 41 MG CHOLESTEROL.

Pear Tatin

Inspired by the French "tarte Tatin," an upside-down apple tart thought to have been created by a pair of sisters named Tatin. Their original would have been loaded with butter. This light biscuit tatin inverts to a glorious golden round with juices dripping down the pears, which taste almost candied. It is an adaptation of a recipe from EATING WELL's food stylist Anne Disrude.

PEAR TOPPING

- 2 tsp. vegetable oil, preferably canola oil
- ⅓ cup packed light brown sugar
- 1 Tbsp. coarsely chopped walnuts
- 2 firm ripe pears, such as Anjou or Bosc, peeled, cored and cut in ¼-inch-thick slices

BISCUIT

- ¾ cup plus 2 Tbsp. all-purpose white flour
- ¼ cup plus 2 Tbsp. yellow or white cornmeal, preferably stone-ground
- 3 Tbsp. sugar
- 1 tsp. baking powder
- 1 tsp. baking soda
- ¾ tsp. ground cinnamon
- ½ tsp. salt
- 1 Tbsp. cold unsalted butter, cut into pieces
- 1 Tbsp. vegetable oil, preferably canola oil
- ⅓ cup nonfat plain yogurt

To make pear topping: Place rack in the lower third of the oven; preheat to 425 degrees F. Heat oil in a 7- or 8-inch nonstick, ovenproof skillet over medium heat. Add brown sugar and cook, stirring, for 1 to 2 minutes, or until the sugar has partially melted. Remove from heat, scatter walnuts in skillet. Arrange pears in the pan in a circular pattern. Set aside.

To make biscuit and bake *tatin*: In a medium-sized mixing bowl, stir together flour, cornmeal, sugar, baking powder, baking soda, cinnamon and salt. Using a pastry cutter or two knives, cut in butter and oil until the mixture resembles coarse meal. In a small bowl, combine yogurt and ⅓ cup cold water. Make a well in the center of the dry ingredients, pour in yogurt mixture and with a fork, stir until just combined. Drop spoonfuls of the dough evenly over the pears.

Place the skillet on a baking sheet and bake for 20 to 25 minutes, or until a toothpick inserted into the center comes out clean. Cool on a rack for 2 to 3 minutes, run a knife around the edge of the skillet and invert the cake onto a plate. Cut into wedges and serve warm.

Serves 6.

235 CALORIES PER SERVING: 4 G PROTEIN, 7 G FAT, 41 G CARBOHYDRATE; 404 MG SODIUM; 5 MG CHOLESTEROL.

Upside-Down Pear Gingerbread

Remember old-fashioned upside-down cakes? In this version, fragrant pears bake under a gingerbread batter, making for a lovely presentation with a minimum of effort.

1	Tbsp. butter, melted		1	tsp. ground ginger
3	Tbsp. light brown sugar		½	tsp. ground allspice
3	firm ripe pears, such as Bartlett or Bosc		¼	tsp. ground nutmeg
1	Tbsp. fresh lemon juice		½	cup sugar
1¼	cups sifted cake flour		2	large egg whites
½	tsp. baking powder		½	cup skim-milk buttermilk
½	tsp. baking soda		¼	cup molasses
½	tsp. salt		2	Tbsp. vegetable oil, preferably canola oil
2	tsp. ground cinnamon			

Position rack in the lower part of the oven; preheat to 375 degrees F. Coat the inside of an 8-inch square baking pan with nonstick cooking spray.

Pour butter into the prepared pan and tilt to coat the bottom evenly. Sprinkle brown sugar over the butter. Peel, halve and core pears. Brush with lemon juice. Cut a pear half crosswise into ⅛-inch-thick slices. Keeping the slices together, slide a metal spatula underneath and invert the sliced pear half onto your hand, pressing to fan slightly. Place it, rounded side down, over the brown sugar in the baking dish. Repeat with the remaining pear halves. Bake, uncovered, for 15 minutes.

Meanwhile, sift together flour, baking powder, baking soda, salt, cinnamon, ginger, allspice and nutmeg into a bowl. Stir in sugar. In a large bowl, whisk together egg whites, buttermilk, molasses and oil. Add the flour mixture to the egg white mixture and stir with a wooden spoon or rubber spatula just until blended. When the pears have baked for 15 minutes, pour the batter evenly over top. Bake for 30 to 35 minutes, or until a cake tester inserted in the center comes out clean. Loosen edges. Invert a serving platter on top of the baking pan and, grasping firmly with hands protected with oven mitts, quickly turn the cake and platter over. Remove the baking dish. Remove any pear slices that adhere to the pan and replace them on top of the cake. Let cool for at least 10 minutes, cut into squares and serve warm.

Serves 9.

214 CALORIES PER SERVING: 3 G PROTEIN, 5 G FAT, 42 G CARBOHYDRATE; 225 MG SODIUM; 4 MG CHOLESTEROL.

Italian Fruit Cake

A very thin slice of this dark fig and nut cake is all you need at the end of a meal.

2½ cups dry red wine
2 Tbsp. plus ½ cup sugar
2 cups dried figs
½ cup golden raisins
⅓ cup blanched slivered almonds, toasted (*page 32*) and chopped
⅓ cup walnuts, chopped
⅓ cup chopped candied citron

3 oz. unsweetened baking chocolate, grated
2 Tbsp. honey
¾ cup all-purpose white flour
½ cup fine dry unseasoned breadcrumbs
1 Tbsp. grated orange zest
1 tsp. ground cinnamon
½ tsp. freshly grated nutmeg
¼ cup canola or olive oil (not extra-virgin)

Preheat oven to 375 degrees F. Coat an 8½-inch springform pan with nonstick cooking spray.

In a small saucepan, combine wine with 2 Tbsp. sugar. Boil for 15 to 20 minutes, or until reduced to ¾ cup. Let cool. Meanwhile, in a small saucepan, cover figs with water. Bring to a simmer and cook for 15 to 20 minutes, or until the figs are moist and plump. Drain and chop coarsely. Set aside. In a small bowl, cover raisins with warm water. Let soak for about 5 minutes. Drain, pressing to release excess moisture.

In a large bowl, mix together figs, raisins, almonds, walnuts, citron, chocolate and honey. In a medium-sized bowl, stir together ½ cup sugar, flour, breadcrumbs, orange zest, cinnamon and nutmeg and add to the almond mixture. Gradually stir oil and the reduced wine into the mixture. Spoon the batter into the prepared pan and smooth the top. Bake for 40 to 50 minutes, or until the cake is firm to the touch. Let cool in the pan on a rack. Cover and let stand overnight to allow flavor to deepen before serving. (*The cake can be prepared ahead and stored, in an airtight container, for up to 2 weeks.*)

Makes 24 slices.

220 CALORIES PER SLICE: 3 G PROTEIN, 8 G FAT, 36 G CARBOHYDRATE; 36 MG SODIUM; 0 MG CHOLESTEROL.

Italian Fruit Cake, opposite

Eight-Cup-High Apple Pie, page 228

Luscious Lemon Squares, page 237

223

Banana Cream Pie, opposite

Banana Cream Pie

*Like a lot of traditional American desserts, most banana cream pies are loaded with fat and calories.
In this version, zwieback and gingersnap crumbs, mixed with oil, water and a small amount
of butter, make a light crust. A meringue topping replaces the whipped cream.*

CRUST

⅔ cup zwieback crumbs (8 biscuits)
½ cup gingersnap crumbs (8 cookies)
2 Tbsp. vegetable oil, preferably canola oil
1 Tbsp. butter, softened
½ tsp. ground ginger

FILLING

1 tsp. unflavored gelatin
1 cup skim milk
2 large eggs, separated
2 Tbsp. all-purpose white flour
1 Tbsp. finely chopped candied ginger
2 tsp. pure vanilla extract
1 large egg white
½ cup sugar
2 large or 3 small ripe, firm bananas, peeled
   and sliced
1 Tbsp. fresh lime juice

To prepare crust: Preheat oven to 375 degrees F. Lightly coat a 9-inch pie plate or loose-bottom tart pan with nonstick cooking spray. In a food processor, combine zwieback and gingersnap crumbs, oil, butter, ground ginger and 1 Tbsp. water. Process until the crumbs clump together. Press the crumb mixture into the bottom and up the sides of the prepared pan. Bake for 10 minutes, or until lightly browned. Cool on a rack.

To prepare filling: In a small saucepan, sprinkle gelatin over 2 Tbsp. water. Let stand for 5 minutes, or until softened. Stir over low heat until the gelatin is dissolved.

Meanwhile, in a bowl, whisk together 2 Tbsp. milk, egg yolks and flour until smooth. In a heavy saucepan, scald the remaining milk. Whisk the scalded milk into the yolk mixture in a steady stream. Return the mixture to the pan and cook over medium heat, whisking constantly, for 1½ to 2 minutes, or until the mixture bubbles and thickens. Remove from the heat and whisk in the dissolved gelatin, candied ginger and vanilla. Refrigerate while you make the meringue.

Place 3 egg whites in a mixing bowl. Set it over a pan of hot water and stir until warmed slightly.

In a small saucepan, combine sugar with ⅓ cup water. Bring to a boil, stirring occasionally. Cook over medium-

high heat, without stirring, until the syrup registers 240 degrees F and is at the soft-ball stage (when a bit of syrup dropped into ice water forms a pliable ball), about 5 minutes. Remove syrup from heat. Set aside.

In a large mixing bowl, beat egg whites with an electric mixer just until soft peaks form. Return the syrup to the heat until it boils. Gradually pour hot syrup into egg whites but not directly onto the beaters, beating constantly. Continue beating until egg whites are cool and very stiff, about 5 minutes.

Fold 1 cup of the meringue into the yolk mixture. Refrigerate until slightly thickened, about 5 minutes. Set the remaining meringue aside.

To assemble pie: Preheat the broiler. Toss bananas with lime juice and arrange over the bottom of the crust. Spoon the yolk mixture evenly over the bananas. Spoon the reserved meringue evenly over the filling and swirl decoratively with the tip of a metal spatula. *Alternatively, using a piping bag fitted with a basket tip, pipe the reserved meringue on top of the filling in overlapping rows to form a lattice.* Place the pie under the broiler for 1 to 2 minutes, or until lightly browned. Let cool to room temperature, then refrigerate until the filling has set, for 5 to 8 hours.

Serves 8.

228 CALORIES PER SERVING: 5 G PROTEIN, 9 G FAT, 33 G CARBOHYDRATE; 90 MG SODIUM; 59 MG CHOLESTEROL.

Light Lemon Meringue Pie

Smooth and soothing; a great classic pie right down to the crust,
redefined with a generous amount of lemon and fewer egg yolks in the filling.

CRUST

1	cup all-purpose white flour
1	Tbsp. sugar
⅛	tsp. salt
1	Tbsp. butter
3	Tbsp. vegetable oil, preferably canola oil

FILLING

1¼	cups sugar
¼	cup cornstarch
¼	tsp. salt
½	cup fresh lemon juice
1½	Tbsp. grated lemon zest
1	large egg
1	large egg white
2	tsp. butter

MERINGUE

3	large egg whites
¼	tsp. cream of tartar
	pinch of salt
½	cup sugar
1	tsp. pure vanilla extract

To make crust: Set oven rack at lowest level; preheat oven to 425 degrees F. In a medium-sized bowl, stir together flour, sugar and salt. In a small saucepan, melt the butter over low heat. Cook for about 30 seconds, swirling the pan, until the butter is a light, nutty brown. Pour into a small bowl and let cool. Stir in oil. Using a fork, slowly stir the butter-oil mixture into the flour until mixture is crumbly. Gradually stir in enough ice water (1 to 2 Tbsp.) so that the dough will hold together in a ball. Press the dough into a flattened disk.

Place between two sheets of plastic wrap and roll into a circle about 12 inches in diameter. Remove the top sheet and invert the dough over a 9-inch pie plate. Remove the remaining wrap. Fold the edges under at the rim and crimp. Line the shell with a piece of foil or parchment paper and fill with pie weights or dried beans. Bake for 10 minutes, remove the weights or beans, and bake for 8 to 10 more minutes, or until the crust is golden. Cool the pie shell on a rack while you make the filling. Reduce the oven temperature to 350 degrees.

To make filling: In a medium-sized heavy saucepan, whisk together sugar, cornstarch and salt. Gradually whisk in 1½ cups boiling water. Place the saucepan over medium-high heat and bring to a boil, whisking constantly. Reduce heat to medium-low and cook, stirring, for 1 minute. Remove from the heat.

In a small bowl, whisk together lemon juice, zest, egg and egg white. Whisk a small amount of the hot sauce into the egg mixture, then whisk this mixture back into the sauce. Return to a simmer over medium heat, stirring, then cook for an additional 30 seconds. Stir in the butter until melted and pour into the baked pie shell. Set aside while you prepare meringue.

To make meringue: In a large bowl, beat the egg whites with an electric mixer on medium speed until frothy. Add the cream of tartar and salt and beat at high speed until soft peaks form. Slowly add the sugar, beating constantly, until the mixture holds stiff, shiny peaks. Beat in the vanilla. Spread the meringue over the hot filling, sealing to edge of crust. With a metal spatula, knife or back of a spoon, make attractive peaks. Bake for 15 minutes, or until the top is lightly browned. Cool the pie on a rack until it is room temperature, about 2 hours.

Serves 8.

322 CALORIES PER SERVING: 4G PROTEIN, 8 G FAT, 60 G CARBOHYDRATE; 161 MG SODIUM; 33 MG CHOLESTEROL.

Key Lime Pie

The traditional condensed-milk filling is lightened with yogurt;
a golden meringue topping gives the pie a decorative flourish.

GRAHAM CRACKER CRUST
1 large egg white
1¼ cups graham cracker crumbs (12 crackers)
1½ Tbsp. butter, melted
1½ Tbsp. vegetable oil, preferably canola oil

FILLING
1 14-oz. can sweetened condensed milk
⅔ cup low-fat plain yogurt
2 tsp. grated lime zest
½ cup fresh lime or key lime juice (4 to 5 limes)
1½ tsp. unflavored gelatin

MERINGUE
⅔ cup sugar
2 large egg whites
¼ tsp. cream of tartar
1 tsp. pure vanilla extract
lime slices for garnish

To make crust: Preheat oven to 350 degrees F. Spray a 9-inch pie plate with nonstick cooking spray. In a medium-sized bowl, beat egg white lightly with a fork until frothy. Add graham cracker crumbs, butter and oil and blend with your fingertips until thoroughly combined. Press the mixture in an even layer on the bottom and sides of the pie plate. Bake for 10 minutes, or until lightly browned. (Do not be concerned if there are small cracks.) Cool on a rack.

To make filling: In a medium-sized bowl (preferably metal), whisk together sweetened condensed milk, yogurt, lime zest and juice. In a small, heavy saucepan, sprinkle the gelatin over 2 Tbsp. cold water. Let soften for 1 minute. Heat over low heat, stirring, until the gelatin is dissolved. Whisk into the lime mixture. Set the bowl over of a larger bowl of ice water, stirring occasionally, until it begins to thicken, 15 to 20 minutes. Turn into the pie shell and place the pie in the freezer to chill.

To make the meringue: Preheat the broiler. Place egg whites in a large bowl. Set it over a pan of hot water and stir for a few minutes until warmed slightly. In a small saucepan, combine sugar with ½ cup water. Bring to a boil, stirring occasionally. Cook over medium-high heat, without stirring, until syrup registers 240 degrees F and is at the soft-ball stage (when a bit of syrup dropped into ice water forms a pliable ball), about 5 minutes. Remove syrup from heat. Set aside.

In a large mixing bowl, beat egg whites with an electric mixer on medium speed until frothy. Add cream of tartar and beat on high speed just until soft peaks form. Return the syrup to the heat until it boils. Gradually pour hot syrup into egg whites but not directly onto the beaters, beating constantly. Continue beating until egg whites are cool and very stiff, about 5 minutes. Blend in vanilla.

Remove the pie from the freezer and spread the meringue over top, sealing to the edge of the crust and swirling roughly on top. Place the pie under the broiler for 1 to 2 minutes, or until lightly browned. Let cool to room temperature, then refrigerate until the filling has set, for 5 to 8 hours. Garnish with fresh lime slices.

Serves 8.

331 CALORIES PER SERVING: 7 G PROTEIN, 10 G FAT, 54 G CARBOHYDRATE; 176 MG SODIUM; 24 MG CHOLESTEROL.

Eight-Cup-High Apple Pie

*This double-crust pie is best when made with at least three different kinds
of apples, preferably a combination of sweet and tart varieties.
The buttery-tasting pastry contains little saturated fat.*

CRUST

  2 Tbsp. butter
½ cup vegetable oil, preferably canola oil
2½ cups all-purpose white flour
  2 Tbsp. sugar
  1 tsp. salt
4-6 Tbsp. cold skim milk

FILLING

½ cup brown sugar
¼ cup plus ½ tsp. sugar
1-2 Tbsp. all-purpose white flour (depending on the juiciness of the apples)
  1 tsp. ground cinnamon
    pinch salt
3½ lbs. apples, peeled, cored and cut into ½-inch-thick slices (about 8 cups)
  1 Tbsp. fresh lemon juice
½ tsp. pure vanilla extract
  1 Tbsp. skim milk

To make crust: In a small saucepan, melt butter over low heat. Cook until light nutty brown, about 1½ to 2 minutes. Do not burn. Pour the butter into a pie plate. Add oil and 1 cup flour; blend with a fork until smooth. Freeze 30 minutes. In a large bowl, combine remaining 1½ cups flour, sugar and salt; place in the freezer for 30 minutes.

Working quickly with a pastry cutter or two knives, cut the cold oil-flour mixture into the cold flour-salt mixture until the fat is in pea-sized lumps. Sprinkle cold milk over the dough, 1 Tbsp. at a time, stirring lightly with a fork, and adding just enough so the dough holds together. Gently knead the dough until it is smooth and holds together. Form the dough into two flattened disks, one slightly larger than the other. Wrap in plastic and refrigerate for 30 minutes.

To make filling and bake pie: Position rack in lower third of oven and preheat to 425 degrees F. In a large bowl, mix together brown sugar, ¼ cup granulated sugar, flour, cinnamon and salt. Add apples and toss to coat. Stir in lemon juice and vanilla and set aside.

Place the large piece of dough between 2 unfloured sheets of wax paper and roll it out into an 11-inch circle, turning and readjusting paper as necessary to eliminate any wrinkles. Peel off the top sheet and turn crust into a 9-inch pie plate. Gently press the crust into the bottom of the pie plate and peel off wax paper. If the pastry cracks or breaks, patch it with scraps of dough. Arrange apples in pastry, roll out the smaller piece of dough in the same manner and lay it over the apples. Fold the edges of the bottom pastry over the top crust and crimp edges together. Lightly brush the pie with milk and sprinkle with remaining ½ tsp. sugar. Cut several slits in the top crust and place the pie on a baking sheet.

Bake for 15 minutes. Reduce heat to 350 degrees F and bake until the pastry is golden and the apples are tender, about 40 to 45 minutes. Cool on a rack before serving.

Serves 12.

325 CALORIES FOR EACH OF 12 SERVINGS: 3 G PROTEIN, 12 G FAT, 54 G CARBOHYDRATE; 204 MG SODIUM; 5 MG CHOLESTEROL.

Pumpkin Pie

With a fraction of the fat, this is not your mom's pumpkin pie.
But it has the rich, subtle spices of the classic and a delicate, faintly sweet crust.

CRUST

- 1 cup all-purpose white flour
- 1 Tbsp. sugar
- ⅛ tsp. salt
- 1 Tbsp. butter
- 3 Tbsp. vegetable oil, preferably canola oil

FILLING

- 1 cup canned pumpkin puree
- 2 large eggs, lightly beaten
- 2 cups evaporated skim milk
- 1 tsp. pure vanilla extract
- ¾ cup packed dark brown sugar
- 1 Tbsp. cornstarch
- 1 tsp. ground cinnamon
- 1 tsp. ground ginger
- ¼ tsp. freshly grated nutmeg
- ¼ tsp. salt

To make crust: In a medium-sized bowl, stir together flour, sugar and salt. In a small saucepan, melt the butter over low heat. Cook for about 30 seconds, swirling the pan, until the butter is a light, nutty brown. Pour into a small bowl and let cool. Stir in oil. Using a fork, slowly stir the butter-oil mixture into the flour until the mixture is crumbly. Gradually stir in enough ice water (1 to 2 Tbsp.) so that the dough will hold together. Press the dough into a flattened disk.

Place between two sheets of plastic wrap and roll into a circle about 12 inches in diameter. Remove the top sheet and invert the dough over a 9-inch pie plate. Remove the remaining wrap. Fold the edges under at the rim and crimp. Chill the pastry while you prepare the filling. *(The crust can be prepared ahead and stored, cov-ered, in the refrigerator for up to 2 days or in the freezer for up to 1 month.)*

To make filling: Position rack in lower third of the oven; preheat to 425 degrees F. In a medium-sized bowl, whisk together pumpkin, eggs, milk and vanilla. In a small bowl, combine brown sugar, cornstarch, cinnamon, ginger, nutmeg and salt. Rub through a sieve into pumpkin mixture and whisk until incorporated.

Pour the filling into the prepared crust and bake for 12 minutes. Reduce heat to 350 degrees F and bake for 35 to 40 more minutes, or until the filling is set and a knife inserted in the center comes out clean. During baking, cover edges with foil if they are browning too quickly. Cool on a rack.

Serves 8.

283 CALORIES PER SERVING: 8 G PROTEIN, 8 G FAT, 45 G CARBOHYDRATE; 212 MG SODIUM; 60 MG CHOLESTEROL.

Cranberry-Raisin Tart

*Gleaming like a jewel, this glazed cranberry tart is decorated with pastry holly leaves.
If you prefer, you can use 2 cups cranberries and 1 cup frozen,
unsweetened raspberries in place of 3 cups cranberries.*

CRUST

- 2 Tbsp. butter
- ½ cup vegetable oil, preferably canola oil
- 2½ cups all-purpose white flour
- 2 Tbsp. sugar
- 1 tsp. salt
- 4-6 Tbsp. cold skim milk

FILLING & GLAZE

- 3 cups fresh or frozen cranberries, picked over, rinsed and patted dry (12 oz.)
- 1 cup raisins
- 1 Tbsp. grated orange zest
- ½ cup fresh orange juice (1 orange)
- ¾ cup plus 2 Tbsp. sugar
- ½ cup packed dark brown sugar
- 2 Tbsp. quick-cooking tapioca
- ½ tsp. ground cinnamon
- ½ tsp. ground nutmeg
- 1 large egg white
- ½ cup orange marmalade
- ⅓ cup chopped walnuts
- ½ cup red-currant jelly

To make crust: Follow directions for crust in the recipe for Eight-Cup-High Apple Pie *(page 228)* except form the dough into one ball instead of two.

Unwrap the dough and place it between two unfloured sheets of wax paper. Roll it out into a 12½-inch circle, turning and readjusting paper as necessary to eliminate any wrinkles. Peel off the top sheet and turn the crust into the bottom of an 11-inch tart pan with removable bottom or a 10-inch pie pan. Gently press the dough into the bottom and peel off the wax paper. Trim any overhanging dough and crimp the edges or press them into the tart pan. (If the pastry cracks, patch it with scraps.) Roll out any dough scraps and cut out three holly leaves. Cover crust and leaves with plastic wrap and freeze until needed. *(The crust and leaves can be prepared up to 1 month ahead, wrapped in plastic wrap and frozen. Do not thaw before baking.)*

To make filling and bake pie: Position rack in the lower third of the oven, preheat oven to 425 degrees F.

In a medium-sized bowl, stir together cranberries, raisins, orange zest, orange juice, ¾ cup sugar, brown sugar, tapioca, cinnamon and nutmeg. Brush a little egg white over the bottom of the pastry crust. Warm marmalade slightly and spread over the crust. Sprinkle on walnuts. Top with the cranberry mixture. Brush a little egg white over the holly leaves and arrange them in the center of the tart.

Bake for 15 minutes. Reduce the temperature to 350 degrees F and bake for 30 to 40 minutes longer, or until the pastry is golden brown. If the pastry browns too quickly, shield it with foil. Cool completely on a rack.

Warm jelly until melted and brush over the tart, avoiding the leaves. Refrigerate for about 10 minutes, or until the glaze has set. *(The tart can be held at room temperature for up to 8 hours.)* If using a tart pan, remove sides before serving.

Serves 16.

259 CALORIES PER SERVING: 2 G PROTEIN, 10 G FAT, 43 G CARBOHYDRATE; 160 MG SODIUM; 5 MG CHOLESTEROL.

Oatmeal Cookies

Prune puree is used to replace most, but not all, of the fat in these wholesome cookies. Some fat is required for taste and texture. Fruit-juice concentrate is available at health-food stores.

½ cup prune puree *(page 187)*
2 Tbsp. unsalted butter, at room temperature
2 Tbsp. vegetable oil, preferably canola oil
1½ cups fruit-juice concentrate
1 Tbsp. pure vanilla extract

3¼ cups whole-wheat pastry flour
1 cup rolled oats
1 tsp. baking soda
½ tsp. salt

Spray two baking sheets with nonstick cooking spray or line with parchment paper. Preheat oven to 350 degrees F. In a large bowl, whisk together prune puree, butter and oil until smooth. Gradually whisk in fruit-juice concentrate and vanilla.

In a small bowl, stir together flour, rolled oats, baking soda and salt. Add the flour mixture to the prune mixture and mix with a wooden spoon until blended. Drop by rounded tablespoonfuls onto the prepared baking sheets, spacing the cookies about 1½ inches apart. Bake one sheet at a time for 12 to 15 minutes, or until lightly browned. Transfer cookies to racks and let cool.

Makes about 3 dozen cookies.

86 CALORIES PER COOKIE: 2 G PROTEIN, 2 G FAT, 16 G CARBOHYDRATE; 62 MG SODIUM; 2 MG CHOLESTEROL.

Devil's Food Cookies

*If these devilishly chocolatey cookies don't get gobbled the day
they are baked, store them, well wrapped, in the freezer.*

1½ cups sugar
½   cup prune puree *(page 187)*
½   cup nonfat plain yogurt
¼   cup vegetable oil, preferably canola oil
2   large egg whites, beaten lightly with a fork

1½ cups sifted cake flour
1   cup unsweetened cocoa powder
½   tsp. salt
½   tsp. baking soda
½   tsp. instant coffee granules

Preheat oven to 350 degrees F. Line baking sheets with parchment paper or coat with nonstick cooking spray.

In a medium-sized bowl, whisk together sugar, prune puree, yogurt, oil and egg whites. In a medium-sized bowl, stir together flour, cocoa, salt, baking soda and instant coffee. Using a wooden spoon, stir the dry ingredients into the wet, mixing just until blended. Drop the dough by heaping tablespoonfuls onto a prepared baking sheet, spacing cookies about 1½ inches apart. Bake for 12 to 14 minutes, or until the tops spring back when touched lightly. Transfer cookies to wire racks and cool.

Makes 2 dozen large cookies.

43 CALORIES PER COOKIE: 1 G PROTEIN, 1 G FAT, 9 G CARBOHYDRATE; 29 MG SODIUM; 1 MG CHOLESTEROL.

"Ice Cream" Sandwiches

Soften 3 cups Extraordinary Low-Fat Vanilla "Ice Cream" *(page 197)* or nonfat frozen vanilla yogurt in the refrigerator for ½ hour. Place 12 Devil's Food Cookies, rounded-side down on the work surface. Scoop about ¼ cup "ice cream" or frozen yogurt onto each one and top with another cookie. Wrap the sandwiches individually in plastic wrap and freeze for 1 hour, or until firm. Store in the freezer for up to 2 weeks. Soften slightly before serving.

Makes 1 dozen ice cream sandwiches.

Ginger Crisps

Gingery flavor and a subtle lemon note make these crisps perfect with tea.
They also make great "dunking" cookies.

2   Tbsp. vegetable oil, preferably canola oil
2   Tbsp. butter, softened
1   cup packed dark brown sugar
1   large egg
2   tsp. grated lemon rind
1¼   cups all-purpose white flour
¼   cup cornstarch

2   tsp. ground ginger
1   tsp. ground cinnamon
1   tsp. baking powder
½   tsp. baking soda
¼   tsp. salt
1   Tbsp. sugar for sprinkling (optional)

Preheat oven to 350 degrees F. Prepare baking sheets by lining them with parchment or lightly spraying with nonstick cooking spray. In a large bowl cream oil, butter, sugar, egg and lemon rind with an electric mixer until smooth. In a medium-sized bowl, sift together flour, cornstarch, ginger, cinnamon, baking powder, baking soda and salt. Stir into the creamed mixture just until combined.

Divide dough into 2 portions. On a floured surface, roll out each portion to a thickness of slightly more than $1/16$ inch. If desired, sprinkle with the sugar, lightly pressing it in with the rolling pin. Cut out shapes with a cookie cutter and place ¼ inch apart on the prepared baking sheets. Bake one sheet at a time for 10 to 12 minutes, or until lightly colored. Let cool 2 minutes, then remove cookies to a rack to cool. *(Cookies can be stored in an airtight container for up to 1 week.)*

Makes about 3 dozen cookies.

57 CALORIES PER COOKIE: 1 G PROTEIN, 2 G FAT, 10 G CARBOHYDRATE; 46 MG SODIUM; 8 MG CHOLESTEROL.

Molasses-Spice Cookies

Great little cookies to have with coffee or tea.

¾   cup molasses
¾   cup nonfat plain yogurt
½   cup sugar
2   Tbsp. vegetable oil, preferably canola oil
2½   cups sifted cake flour
1½   tsp. ground cinnamon

1½   tsp. ground ginger
½   tsp. baking soda
½   tsp. ground mace
½   tsp. ground cloves
½   tsp. salt

Preheat oven to 350 degrees F. Line baking sheets with parchment paper or spray with nonstick cooking spray. In a large bowl, whisk together molasses, yogurt, sugar and oil until smooth. In a medium-sized bowl, stir together flour, cinnamon, ginger, baking soda, mace, cloves and salt. Using a wooden spoon, stir the dry ingredients into the wet, mixing just until blended.

Drop the dough by tablespoonfuls onto the prepared baking sheets, spacing cookies about $1\frac{1}{2}$ inches apart. Bake for about 15 to 20 minutes, or until browned. Transfer cookies to a rack and let cool.

Makes about 3 dozen cookies.

63 CALORIES PER COOKIE: 1 G PROTEIN, 1 G FAT, 13 G CARBOHYDRATE; 44 MG SODIUM; 1 MG CHOLESTEROL.

Brandy Snaps

These spicy, buttery crisps are a delightful accompaniment to frozen desserts.

¼ cup packed brown sugar
¼ cup dark corn syrup
¼ cup brandy
2 Tbsp. unsalted butter
2 Tbsp. vegetable oil, preferably canola oil

2 tsp. molasses
¼ tsp. ground ginger
¼ tsp. ground cinnamon
⅔ cup all-purpose white flour

Preheat the oven to 400 degrees F. Coat a baking sheet with nonstick cooking spray. In a medium-sized saucepan, combine brown sugar, corn syrup, brandy, butter, oil, molasses, ginger and cinnamon. Bring to a boil over medium heat and boil for 1 minute. Remove from heat; cool for 1 minute. Whisk in flour until smooth.

Drop heaping teaspoons of batter (about 5 per sheet) 4 inches apart onto the prepared baking sheet. Bake for 6 to 8 minutes or until golden brown, and lacy holes have formed. Cool for about 1 minute. With a metal spatula, remove the cookies from the baking sheet and immediately wrap them around a wooden spoon handle. (If the cookies become too firm to shape, return them to the oven to soften.) When the cookies are firm, transfer to wire racks. Continue until all the batter is baked. *(The cookies can be stored in an airtight container for up to 1 week.)*

Makes about 16 cookies.

72 CALORIES PER COOKIE: 1 G PROTEIN, 3 G FAT, 8 G CARBOHYDRATE; 17 MG SODIUM; 4 MG CHOLESTEROL.

Almond Tuiles

Tuiles is French for "tiles." These wafer-thin cookies are so named because they are molded to a U-shape while still hot from the oven and, when cool, are stacked on a serving tray so that they resemble the curved, clay roof tiles typical of southern France.

2 large egg whites
½ cup sugar
⅓ cup all-purpose white flour
¼ cup unsalted butter, melted

1 Tbsp. pure vanilla extract
½ tsp. ground cinnamon
¼ tsp. salt
½ cup sliced blanched almonds

Line 2 baking sheets with parchment paper. In a mixing bowl, whisk together egg whites, sugar, flour, butter, vanilla, cinnamon and salt until just blended. Stir in almonds with a rubber spatula. Cover with plastic wrap and refrigerate for 1 hour.

Preheat oven to 325 degrees F. Drop scant teaspoonfuls of chilled batter onto the baking sheets, allowing 12 to a sheet. Using a long-bladed spatula or a table knife, gently smooth batter into thin circles. Bake, one baking sheet at a time, until the cookie edges are golden brown, about 10 to 12 minutes. While the cookies are still hot remove them from the pan one by one and curl each around a rolling pin. Cool. *(The cookies can be stored in an airtight container for up to 2 days. If they lose their crispness, place them in a 275-degree F oven for 1 minute.)*

Makes about 4 dozen cookies.

55 CALORIES PER 2 COOKIES: 1 G PROTEIN, 3 G FAT, 6 G CARBOHYDRATE; 46 MG SODIUM; 5 MG CHOLESTEROL.

Chocolate-Meringue Drop Cookies

*In response to all the readers who asked the EATING WELL Test Kitchen
to revise their favorite buttery chocolate chip cookie recipe, we offer these irresistible meringue cookies.
We haven't found (at least not yet) a low-fat formula for the traditional butter-based cookie.
But you may find these even more addicting.*

¾ cup hazelnuts or blanched almond slivers, toasted *(page 32)*
1 oz. bittersweet or semisweet chocolate (not unsweetened), finely chopped
6 Tbsp. unsweetened cocoa powder
3 Tbsp. all-purpose white flour
3 large egg whites, at room temperature

⅛ tsp. salt
1 tsp. instant coffee granules
2 cups confectioners' sugar
½ tsp. pure vanilla extract
⅛ tsp. pure almond extract (increase to ¼ tsp. if almonds are used)

Preheat oven to 325 degrees F. Line two large baking sheets with parchment paper. Remove and discard any loose bits of hull from hazelnuts, if using, by rubbing them between hands or in a clean kitchen towel. Coarsely chop nuts. Stir together nuts, chocolate, cocoa and flour; set aside.

Reduce oven temperature to 275 degrees F. In a large mixing bowl, with mixer on low speed, beat egg whites for about 30 seconds. Gradually raise speed to high and beat until whites are frothy and opaque. Add salt and coffee and continue beating until soft peaks begin to form. Gradually beat in confectioners' sugar. Scrape down the sides of the bowl several times. Add vanilla and almond extract. Continue beating until mixture stands in very stiff, but not dry, peaks. Using a rubber spatula, fold about ⅓ of the nut mixture into the whites. Add remaining nuts to whites and continue folding them in, just until ingredients are thoroughly blended.

Immediately drop cookies by large teaspoonfuls about 1½ inches apart on the prepared baking sheets. Place the baking sheets on separate racks of the oven and bake for 20 to 25 minutes, or until cookies are dry and firm on top when pressed. Reverse pans halfway through to ensure even baking. Cool the baking sheets on racks. Gently peel cookies from paper. *(Store in an airtight container for up to 1 week.)*

Makes about 2½ dozen cookies.

57 CALORIES PER COOKIE: 1 G PROTEIN, 2 G FAT, 9 G CARBOHYDRATE; 15 MG SODIUM; 0 MG CHOLESTEROL.

Brown Sugar-Pecan Meringue Cookies

These cookies, topped with grated chocolate and chopped nuts, are slightly soft and chewy.

1 cup pecans, toasted *(page 32)* and finely chopped
2 Tbsp. all-purpose white flour
4 large egg whites, at room temperature
¼ tsp. cream of tartar
⅛ tsp. salt
1⅔ cups packed light brown sugar
½ tsp. pure vanilla extract
1½ oz. bittersweet or semisweet chocolate (not unsweetened), grated or very finely chopped

Preheat oven to 225 degrees F. Line two large baking sheets with parchment paper. Stir ¾ cup pecans together with flour. In a large mixing bowl, with mixer on low speed, beat egg whites for about 30 seconds. Gradually raise speed to high and beat until frothy and opaque. Add cream of tartar and salt and beat until soft peaks begin to form. Gradually beat in sugar. Add vanilla. Scraping down the sides of the bowl several times, continue to beat until the mixture stands in stiff but not dry peaks. Using a rubber spatula, quickly fold nut-flour mixture into whites.

Immediately drop batter by rounded teaspoonfuls onto the prepared baking sheets, spacing cookies about 1 inch apart. Using a table knife and working in a circular motion, smooth the tops slightly. Bake for 25 to 35 minutes, or until cookies are slightly warm on top. Reverse pans halfway through to ensure even baking. (A shorter baking time will yield softer cookies; longer baking, slightly crisper ones.) Remove pans from oven and sprinkle chocolate over cookies. Bake for about 30 seconds more to melt chocolate slightly. Sprinkle with remaining ¼ cup chopped pecans. Cool the baking sheets on racks. Let stand until chocolate sets or put cookies in the refrigerator about 5 minutes to hasten setting. Gently peel cookies off paper. *(Store in an airtight container, with wax paper between the layers, for up to 4 days.)*

Makes about 3 dozen cookies.

70 CALORIES PER COOKIE: 1 G PROTEIN, 3 G FAT, 12 G CARBOHYDRATE; 17 MG SODIUM; 0 MG CHOLESTEROL.

Sighs

These melt-in-your-mouth treats are as light as a sigh.

2 large egg whites
¼ tsp. cream of tartar
¼ tsp. salt
1 cup sugar
¾ cup toasted blanched slivered almonds *(page 32)*

Preheat oven to 250 degrees F. Line two baking sheets with parchment paper or brush them with oil and dust with flour, shaking off excess.

In a large mixing bowl, beat egg whites with electric mixer until foamy. Add cream of tartar and salt; beat until soft peaks form. Gradually add sugar, beating until stiff, but not dry, peaks form. Fold in the almonds. Drop the batter by heaping tablespoons onto the prepared baking sheets. Bake on separate racks for about 1½ hours, or until light golden and firm to the touch. Reverse pans halfway through to ensure even baking. Transfer cookies to a rack and let cool. *(The cookies can be prepared ahead and stored in an airtight container for up to 1 week.)*

Makes about 2 dozen cookies.

53 CALORIES PER COOKIE: 1 G PROTEIN, 2 G FAT, 9 G CARBOHYDRATE; 27 MG SODIUM; 0 MG CHOLESTEROL.

Luscious Lemon Squares

This bake-sale bestseller from Anita Wilson deserved a fix. It was easy to cut the yolks from the filling but trickier to slim down the shortbread crust. We managed to trim the overall fat by half and maintain the tender crust. These are best served the day they are made.

CRUST

- 1 cup sifted cake flour
- ¼ cup confectioners' sugar
- 2 oz. reduced-fat cream cheese (¼ cup)
- 3 Tbsp. vegetable oil, preferably canola oil

FILLING

- 3 large egg whites
- ¾ cup sugar
- 1½ Tbsp. grated lemon zest
- 2 Tbsp. all-purpose white flour
- ½ tsp. baking powder
- ¼ tsp. salt
- ⅓ cup fresh lemon juice (1 large lemon)
  confectioners' sugar for dusting over top

To make crust: Preheat oven to 350 degrees F. Coat the inside of an 8-inch square baking pan with nonstick cooking spray; set aside.

In a large bowl, stir together cake flour and confectioners' sugar. Using a pastry blender or your fingertips, cut cream cheese into the flour mixture until crumbly. Gradually add oil, stirring with a fork. Toss with fingertips until evenly moistened. (The mixture will be crumbly.) Press into the bottom of the prepared baking pan. Bake for 20 to 25 minutes, or until light golden.

To make filling: In a mixing bowl, beat egg whites, sugar and lemon zest together with an electric mixer until smooth. In a small bowl, stir together all-purpose flour, baking powder and salt. Add to the egg-white mixture and beat until blended. Beat in lemon juice. Pour over the hot crust and bake for about 20 minutes longer, or until the top is light golden and set. Let cool in the pan on a rack. Spray a sharp knife with nonstick cooking spray and cut into squares. Dust with confectioners' sugar.

Makes 16 squares.

100 CALORIES PER SQUARE: 2 G PROTEIN, 3 G FAT, 17 G CARBOHYDRATE; 74 MG SODIUM; 2 MG CHOLESTEROL.

R_x *Anita Wilson of Chico, California*

Better-For-You Brownies

*Applesauce and corn syrup allow these brownies
to boast of just 4 grams of fat per square.*

1 oz. unsweetened chocolate
1 cup sifted cake flour
¾ cup unsweetened cocoa powder
½ tsp. salt
3 large egg whites
2 large eggs
1¼ cups sugar

¾ cup dark corn syrup
¾ cup unsweetened applesauce, at room temperature
¼ cup vegetable oil, preferably canola oil
1 Tbsp. pure vanilla extract
2 Tbsp. walnuts, toasted *(page 32)* and chopped

Preheat oven to 350 degrees F. Coat a 9-by-13-inch baking pan with nonstick cooking spray.

Melt chocolate in a small bowl over hot, not boiling water or in a microwave oven at medium (50 percent) power. Set aside.

In a medium-sized bowl, stir together flour, cocoa and salt. In a large bowl, whisk together egg whites and eggs. Add sugar, corn syrup, applesauce, oil and vanilla.

Whisk in the chocolate. Add the flour mixture to the egg mixture and stir with a wooden spoon until blended.

Pour into the prepared pan and sprinkle with walnuts. Bake for 30 to 35 minutes, or until a cake tester inserted in the center comes out clean. Let cool in the pan on a rack. Cut into squares.

Makes 2 dozen brownies.

129 CALORIES PER BROWNIE: 2 G PROTEIN, 4 G FAT, 23 G CARBOHYDRATE; 64 MG SODIUM; 18 MG CHOLESTEROL.

Cottage Cheese Rugelach

*Expect some of the filling to ooze out during baking,
but don't worry—there will still be plenty inside the cookie.*

DOUGH

- 2 cups nonfat cottage cheese, pressed to yield 1 cup *(page 26)*
- 4 oz. reduced-fat cream cheese (½ cup)
- ½ cup sugar
- 2 Tbsp. vegetable oil, preferably canola oil
- 2 Tbsp. butter, softened
- 1 tsp. pure vanilla extract
- 3 cups sifted cake flour
- ½ tsp. salt

FILLING

- ½ cup packed light brown sugar
- 2 Tbsp. Grape-Nuts cereal
- 2 Tbsp. walnuts, toasted *(page 32)* and chopped
- 1 tsp. ground cinnamon
- ½ cup dried currants

To make dough: In a medium-sized bowl, beat the cottage cheese, cream cheese, sugar, oil, butter and vanilla with an electric mixer until light and fluffy. Mix together flour and salt and add to the cheese mixture; stir with a wooden spoon until just blended. Wrap dough in wax paper, then in plastic wrap, and chill 2 to 3 hours or preferably overnight.

To make filling: In a small bowl, stir together brown sugar, Grape-Nuts, walnuts and cinnamon. Cover and set aside.

Set oven rack in upper portion of oven; preheat oven to 350 degrees F. Prepare two baking sheets by coating with nonstick cooking spray or lining with parchment paper.

To form and bake rugelach: Divide the dough into four equal parts. On a lightly floured surface, roll each portion into a 10-inch-diameter circle. (Keep remaining dough chilled until ready to use.) Sprinkle with one-quarter of the brown-sugar mixture and 2 Tbsp. currants, pressing slightly so that the filling adheres. Cut the circle into 8 wedges. Beginning at the widest end, roll up each wedge and curve into a crescent. Place on a prepared baking sheet. Repeat with the remaining dough.

Bake for 20 to 25 minutes or until tops are light brown. Immediately transfer to a rack and let cool.

Makes 32 rugelach.

103 CALORIES PER RUGELACH: 4 G PROTEIN, 3 G FAT, 16 G CARBOHYDRATE; 67 MG SODIUM; 4 MG CHOLESTEROL.

℞ *Allison Toppel of Las Vegas, Nevada*

Sources

A few of the ingredients used in the recipes in the RECIPE RESCUE COOKBOOK may be unfamiliar to some readers or not available at local supermarkets, depending on the region. Call a nearby health-food store or Asian specialty shop, and if the item is not readily available, try the mail-order purveyors listed here.

Arborio Rice. This Italian-grown grain is a must for risotto because the high-starch kernels add creamy texture. Arborio is found in most supermarkets, Italian markets and health-food stores.

Asiago Cheese. An Italian semi-firm cheese suitable for grating, available at specialty cheese shops and gourmet stores.

Chipotle Peppers Packed in Adobo Sauce. Smoked jalapeño peppers packed in a tomato sauce. They are available from:

> **Dean & DeLuca, Inc.**
> Mail Order Department
> 560 Broadway
> New York, NY 10012
> 800-221-7714

Dried Cranberries. A sweetened, dried form of cranberries can be used in the same dishes you would use raisins. Dried cranberries are showing up on supermarket shelves, or order by mail:

> **American Spoon Foods**
> 1668 Clarion Avenue
> P.O. Box 566
> Petoskey, MI 49770
> 800-222-5886

Dutch-Processed Cocoa. Many consider its flavor to be the highest quality. The cocoa is alkalized during manufacture. Dutch-processed should not be used in devil's food recipes where the reaction of baking soda and acid in cocoa is essential.

Fermented Black Beans. A Chinese specialty of small black soybeans preserved in salt, then canned or placed in plastic bags. Available in Asian markets.

Five Spice Powder. A standard ingredient in Chinese cooking, it is usually an equal mixture of cinnamon, cloves, fennel seed, star anise and Sichuan peppercorns, available at Asian markets and most supermarkets.

Green Lentils from Le Puy. These richly flavored lentils from south central France are highly regarded. They hold their nearly round shape after cooking due to their high oil content. This makes them ideal for salads and other dishes. Available at some gourmet specialty shops and by mail from:

> **Dean & DeLuca, Inc.**
> Mail Order Department
> 560 Broadway
> New York, NY 10012
> 800-221-7714

Guava Jelly & Guava Nectar. Preserves from the tropical fruit, available in many supermarkets and in Hispanic groceries.

Juniper Berries. The hallmark flavoring of gin, juniper berries are the dried fruits of the evergreen shrub. Juniper berries lend a spicy, pine flavor that complements robust meat dishes. They are available in the spice section of most supermarkets.

Parmigiano-Reggiano. This is Italy's top-quality grating cheese from Parma; it is aged two years or more, in

comparison to American Parmesans, which are aged about 14 months.

Shiitake Mushrooms. These Japanese and Korean mushrooms are now cultivated in North America and often can be found fresh and dried in the produce sections of supermarkets year-round.

Sichuan Pepper. Not actually a peppercorn, rather the berry of a prickly ash tree. Found in Asian markets and specialty stores.

Whole-Wheat Pastry Flour. A fine-textured, soft-wheat flour with a high starch content that retains the wheat germ, which means it has a higher fiber content than white flours. Pastry flours make tender cakes and pastries. Available at some health-food stores. Organically grown, stone-ground flour is available by mail from:

Morgan's Mills
RD2, Box 4602
Union, ME 04862
207-785-4900

Yukon Gold Potatoes. A yellow-fleshed, tan-skinned, medium-sized potato beginning to be available at large supermarkets and in season at farmers' markets.

Metric Conversion Guidelines

These guidelines were developed to simplify the conversion from Imperial measures to metric.
The numbers have been rounded for convenience. When cooking from a recipe,
work in the same system throughout the recipe; do not use a combination of the two.*

METRIC SYMBOLS

Celsius: C	gram: g
liter: L	centimeter: cm
milliliter: mL	millimeter: mm
kilogram: kg	

SOME COMMON CAN/PACKAGE SIZES

VOLUME		MASS	
4 oz.	114 mL	4 oz.	113 g
10 oz.	284 mL	5 oz.	142 g
14 oz.	398 mL	6 oz.	170 g
19 oz.	540 mL	7¾ oz.	220 g
28 oz.	796 mL	15 oz.	425 g

OVEN TEMPERATURE CONVERSIONS

IMPERIAL	METRIC
250 F	120 C
275 F	140 C
300 F	150 C
325 F	160 C
350 F	180 C
375 F	190 C
400 F	200 C
425 F	220 C
450 F	230 C
500 F	260 C

LENGTH

IMPERIAL	METRIC
¼ inch	5 mm
⅓ inch	8 mm
½ inch	1 cm
¾ inch	2 cm
1 inch	2.5 cm
2 inches	5 cm
4 inches	10 cm

VOLUME

IMPERIAL	METRIC
¼ tsp.	1 mL
½ tsp.	2 mL
¾ tsp.	4 mL
1 tsp.	5 mL
2 tsp	10 mL
1 Tbsp.	15 mL
2 Tbsp.	25 mL
¼ cup	50 mL
⅓ cup	75 mL
½ cup	125 mL
⅔ cup	150 mL
¾ cup	175 mL
1 cup	250 mL
4 cups	1 L
5 cups	1.25 L

MASS (WEIGHT)

IMPERIAL	METRIC
1 oz.	25 g
2 oz.	50 g
¼ lb.	125 g
½ lb. (8 oz.)	250 g
1 lb.	500 g
2 lb.	1 kg
3 lb.	1.5 kg
5 lb.	2.2 kg
8 lb.	3.5 kg
10 lb.	4.5 kg
11 lb.	5 kg

*Developed by the Canadian Home Economics Association and the American
Home Economics Committee

Recipe & Photography Credits

Recipes previously published in EATING WELL *Magazine*

Nancy Baggett: Apple-Oat Muffins, p. 31; Rum-Raisin Spice Muffins, p. 37; Enlightened-Banana Breakfast Muffins, p. 38; Blueberry Muffins, p. 38; Quick Corn Bread, p. 43; Apricot-Orange Loaf, p. 46; Curried Seafood Bisque, p. 66; Frozen Lemon Mousse, p. 185; Devil's Food Layer Cake, p. 208; Enlightened Black Forest Cherry Torte, p. 210; Marbled Pound Cake, p. 216; Chocolate Meringue Drop Cookies, p. 235; Brown Sugar-Pecan Meringue Cookies, p. 236. Sidebar, p. 212.

Bruce Beck: Oven-Steamed Flounder With Cantonese Flavors, p. 172; Sidebar, p. 168.

Shirley King: Braised Monkfish, p. 171.

Susan Loomis: Eight-Cup-High Apple Pie, p. 228.

Mary Ludwig: Quick-Rising Dough, p. 108; Pesto Pizza, p. 108; Wild Mushroom & Sage Pizza, p. 109; Pizza Primavera, p. 110; Caramelized Onion Pizza, p. 110; Tex-Mex Pizza, p. 112; Eggplant Pizza, p. 111.

Mäni's Bakery, Los Angeles: Oatmeal Cookies, p. 231.

Perla Meyers: Fricassee of Salmon With Cucumbers & Dill, p. 167; Sauté of Shrimp With Fragrant Indian Spices, p. 173.

Bill Neal: Mama's Potato Salad, p. 85.

Susan G. Purdy: Lemon Soufflé, p. 178; Cranberry Raisin Tart, p. 230; Sidebar p. 179.

Steven Raichlen: Angel Food Cake With Eggnog Spices, p. 212; Banana Cream Pie, p. 225.

Mary Randelman: Roast Chicken With Guava Glaze, p. 159.

Franco Romagnoli: Baked Stuffed Onions, p. 99; Italian Fruit Cake, p. 220; Sighs, p. 236.

Richard Sax: Potato & Smoked Fish Frittata, p. 24; Blueberry Cornmeal Loaf, p. 44; Chicken Paprikash, p. 152; Turkey-Stuffed Cabbage Rolls With Sauerkraut, p. 157; Indian Pudding, p. 188; Oeufs à la Neige, p. 191; Peach Melba Shortcake, p. 192; Cherry & Nectarine Cobbler, p. 193; Plum-Berry Crisp, p. 194; Patty's Cake, p. 217; Pear Tatin, p. 218.

Regina Schrambling: Southwestern Three-Bean Salad, p. 86; Garden Vegetable Salad With Roasted Scallion Dressing, p. 87; Braised Winter Vegetables With Thyme, p. 101; Bulgur With Celery and Sage, p. 123; Braised Beef With Brandy & Mustard, p. 136; Braiseworthy Lamb Shanks With Roasted Garlic & White Beans, p. 137; Sidebar, p. 136.

Martha Rose Shulman: Black Bean Chili, p. 129; Black Bean Frijoles, p. 131.

Nina Simonds: Roasted Summer Vegetables, p. 100; Stir-Fried Vegetables in Black Bean Sauce, p. 133; Almond Tuiles, p. 234.

William Weaver: Turkey With Madeira Gravy, p. 158.

John Willoughby: Pork Tenderloin With Braised Red Cabbage, p. 139; Stir-Fried Pork With Cauliflower & Broccoli, p. 140; Swordfish Steaks With Middle Eastern Flavors, p. 166; Sidebar, p. 166; Sidebar p. 171.

Rx Recipes submitted by EATING WELL readers

Jan Anderson *(Eugene, OR)*: Cauliflower With New Mornay Sauce, p. 104.

Sybil Basnight *(Manteo, NC)*: Outer Banks Crab Gratin, p. 174.

Angelo and Sue Bologna *(Santa Monica, CA)*: Carrot Cake, p. 215.

Debbie Boyken *(Denville, NJ)*: Stollen, p. 48.

Bonnie Cady *(Harpers Ferry, WV)*: Lemony Stuffed Fillet of Sole, p. 168.

Ellen W. Davis *(California, MD)*: Pumpkin-Wheat Bread, p. 42.

Susan P. Fillion *(Baltimore, MD)*: Clear-Conscience Waffles, p. 20.

Jan Heffington *(Morrison, CO)*: Sour Cream Mushroom Soup, p. 73.

Eleanor Henderson *(Brick, NJ)*: Extraordinary Low-Fat Vanilla "Ice Cream", p. 197.

Cindy Hendrick *(Bloomington, MN)* and Sandy Dreschler *(Smithtown, NY)*: Corn Pudding, p. 105.

Susan Kirby *(Buffalo, NY)*: New Generation Granola, p. 27.

David A. Klueter *(Fairfax, VA)*: Spaghetti alla Carbonara, p. 116.

Marlene Kohlenberg *(Oak Park, MI)*: Simple Noodle Kugel, p. 195.

Mary Jo Marsh *(Antigo, WI)*: Quiche Lorraine Light, p. 22.

Jenifer Jill Mathers *(East Burke, VT)*: Green Bean Casserole Sans the Cans, p. 98.

Edna McNamara *(Bedminster, NJ)*: Proper Scottish Oat Scones, p. 40.

Donna T. Meinecke *(Denton, TX)*: Cinnamon Rolls, p. 47.

Pam Miller *(Fairfax, VA)*: One-Step, One-Hour Lasagna, p. 119.

Susan J. Niemczyk *(Washington, D.C.)*: Reformed Chocolate Mousse, p. 180.

Beverly Parker *(Austin, TX)*: Zucchini-Oatmeal Muffins, p. 32.

Amy Simon *(Hampstead, NH)*: Macaroni & Cheeses, p. 120; Glazed Cheesecake With Fruit, p. 213.

N. Thies *(Osceola, MO)*: Spinach Pesto Appetizer, p. 55.

Allison Toppel *(Las Vegas, NV)*: Cottage Cheese Rugelach, p. 239.

Elizabeth Truden *(Cleveland Heights, OH)*: English Trifle, p. 189.

Ardath Weaver *(Raleigh, NC)*: New Year's Black-Eyed Peas, p. 132.

Ora Williamson *(Silver Spring, MD)*: Hot Crab Dip, p. 52.

Anita Wilson *(Chico, CA)*: Luscious Lemon Squares, p. 237.

Frances Winick *(Tucson, AZ)*: Pastitsio, p. 141.

Mary Wood *(New York, NY)*: Plum Pudding, p. 186.

Nancy Zager *(Stamford, CT)*: New "Veau" Veal Stew, p. 142; Chocolate Cheesecake Renewal, p. 214.

Photographers

Angelo Caggiano: p.147, p. 221.

Brian Hagiwara: p. 146, p. 148, p. 201, back cover (left and center).

Steven Mark Needham: front cover, p. 36, p. 71, p. 92, p. 125, p. 126, p. 127, p. 181, p. 182, p. 183, p. 184, p. 202, p. 203, p. 222.

Alan Richardson: p. 70, p. 72, p. 91, p. 223, p. 224, back cover (right).

Maria Robledo: p. 33, p. 90.

Ellen Silverman: p. 34, p. 35, p. 69, p. 128.

Jerry Simpson: p. 145, p. 204.

Mark Thomas: p. 89.

Index

>>>>𝓥<<<<

Page numbers in italics indicate photographs.

More Cookbooks from Camden House

THE EATING WELL COOKBOOK
Edited by Rux Martin, Patricia Jamieson and Elizabeth Hiser
ISBN 0-944475-22-1 $17.95 paperback
ISBN 0-944475-19-1 $24.95 hardcover

Steven Raichlen's
HIGH-FLAVOR, LOW-FAT COOKING
ISBN 0-944475-31-0 $18.95 paperback
ISBN 0-944475-32-9 $24.95 hardcover

WHOLEHEARTED COOKING:
Simply Delicious Low-Fat Recipes
By Terry Blonder
ISBN 0-944475-46-9 $17.95 paperback
ISBN 0-944475-45-0 $22.95 hardcover

FOR GOODNESS' SAKE:
An Eating Well Guide to Creative Low-Fat Cooking
By Terry Blonder
ISBN 0-944475-08-6 $14.95 paperback

THE STONYFIELD FARM YOGURT COOKBOOK
By Meg Cadoux Hirshberg
ISBN 0-944475-13-2 $17.95 paperback

SIMMERING SUPPERS
Edited by Rux Martin & JoAnne Cats-Baril
ISBN 0-944475-69-2 $16.95
ISBN 0-944475-81-1 $21.95

THE HARROWSMITH COUNTRY LIFE BAKING BOOK
Edited by Sandra J. Taylor
ISBN 0-944475-28-0 $18.95

Available at Your Local Bookstore

Patricia Jamieson is EATING WELL's Test Kitchen Director, overseeing the development and testing of over 1,500 recipes a year. Trained at LaVarenne cooking school in France, she fine-tuned her skills at several Parisian restaurants. She writes the *Rx for Recipes* column in EATING WELL Magazine, and appears frequently on CNN's "On the Menu" show, demonstrating healthful recipes from the magazine.

Cheryl Dorschner is a freelance editor, researcher and writer for several book and magazine publishers. She has worked for EATING WELL, *Harrowsmith Country Life, Country Journal* and *National Gardening* magazines. This is her twelfth book. She lives in Williston, Vermont.